# From our special correspondent

# From our

## R. J. Wilkinson-Latham

# special correspondent

## Victorian war correspondents and their campaigns

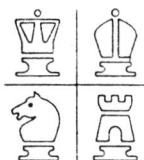

HODDER AND STOUGHTON
LONDON   SYDNEY   AUCKLAND   TORONTO

# For Christine

*. . . the duty of a war correspondent is primarily to chronicle incident.*
Winston S. Churchill in a dispatch to the *Daily Telegraph*
23 September 1897

*British Library Cataloguing in Publication Data*
*Wilkinson-Latham, Robert John*
*From our special correspondent.*
*1. War correspondents — Great Britain*
*I. Title*
*070.4'49'90981          PN4823*
*ISBN 0-340-23457-1*

*for Hodder and Stoughton Limited, Mill Road,*
*Dunton Green, Sevenoaks, Kent by Stephen Austin*
*and Sons Limited, Hertford. Designed by Bernard*
*Crossland Associates.*
*Hodder and Stoughton Editorial Office:*
*47 Bedford Square, London WC1B 3DP*

# Contents

# List of illustrations

7

*List of illustrations*

9

*List of
illustrations*

# Acknowledgements

It would certainly not have been possible to write this book without the untiring help of the individuals and organizations mentioned below who either provided information, answered numerous queries or put me on the track of suitable material. To them my deep thanks.

Gordon Phillips, *The Times*; E. H. Marsh, *Daily Telegraph*; Chief Librarian, Associated Newspapers Group Ltd.; the Staff of the Reading Room, National Army Museum; the Staff of the Reading Room, British Newspaper Library, Colindale, and British Library; Mrs. Pat Hodgson; E. T. Floyd Ewin, MVO, OBE, MA, Registrar and Receiver of St. Paul's; Robin Gibson, Assistant Keeper, National Portrait Gallery.

My brother aided considerably in the research and daily handed me sheaves of paper containing the names and biographical details of war correspondents. I must also acknowledge Mrs. Margaret Craven and Mrs. Angela Woods for their superb typing of the drafts and final manuscript.

The author and publisher wish to thank the following for permission to reproduce photographs: National Army Museum, London; Radio Times Hulton Picture Library, London; New York Public Library, New York; Library of Congress, Washington D.C.; Kunstall, Hamburg; National Portrait Gallery, London; E. Lucas, Cannes.

# Introduction

*It was above all necessary that England at breakfast should be amused and thrilled and interested . . .*
Rudyard Kipling

Ever since the appearance of the first printed newspapers, one of which was thought to have been the *Weekly News* which sold on the London streets in 1622, a new and powerful means of mass communication was established. This enabled news from other parts of the country or the known world to be collected together in one publication to reach a wider and more varied public than had hitherto been known. Merchants were not slow to realize that this new medium offered an entirely new 'market place' for their products or services, even though their advertisements were heavily taxed, while the more educated and intelligent were quick to see the newspaper as a powerful political and social weapon.

Newspapers greatly reflected the society they were designed to serve and mirrored the everyday conditions of life in a community or country, their attitudes and political and social climate. The problem of the proprietors was how to fill their newspapers with interesting news and opinions to outwit their rivals and sell more copies. During the eighteenth century, Britain was already spreading her influence beyond Europe and gathering colonies rapidly, so the demand at home was for news, views, and impressions of these newly acquired or discovered places that few readers had heard of, let alone visited. This increase in demand for relatively cheap reading matter caused an upsurge in the number of newspapers that appeared.

The powerful influence and popularity of the press in political matters can be judged by the fact that the government imposed a duty on paper and newsprint, hoping by this means to make newspapers too expensive for the working class and to check any social unrest that might be caused by extremist newspapers. Untaxed newspapers were seized and the editors and vendors thrown into prison. By law, paper was delivered for a London newspaper to Somerset House where each sheet was stamped in the corner in red with a die bearing the duty. French papers also attracted a duty of ten per cent of the selling price in the form of a *timbre* in blue in the upper right corner of the front page. The stamp was reduced from 4*d.* to 1*d.* in September 1836 and two months later had the name of the newspaper included in the design to prevent proprietors 'buying' too many to give a false idea of their circulation. The stamp lingered until 1855 and the duty on paper until 1861, when the 'tax on Knowledge', as Gladstone called it, was repealed. The stamp impressed on the top front right corner of a newspaper also meant that it could be sent through the post free of charge and many owners would never know their paper's true readership because of this. Small syndicates of three or four people formed to take, say *The Times*, and passed it on post free after reading to the next person, in effect reducing the individual cost from 5*d.* to 1*d.* Many large towns and cities also had coffee-houses and news-rooms where papers could be read for 1*d.* and bought at half price the day before the appearance of the new edition. Newsagents also ran a scheme for lending newspapers.

In 1715, there were such newspapers as the *Scots Courant*, the *Weekly Packet*, and the *Flying Post* as well as many others with names that emphasized either speed in newsgathering or critical and probing reports and comments. Besides the advertisements, which had now become a common feature in most newspapers, the bulk of the columns in the London papers, for example, was made up of local news, happenings at Court, the dramas enacted at the law courts and assizes, bankruptcy and crime as well as a social calendar of events, past, present, and future. Social and political comment was a large column filler and a glance at the relevant pages would reveal the newspaper's political leanings. Foreign news was also featured, usually as and when it arrived and normally gleaned from foreign newspapers. During a period of war or other important crisis, more space was given over to reproducing the official dispatches, at least those the government wanted made public, and letters from correspondents on the spot.

Throughout the seventeenth and eighteenth centuries, foreign news had usually been provided by letters from travellers, merchants, diplomats, or soldiers on a 'part-time' basis and any examination of newspapers, for the year 1745 for example, will reveal numerous references and quotations from letters. The Jacobite rebellion had broken out in Scotland and the *Universal Spectator* of 23 November 1745 quoted a letter from the Mayor of Carlisle recounting the surrounding of the city by the Highland rebels and their demands to the mayor to capitulate. Not all letters were written with the express intention of publication and many were 'passed on' to the newspapers by the recipients because they thought the contents either interesting or of monetary value. In the closing years of the nineteenth century, Winston Churchill, when covering the Sudan campaign of 1898 as an officer attached to the 21st Lancers, used this guise of private letter-writing to have his account published in the *Morning Post* and the 'my dear' with which every letter opened was none other than the newspaper's editor, Oliver Borthwick.

During war or troubled times of political upheaval and crisis the press was not entirely free to print its views, especially if they were critical of or opposed to the government policies. The *Westminster Journal* of 14 December 1745 records the searching of '... Several printing Houses ... by His Majesty's Messengers for treasonable Libels ...'. If the press were on occasion responsible for saying too much, the government was also guilty of saying too little or withholding news. A case in question was the defeat of the British force at the battle of New Orleans in January 1815 which received little if any coverage in the newspapers, those that did mention it proclaiming it a British victory. The escape of Napoleon from Elba in February and his subsequent rule of a 'Hundred Days' culminating in his final defeat at Waterloo on 18 June 1815 had received the majority of the coverage and had eclipsed the American victory. *Cobbett's Weekly Political Register*, a decidedly anti-government paper, recorded on 8 July 1815 that:

> ... the country people in England, and a great many of the townspeople, *never know* anything of such defeats. The London newspapers, which alone have a very wide circulation are employed in the spreading of falsehood and the suppressing of the truth.

Machinery for printing the *Illustrated London News* (from the *Illustrated London News,* 30 August 1879).

Cobbett's opinion of the press was not high and he declared that the '. . . Country newspapers, with very few exceptions, are the mere gutters, through which pass a part only of the filth of the more copious London sewers . . .'.

During the eighteenth century, the London reader had a wide choice of newspapers such as the *Daily Post*, the *Examiner*, the *Penny London Post*, the *London Gazette*, the *Westminster Journal*, the *Daily Advertiser*, and in 1785 the *Daily Universal Register* which in 1788 would become the famous, powerful, and influential *Times* of Printing House Square. Each filled their pages as best they could and some were not adverse to reprinting items which appeared in rival newspapers the day before, due to the limited sources of information.

If the gathering and transmitting of news was slow and erratic, the methods of printing were equally so. In spite of growing industrialization in Britain, the printing trade still relied on hand composition of type and hand-operated presses with which to print. Illustrations were exceedingly few before the appearance of Herbert Ingram's *Illustrated London News*, the first issue of which was published on Saturday, 14 May 1842, priced 6*d*. and containing thirty illustrations as well as news, views and comment. Illustrations had appeared before in the press but were usually crude by comparison with those of the *Illustrated London News*. The *Weekly Chronicle* used sensational pictures but not as a regular feature and the *Observer* on the occasion of Queen Victoria's coronation published a rather poorly executed engraving of the scene in Westminster Abbey. With the advice of two wood block engravers, Henry and Frank Vizetelly, Ingram launched his unique newspaper that would be copied by many others in various countries but never equalled. It is interesting to note that both Vizetelly brothers became war artists and correspondents to the *Illustrated London News*. During the siege of Paris in 1871, both Henry and his son Ernest, who was eighteen at the time and later claimed to be the youngest war correspondent on record, supplied news and views to Ingram.

Wood blocks were exclusively used for illustrations and the artist's sketch was traced on to the box or cherry wood block prior to engraving. To obtain large pictures, a number of wood blocks were bolted together, the picture traced on, the block disassembled and the pieces handed to a number of engravers to enable the block to be made in time.

The *Graphic* in 1882 described the blockmaking process for its readers:

> The process of electrotyping may be briefly described as follows. The wood block is placed in a bed of wax, which has been melted, and allowed to cool until it has arrived at the proper consistency. It is then submitted to a great pressure in a press of hydraulic or other construction, and in this way a *facsimile* of the original is produced, but with every detail reversed. This wax impression is then covered with a thin coating of black lead, such being a good conductor of electricity, and is hung by means of a brass rod in a large bath filled with a solution of sulphate of copper, sulphuric acid, &c. Side by side with this bath is a powerful battery of Smee's construction, that is to say, zinc and platinized silver in dilute sulphuric acid. The current generated by this battery is put into connection with the wax mould hung in the bath, and also with a sheet of copper also hung there side by side with the mould. The effect of the electricity is in the first place to decompose the copper, and in the second place to attract the particles of copper to the mould. In a short time a thin coating of copper has formed upon the mould, of which it is again the reverse, and consequently the exact facsimile of the original block.

After 1851 a more exact and almost photographic impression could be produced using Scott Archer's photographic collodion process whereby the photograph or photographed drawing could be produced on the surface of the wood block without the need of tracing. In 1858, the *Illustrated London News* of 5 June noted that 'Mr. J. Cavtentein's photographs on wood for the purpose of engraving are deserving of attention'.

It was not until 4 March 1880 that a photograph printed by the new halftone method (as used for illustrations in this book) appeared in the *New York Daily Graphic* followed in October by one in *Leipziger Illustrierte*, but development of this process was slow and the engraved wood block and line drawing still largely prevailed. Photography, which would later almost eclipse the war artist, was first perfected in 1839 by a Frenchman named Louis Daguerre but the basis of modern photography was a process invented by W. H. Fox Talbot in 1841 known as the Calotype. This system was used by John MacCosh, a surgeon in the Bengal Army who is credited with being the first war photographer. During the Second Sikh War (1848-9) he managed to take small portraits of officers and men but during the Second Burma War

Typical bookseller's account of the 1850s showing the newspapers and periodicals available. It also shows the common practice of advertising newspaper lending.

(1853-4) he had perfected his technique to enable him to photograph the captured cities of Rangoon and Prome. In 1848, a new process using albumen on glass was introduced and three years later the more advanced wet plate or wet collodion process, but even with this photographers such as Roger Fenton in the Crimea, commissioned by Thomas Agnew the Manchester print specialists, could only work near their special vans so that they could develop the plates before the sensitizing chemicals dried. Carol Popp de Szathmari, a photographer with the Russian troops, also suffered the same handicaps. By the mid 1870s a dry plate or gelatin emulsion process enabled plates to be stored ready for many months, but the real breakthrough came in 1888 when the celluloid roll film appeared together with George Eastman's Kodak camera. Even with this new improvement, photographers appeared to have had little success in capturing battle action pictures until the Omdurman campaign of 1898 and Boer War (1899-1902) and the illustrated newspapers still continued to rely mainly on the talented skill of their war artists to portray events.

The *Daily Graphic,* the first illustrated daily paper, founded in 1890, used mainly wood block and line illustrations but condescended to publish a halftone of a photograph in 1891. Halftone, a process of reproducing photographs by the use of a screen of dots, was 'invented' by Stephen Hargan in America in 1880 and in Germany by Meisenbach in 1882, although since the early days of photography, printers and photographers had struggled to perfect a suitable method for printed reproductions. A number of newspapers attempted to perfect methods suitable for their presses, one being the *Bradford Telegraph* which patented a halftone process in 1883. By 1897, however, the halftone process was widely in use, even for reproducing the drawings of the war artists, but it was not until January 1904 that the first daily paper to be exclusively illustrated with photographs, the *Daily Mirror*, appeared. It was not until the 1920s that daily newspapers, as opposed to illustrated papers, started to include photographs.

After 1800 a number of improvements were made in printing but these were mainly confined to the presses rather than the actual composition. Attempts had been made at the beginning of the nineteenth century to construct a machine which would select pre-cast type but it proved neither efficient nor practical. Type still continued to be set by highly skilled compositors until the mid 1880s when Ottmar Merganthaler developed the Linotype machine which was capable of casting single lines of type to the instructions of the operator who tapped out the text on a keyboard. Two years later, a similar machine, which cast individual letters and placed them on a 'galley', was invented. An improvement in the casting of type was made by a journalist, Frederick Wicks, whose 'Rotary Typecasting Machine' produced type with such rapidity that the inventor claimed that '. . . 3 sufficed to supply *The Times* with a new fount each day for its publication'.

By the 1840s, steam-driven presses were in use in many of the large printing firms, *The Times* having installed Koenig's steam-driven presses by 1814, and the *Illustrated London News* boasted when two new

Paper for the *Illustrated London News* being delivered to Somerset House in London for duty stamps.

modern printing machines were installed on their premises at 198 Strand, London, in 1898 that they had the '... power to produce nearly four times the present circulation' and the machines worked '... at the rate of 2000 perfect impressions an hour'.

Newsgathering was still the main problem of the editors, the more progressive of whom were not content to print the same official dispatches as their rivals. During the early years of the nineteenth century, *The Times*, one of the major influences in British newspapers, decided that a more accurate and interesting account, completely different from that of their rivals, could be obtained by sending an employee of their own to gather on the spot facts and stories, write them up in a dispatch, and send it back by the fastest means to London. *The Times* chose as their special correspondent Henry Crabb Robinson, a lawyer by profession, whom the editor sent firstly to central Europe in 1807 to cover the French campaign there resulting in a series of letters headlined 'From the Banks of the Elbe'. Obviously pleased with their war correspondent, they sent him in the following year to Spain. Arriving at Corunna at the end of July he was deeply impressed by the

*Introduction*

Model of an optical telegraph
system used in many countries
before the advent of F. Morse's
'wire' system. This example is
the system developed by
Edelcrant in Sweden in 1794.

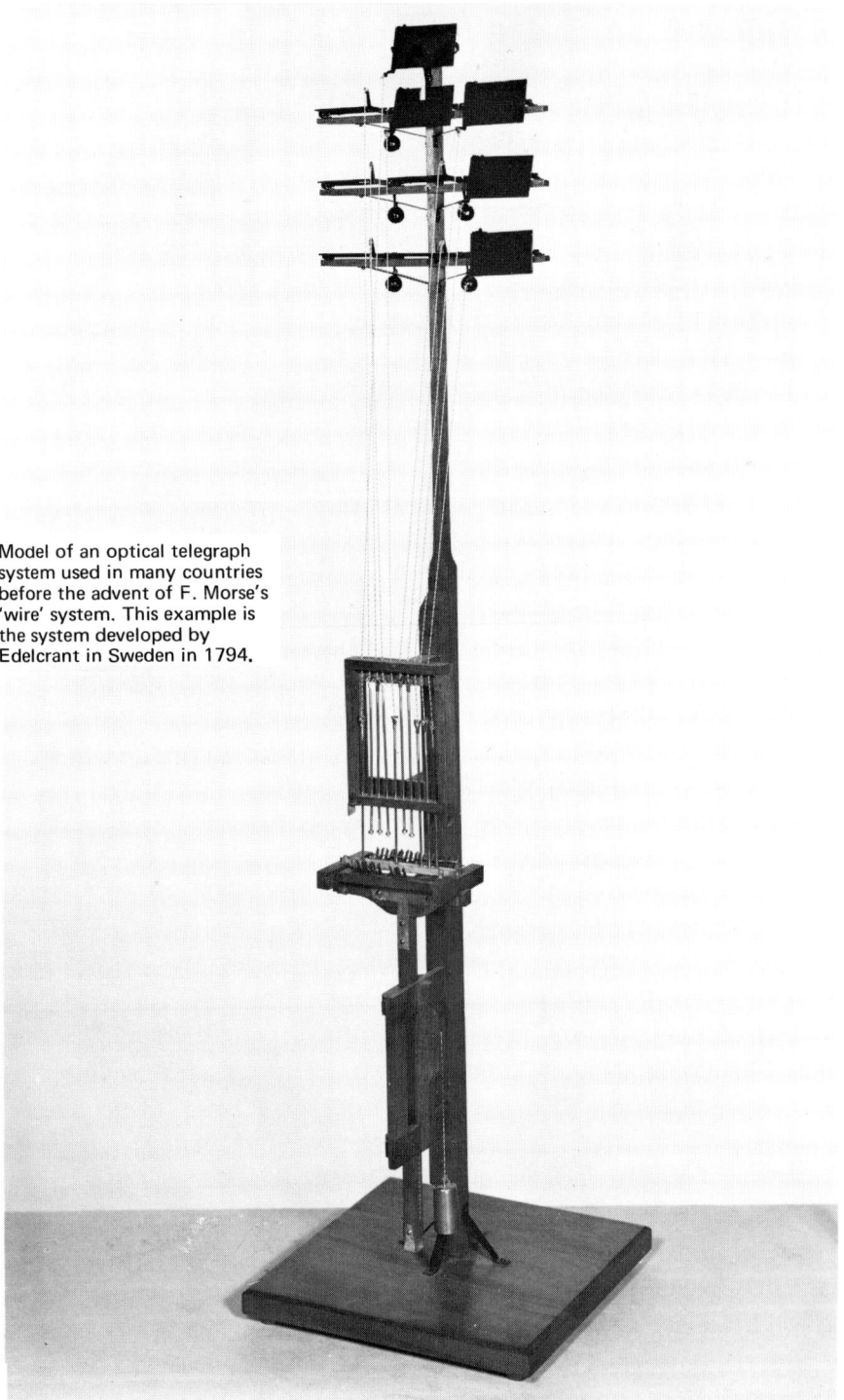

determination of the Spaniards. 'We need not fear the speedy emancipation of the Capital', he reported in his first dispatch, 'and the compression of the French force within the provinces adjoining Bayonne.' By October, Robinson's dispatches had lost much of this air of optimism. At the beginning of the following year as the army retreated towards Corunna, Robinson's dispatches amplified much of the bitterness felt by the officers due to the retreat which they considered '. . . more properly a flight'. Unfortunately for *The Times*, Henry Crabb Robinson did not have the searching or inquisitive mind that would later be the hallmark of William Howard Russell's dispatches and his methods of obtaining information from the seat of war, wrote S. T. Sheppard in an article in the *United Service Magazine* for March 1907, 'may not at the present seem adequate . . .' but they were novel. Robinson tended to base his reports on the local newspapers rather than what he saw himself and even in his last dispatch from Corunna, written on the evening of 16 January 1809 after the French had been repulsed, he did not even mention the death of the Commander-in-Chief, Sir John Moore. When the British troops left the Spanish mainland, Robinson returned to England where, probably wisely, he resumed his career as a lawyer. In 1869, *Diary, Reminiscences and Correspondence of Henry Crabb Robinson*, the first professional war correspondent, were published.

*The Times* was not the only newspaper to discover the value of the special correspondent. In 1809, the *Morning Chronicle* attempted to send a Mr. Finnerty to accompany the expedition being mounted against Antwerp and which ended in disaster in the swamps of Walcheren. The Admiralty were informed that 'Mr. Finnerty, so well known by his violent and factious writings . . .' was actually on board one of the warships waiting to sail under the guise of a private secretary to one of the captains. Lord Castlereagh had him removed and in his bitterness Finnerty later attacked his Lordship and the expedition in no uncertain terms, an outburst that cost him a year in prison for libel.

Further attempts to send correspondents to Portugal and Spain when a new force was dispatched were baulked by the new Commander-in-Chief, Sir Arthur Wellesley, who never allowed any such civilians on any of his campaigns, at the same time deploring any letters from officers that might appear in the newspapers giving intelligence to the enemy. Thomas Heaphy, however, acted as official war artist to the Duke of Wellington from 1812. Napoleon, it was once said, remarked that 'English papers make my best spies' which reflected either the mediocrity of the French intelligence service, the reputation of the London press, or the total lack of censorship on dispatches and letters, which was in fact the case. Not until after the Crimean War would press censorship be introduced and not until the siege of Ladysmith during the Boer War of 1899—1902 would press and letter censorship become the responsibility of a Military Intelligence officer. From Badajoz on 21 November 1809, Wellesley wrote to Lord Liverpool, drawing his attention to:

> the frequent paragraphs in the English newspapers describing
> the position, the numbers, the objects, and the means of
> attaining them, possessed by the armies in Spain and Portugal.
> In some instances the English newspapers have accurately
> stated, not only the regiments occupying a position, but the
> number of men fit for duty of which each regiment was
> composed; and this intelligence must have reached the enemy
> at the same time as it did me, at a moment at which it was
> most important that he should not receive it.

In the Crimea, Lord Raglan was to complain in almost the same words about the London correspondents. In Army Orders of 10 August 1810, Wellesley felt compelled to publish the following because of the leakage of information to the London newspapers:

> . . . the General Officer requests that officers will, for the sake
> of their own reputations avoid giving opinions upon which they
> cannot have a knowledge to enable them to form any. And that
> if they choose to communicate facts to their correspondents,
> regarding the positions of the army, its numbers etc., they will
> urge their correspondents not to publish their letters to the
> newspapers until it shall be certain that the publication of the
> intelligence will not be injurious to the army . . . it may be
> right to give the British public this information, but if they
> choose to have it, they ought to know the price they pay for
> it and the advantage it gives to the enemy.

Editors still did their best to present the news in a varied form and tried to differ from their rivals. 'We have been favoured,' *The Times* of 11 August 1812 announced, 'by a correspondent with a very important document which we this day publish, relative to the effective strength of the French army in the South, previous to the capture of Badajoz . . .' They then reproduced an inaccurate set of outdated figures of the French army, but at least if was different and exciting to readers at home.

Dispatches, which the government issued later to the press, came from the Peninsula by ship to Plymouth and were relayed by coach or rider to London. Brief details of news of great importance were sent to London by 'telegraphic' dispatch. This 'telegraphic' dispatch was not the method now associated with that word but a system of sending signals with flags from post to post within sight of each other. Although faster than the horse, it depended on pre-set stations and good visibility. The heliograph, a system of signalling with mirrors and sunlight, was much used in India and later in South Africa during the nineteenth century when tribesmen and Boers took to cutting the telegraph lines.

The escape of Bonaparte from Elba was reported in the pages of the *Examiner* of 12 March 1815 who received the news '. . . first brought to Mr. Rothchild, the Banker, by one of his clerks, who came post from Paris'. The allied victory on 18 June 1815 at an obscure village in Belgium called Waterloo was reported in *The Times*, never one for banner headlines, on an inside page of their issue of 22 June. The announcement, taken directly from the Duke of Wellington's dispatch informed readers that:

> The Duke of WELLINGTON's dispatch, dated Waterloo, the
> 19th June states, that on the previous day, Bonaparte attacked,
> with his whole force, the British line supported by a Corps
> of Prussians; which attack after a long and sanguinary
> conflict terminated in the complete Overthrow of the
> Enemy's Army . . .

Such, saving the occasional burst into capital letters, was the restrained announcement to the British public of the victory. The *Bristol Mirror* announced the news to its readers on 24 June and other provincial papers, swiftly following the announcement of the London press, headlined the victory. For the next few weeks the details of the battle were elaborated as eye-witness accounts and private letters became available.

During the next forty years, Britain was not engaged in any large-scale war, although there were numerous small wars and expeditions in India, the news of which was taken from official dispatches and letters from correspondents. In Europe, however, the 1830s and 1840s were times of social and political upheaval which was widely reported in the newspapers, the use of 'foreign' correspondents for reliable on the spot reports having now become established.

During this period, another and perhaps more important and far-reaching event occupied the press, that of the social and political implications of the climax of the 'Industrial Revolution'. Since the middle of the eighteenth century, the industrialization of Britain had been gathering momentum, factories springing up and new and more economical methods of manufacture were being instituted. Machines were replacing skilled manpower which led to unrest, unemployment, poverty for some, and the inevitable riots and confrontations with the civil powers. Roads, railways, bridges, and canals now opened up the country resulting in a speed-up of communications which affected the gathering, reporting, and distribution of the news.

In 1830, after George Stephenson's 'Rocket' had triumphed at the Rainhill Trials, the first public railway had been opened and by 1832 gaslight was fast replacing oil lamps and candles in houses and factories. Steam power now drove powerful engines replacing the somewhat uncertain engines driven by watermills. While it was an era of material progress, it was still one of intolerance, untaxed newspapers such as the *Poor Man's Guardian* and the *Cosmopolite* being hounded by the law and the editors, contributors, and sellers being sentenced to prison terms out of all proportion to the misdemeanour. At the close of the nineteenth century, W. T. Stead, the controversial editor of the *Pall Mall Gazette* and later *Review of Reviews* and also the pioneer of the personal interview, considered the supreme outcome of the labour of the nineteenth century was the '. . . production of a Quick-Firing gun capable of pumping tons of explosive shells over four or five miles of country at a rate of twelve shots a minute'. It was a great blow to critical journalism when W. T. Stead was lost aboard the *Titanic* which sank in 1912.

The squabble between Belgium and Holland, about who dominated that country after the Treaty of Vienna, broke into open conflict in 1830 with France and Britain allied together in an attempt to restore the *status quo*. Political bargaining continued until 1832, when the *Newcastle Journal* of 13 October reported that it had received vital news from a special courier from Brussels concerning the possible intervention of an Anglo-French force. War was declared and French troops moved on Antwerp. News of the Dutch withdrawal was printed in the *True Sun*, whose method of newsgathering astounded their rivals. 'IMPORTANT NEWS FROM ANTWERP', the headlines declared, '(JUST ARRIVED BY A CARRIER PIGEON) ANTWERP, MONDAY, NINE A.M.' The newspaper proudly boasted that the news had arrived that morning and that they had '. . . seen a carrier pigeon, bringing probably the same information to the Government'.

In England, speed of communication was being increased by such machines as Hancock's New Steam Carriage, said to have a speed of about ten miles an hour, although *Bell's Weekly Messenger* of 17 September 1832 declared that it '. . . hurried down a declivity at a most enormous rate, probably 50 miles an hour'. This new fast means of communication although aiding on one hand the gathering and reporting of news meant that news of social unrest also spread at an alarming rate. Provincial papers followed those of the capital with rapidity in reporting unrest in the metropolis especially during the Chartist riots when even the government resorted to publishing its own newspaper entitled *Voice of the People*.

During the Carlist War in Spain in 1837, the *Morning Post* sent C. L. Gruneisen, better known as a music critic, while *The Times* employed the services of a Captain Henningsen. Both were captured and deported from Spain. George Borrow in his work *The Bible in Spain* described the correspondents of the English press as being entitled to the:

> . . . appellation of cosmopolites. The activity, energy and courage they display are truly remarkable. I saw them [ he continued ], during the three days in Paris [ 1830 ] mingle with the *canaille* and rabble behind the barriers . . . There they stood, dotting down what they saw in their note books, as unconcernedly as if reporting a Reform meeting in Finsbury Square or Covent Garden, while in Spain they accompanied the Carlists and Christino guerillas in some of their most desperate expeditions, sleeping on the ground, exposing themselves fearlessly to hostile bullets, to the inclemency of winter, and the fierce rays of summer's burning sun.

Yet correspondents did not enjoy any of the privileges of prisoners of war and one Spanish general exclaimed that as Gruneisen had done more harm with his pen than any Carlist generals with their swords, he would have no compunction about shooting all Carlist correspondents.

Railways now opened up the country for the gathering and distribution of news and newspapers. The *Illustrated London News* of

26 February 1848 carried the following story which was a milestone in newspaper distribution:

> One of the most extraordinary achievements in newspaper expressing was performed on Saturday last. A special express, which was arranged by Messrs. W. H. Smith and Son, news-vendors, Strand, left London at 35 minutes past five o'clock in the morning with newspapers of the day, and reached Glasgow at 57 minutes past three in the afternoon . . .

W. H. Smith had already set up a number of records of this nature and his newspaper distribution system was far ahead of any other wholesaler but even so the prohibitive price of newspapers still prevented the London dailies having a wide circulation in the provinces, where local news was more demanded and national news, if a day or so late, could be had in the same local paper. News-rooms in the larger provincial cities and towns flourished with their wide and varied reading, some taking as many as 130 newspapers a day. The high cost, late arrival and paucity of local news still enabled the provincial papers to protect themselves against the richer dailies of the metropolis until the coming of the telegraph. This form of communication made competition on equal terms possible and allowed, as the London press complained, the provincial papers to profit freely from the foreign and war news gathered by them at great expense. This was one of the reasons why some larger provincial papers did not commission their own war correspondents until later in the century, the *Manchester Guardian* first making its own arrangements during the Franco Prussian War and the *Western Morning News* shortly afterwards.

News from Ireland was also prominent in the press in the 1840s following the great potato famine, the expulsion of tenants, and the mass exodus to the Americas and Australia. *The Times* had their own correspondents on the spot, such men as Sidney Godolphin Osborne, later to be one of Florence Nightingale's most ardent supporters, and William Howard Russell, a twenty-eight-year-old Irishman who was studying to be a lawyer. Both men would later meet in the Crimea, the former as a chaplain to the forces and the latter as *The Times*'s special correspondent. The uniqueness of Russell's type of journalism was soon evident to John T. Delane, *The Times*'s progressive editor, who took Russell on as a full-time correspondent in the late 1840s. He was later to establish an important name for himself as *The Times* correspondent in the Crimea and become, as his epitaph in St. Paul's Cathedral states,

'The First and Greatest of War Correspondents'. In 1882, Russell was to remark, '... I wonder what would have come of it all had I followed the quiet path ...'. After the Crimean War, Russell was to be followed by numerous other correspondents who avidly reported wars all over the world for a news- and adventure-hungry public.

The special correspondents were soon to find their task of sending dispatches less arduous. In 1844, F. B. Morse, an artist and portrait photographer, had opened his first telegraph line between Baltimore and Washington and during the next thirty or so years, whole countries and continents were linked by his system. News by 'the wire' now travelled faster than a man could ride or a train could run. In 1848, the Electric Telegraph Company established a line between London and Edinburgh which according to a contemporary journal '... made a saving of one to two hours in the transmission of intelligence'. Before this date, the telegraph had been mainly used by the railway companies for their own internal purposes and in controlling trains. Later, 'the wire' was used to book carriages to meet passengers at certain stations, but by 1848, its advantages were realized and it became very much the machine of the moment. In 1848, the British North America Royal Mail steamer *Niagara* cut the time between Liverpool and North America by crossing the Atlantic in twelve days and nine hours, five days less than the previous record. Later the *Niagara* was utilized for laying the Atlantic telegraph cable.

In 1851, Britain and France were linked by a submarine cable and in 1855, during the Crimean War, Varna was linked to Europe by cable to enable the home governments of France and Britain to be in closer contact with their commanders in the field. The new use of the telegraph, however, appears to have been abused in the Crimea for the Commander-in-Chief, General Simpson, was forced to complain to Lord Panmure at the War Office that '... some telegraphic messages reach us that cannot be sent under due authority and are perhaps unknown to you, although under the protection of your Lordship's name ...'. This referred to a strange message received by General Simpson after midnight on 16 July 1855 which was brought by a dispatch rider. 'Lord Panmure to General Simpson — Captain Jervis has been bitten by a centipede. How is he now?' General Simpson ventured '... to mention this message because there have been two equally trifling, causing inconvenience and worse may come out of such practice with the wires'.

In 1858, the first transatlantic cable was laid for the Atlantic Telegraph Company by the *Agamemnon*. The *Illustrated London News* of 3 April 1858 declared that 'the American Telegraph Co. now sends dispatches from both ends of the line simultaneously, by a single wire . . .', but unfortunately it broke after several weeks and a new cable was not laid until the 1860s. Despite these improvements, news, especially from India and further east, took a considerable time to reach London. In India, where in 1857 the mutiny of the Native Bengal army was raging, news had to be collected and sent to Calcutta where it was put aboard a steamer bound for Suez. At Suez (there being no canal at this time) dispatches were sent overland to Alexandria where they were telegraphed to Malta and from there to Europe and across the Channel to London, the whole journey taking some four weeks. The transportation of telegraphic dispatches was speeded up in 1870 when a cable was laid by the *Great Eastern* between Aden and Bombay.

In Europe and in other continents, lines were being put up as fast as possible with emphasis on direct lines rather than short runs dependent on intermediate stations. The *Illustrated London News* of 22 May 1858 proudly announced, 'The first message direct from Constantinople to London on the 2nd inst. came "in less than no time" — it left at 11.45 in the evening yet arrived at 8.57 the same evening beating the sun by three hours.'

In 1876, Alexander Graham Bell revolutionized communications with his invention of the telephone which, however, was little used by war correspondents. In 1899, Marconi succeeded in sending a radio message across the Channel and two years later sent a wireless signal across the Atlantic. Other inventions based on the telegraph blossomed such as the 'teleautograph' which was capable of transmitting actual handwriting or drawing and Professor David Hugh's 'Printing Telegraph' which was used on all important lines in Europe and the submarine cable between Britain and the Continent.

Although many of these material aids speeded up the time taken for a correspondent's dispatches to reach his editor, news, especially from Africa, America, and India still took weeks to arrive. Although lines were being put up and submarine cables laid, the countryside in which battles and colonial wars were fought was seldom directly serviced by telegraph. Dispatches had to be written, censored, and then taken by a dispatch rider to the nearest telegraph station for transmission to the coast where they were sent over the submarine cable (if one existed) or put aboard the earliest sailing steamer. The captain of the vessel would call at the extremity of a telegraph system linked to Europe or London and send the dispatches. The war artist could not, however, act with the same speed. He was reliant on any available postal system. His drawings and sketches had to be taken, once passed by the censor, to the nearest post office for transmission in the usual way to London. Occasionally sketches were taken to the coast and put aboard a ship which speeded up the time taken for their journey. In many wars and campaigns, a journalist often carried the sketches of a war artist when riding with his dispatches to the nearest telegraph, going on further to the nearest post office as between them there was no competition for a 'first' or 'scoop'. There are many instances of artist and correspondent teaming up together during a campaign in the same cart or using the same tent and servants.

While many correspondents acted as their own dispatch riders, some had special riders such as Godfrey Lagden representing the *Daily Telegraph* who during the Egyptian campaign of 1882 employed the Hon. Maurice Raymond Gifford as a dispatch rider. Godfrey Lagden was later to give up journalism and raise and command the Transvaal Light Infantry. During the Boer War, the Hon. Somers Somerset amongst many others acted as a dispatch rider for *The Times* and a correspondent of the London press remembered that 'This gentleman's carbolic tooth powder was the only antiseptic dressing available and was therefore used in all cases with what results I recommend the *Lancet* to inquire'. Dispatch riders were paid handsomely for their work entailing numerous risks, but there appeared to be few who picked up the full amount offered for a ride. 'A dispatch rider,' wrote Fred W. Unger, a correspondent of the *Daily Express* in South Africa during the Boer War, 'gets nearly a pound a mile but as often as not he does not get very far. Only the other day four of Reuter's dispatch riders were caught by the Boers near Mafeking.' The press agencies such as Reuter's and Laffins were great users of dispatch riders and were amongst the most generous with payments to their men in the field.

The cost of maintaining a correspondent in the field was enormous and only the larger, wealthier, and wide circulation newspapers could afford the expense. Besides the travelling and living expenses, there was the correspondent's salary and probably a hefty bonus at the end of a campaign. Melton Prior, the illustrious and celebrated war artist of the *Illustrated London News*, remembered that Sir William Ingram, the owner, used to call him the 'Illustrated Luxury' because as Prior put it 'I travelled in comfort'. 'I wonder,' he continued, 'what the proprietors of the "dailies" called their representatives, who cost fifteen shillings a word plus comfort.' The fifteen shillings a word referred to by Prior was the cost of telegrams from Egypt to London in 1884. J. C. MacDonald of *The Times* wrote to William Howard Russell after the Indian Mutiny on the subject that '... I reckon that altogether we shall not get out of this job for telegrams alone under £5,000'. The correspondents themselves also added to their newspaper's costs by offering large bonuses to riders to take dispatches through enemy lines or to the telegraph stations before those of their rivals. The race to get the news home first was an expensive one and also risky but the competition between correspondents and their newspapers was such that these risks had to be taken.

The inequality of newsgathering was apparent even before the Crimean War in 1854 when the smaller London and especially local provincial papers had to resort to using the dispatches of the larger and wealthier newspapers of the metropolis, their circulation and finances permitting them to have neither a correspondent nor access to letters from officers on the spot. In a move to remedy this situation, a thirty-three-year-old German, Israel Beer Josephat Reuter, started a telegraphic and pigeon carrying news service in Aachen, Germany, in 1849. So successful was the news gathering and distribution service that Reuter extended it to cover other countries and later every continent. Reuter had first arrived in London in 1858 and soon introduced himself to the editors of the influential London daily newspapers:

> I am a Prussian! [he told James Grant of the *Morning Advertiser*], and have been employed for many years as a courier to several of the Courts of Europe ... and in that capacity have formed personal intimacies with gentlemen connected with most of the European Governments. It has occurred to me that I might, therefore, be able to supply, by telegraph, the daily press of London with earlier and more accurate intelligence of importance, and, at the same time at a cheaper rate than the morning journals are now paying for their telegraphic communications from the Continent.

The *Morning Advertiser* and others were given a fortnight's 'free trial' before having to pay £30 per month if they accepted the service. *The Times* in its aloof fashion at first refused, but later through force of necessity became a delighted subscriber. Reuter soon opened his London office and in conjunction with John Duncan set up a large network for receiving and sending out news. The simple method of paying a subscription guaranteed a newspaper the right to receive and reproduce Reuter's dispatches. Reuter soon spread his tentacles to other continents to provide up-to-the-minute news for his subscribers. In any country or during any conflict, there was always more than one Reuter correspondent on hand. Reuter, the pioneer of news-gathering, moved his headquarters to London and was created a Baron in 1871. Other agencies soon sprang up, based on Reuter, and they too provided the same service.

While the news service provided by the agencies was admirable and enabled editors to keep their fingers on the pulse of what was happening through the short telegraphic messages, it proved for the London papers no substitute for the 'special' who could supply a wordy on-the-spot account or an individual telegraphic dispatch of what was happening. More and more newspapers took to sending out correspondents or arranging with officers and correspondents on the spot to act for them. By the time of the Boer War of 1899, a veritable army of correspondents descended on South Africa from the London, provincial, and foreign press.

The gradual increase in the number of 'gentlemen of the press' was all too apparent to the military authorities and soon the freedom of movement and of dispatches which Russell had enjoyed in the Crimea along with Nicholas Woods and other pressmen was being curtailed by censorship. 'Of all the thankless positions in an army,' wrote an officer during the Sudan campaign of 1882, 'the press censor has the worst. Abused by correspondents at the seat of war, maligned by editors at home and continually found fault with by his superiors with the army for allowing too much to pass . . . .' Telegrams and dispatches had to be countersigned and passed which entailed copious editing before they were allowed to be dispatched and any alterations made afterwards by the correspondent and not authorized were met with severe censure. In Afghanistan in 1879, Lord Roberts discovered that MacPherson of the *Standard* continued to alter his dispatches after Roberts had signed them and following a due warning Roberts recorded that '. . . I felt it to be my duty to send the too imaginative author to the rear'. By the end of the nineteenth century, Archibald Forbes, himself one of the most famous of war correspondents, wrote that:

For better or for worse, the war correspondent as regards a British army in the field, has been stamped out. The journalist who now accompanies an army is a war reporter. He dances in the fetters of the censorship, whose power over him is absolute: it may not only detain or withhold his work, but at discretion may alter it so that he may be made to say the direct reverse of what he wrote. If the position has its humiliations, it also has its compensations. The censorship which makes a slave of the war reporter, *ipso facto* relieves him of all responsibility for the words he writes.

In spite of the increased tightening of restrictions, the 'specials' still managed to send back interesting and exciting accounts of what they saw or experienced. From the Crimea to the Boer War, each small or large war whether British or foreign was followed with equal interest by numerous journalists of the British, American, and European press. During the second half of the nineteenth century, the style of the 'special' altered from the somewhat flowery, over-descriptive yet hard-hitting dispatches of William Howard Russell of *The Times* through a twenty-year period from about 1878 of 'jingoistic' journalism. Eventually, by the time of the Boer War of 1899-1902, war reporting had largely returned to unbiased dispatches and a simple descriptive style as used by G. W. Steevens of the *Daily Mail* and Winston S. Churchill of the *Morning Post*.

Perhaps the most noticeable change in the war correspondents' style during the latter years of the nineteenth century was their attitudes to natives, both friend and foe. From the 1870s, when a growing number of colonial expeditions were mounted, natives were allowed to be either swarming savages or comic coons. This universal descriptive was not only used by war correspondents who always seemed to find places for comic cooks or porters but was a standard recipe for the stories that appeared in the boy's adventure papers such as the *Boy's Own Paper* which appeared in 1879, the *Union Jack* edited by the adventure story writer and one-time war correspondent George Alfred Henty, and many other similar publications. The 'sun drenched, blood stained prose' could never be complete without the native. In the Sudan expedition of 1898, the war correspondents' attitude altered drastically towards the native enemy. Winston S. Churchill described the Dervishes' 'constancy and courage' while G. W. Steevens, the twenty-eight-year-old star correspondent of the *Daily Mail*, was overwhelmed with admiration for the 'fuzzy-wuzzy':

And the Dervishes? [he wrote] The honour of the fight must
still go with the men who died. Our men [he continued,
referring to the battle of Omdurman (1898)], were perfect,
but the Dervishes were superb — beyond perfection. It was the
largest, best and bravest army that ever fought against us for
Mahdism . . .

Later Steevens declared that the British fire was so murderous that 'No
white troops would have faced it for five minutes . . .' The British
army had fought numerous native enemies but the Dervishes were
undoubtedly the most experienced and dangerous. Rudyard Kipling,
the unofficial spokesman for the British soldier, paid Tommy Atkins's
tribute to the Dervishes:

We've fought with many men across the seas,
An' some of 'em was brave an' some was not:
The Paythan an' the Zulu an' Burmese;
But the Fuzzy was the finest o' the lot.
                                    'Fuzzy-Wuzzy'

During the early years of the twentieth century, correspondents found
a changing world. There were still a few minor colonial wars to be
reported but they discovered increasing tensions in Europe leading to
revolutions and what has often been described as the rehearsal for the
First World War, the Balkan War of 1912-13. By early 1914, it seemed
evident that a European war was inevitable and the assassination of
Archduke Ferdinand at Sarajevo started a chain of events that was
impossible to stop. But some of the romanticism attached to the war
correspondent was still alive. As the 'German wolf discards his sheep's
clothing', *The Times* of 2 August 1914 carried on its front page in
the famous personal column the following announcement in the
typical subdued phraseology of that paper. 'WAR—Gentleman, Military,
diplomatic, literary experience offers SERVICES as WAR CORRES-
PONDENT.' War was declared between the major powers of Europe
and the British expeditionary force crossed the Channel to France
accompanied by those newspapermen '. . . stupid enough to follow
Tommy Atkins', as Melton Prior had once remarked where soldier
and correspondent alike found a new, frightening, and different kind
of war.

# 1

# The birth of the modern war correspondent

## (1854–7)

*He works for his paper. He gives his time, his health, his brains, his sleeping hours, and his eating hours, and sometimes his life to get news for it.*
Richard Harding Davis, American journalist and war correspondent.

The thoughts of the British nation were far from war in the year 1851: and few could have imagined what influence certain reporters of war would soon have over those in power. During the previous year, people had cast an indifferent eye over the columns of the newspapers that reported the squabble between Prussia and Denmark on the Schleswig-Holstein problem. But now Britain had emerged from the rather unsteady 1840s into a new decade of prosperity and power, her Empire and influence reaching the four corners of the world. The culmination of this industrial achievement and the main interest of the people was the Great Exhibition of All Nations, better known as the Great Exhibition, which was organized under the patronage of Albert, the Prince Consort. Many nations were invited to display their arts, crafts, and industries and a magnificent steel and glass structure, dubbed the 'Crystal Palace', was built in Hyde Park. The success of the exhibition was never to be equalled and its prestige value for the Victorians was immeasurable.

The Danish War of 1850 had been covered by most newspapers. The custom of allocating special correspondents was now well established and *The Times* sent a thirty-year-old Irishman, William Howard Russell.

This was to be Russell's first taste of war reporting although by this time he had covered nearly every other branch of journalism from parliamentary debates to railways and from civil disturbances to crime. His life story shows how the qualities which he brought to journalism set a new standard and he did his job so well that people were convinced of the need for such a profession at any future time of war.

William Howard Russell was born at Lily Vale in the parish of Tallaght, County Dublin, on 28 March 1820. He saw little of his father in his youth as John Russell's business had collapsed like many others and he and his wife, Mary, sought a new way of life with hopes of prosperity in Liverpool. William was brought up by his grandfather, Captain John Kelly, a retired officer. 'What he was captain of,' wrote Russell later, 'I know not, but there was in the "parlour" a picture of a lad in a red coat with wide lapels of dark blue . . .' Russell soon had a rude awakening to life when he was sent to Dr. Wall's junior school. '. . . As I was vivacious, idle and a good deal spoilt, I was singled out by a morose young tyrant, who imitated, as far as he could, the methods of his chief in signal and painful correction.' His next school was run by the Rev. E. J. Geoghegan, whose academy in Dublin enjoyed a fine reputation.

Russell's first venture into journalism was at the age of sixteen. He had shot a bird which he termed a '. . . curious sort of lark'; he took the body home, sketched it, and setting down a few details sent the information to the *Dublin Penny Journal*. The bird it seems was extremely rare in Ireland and Russell's article was later quoted in every standard work on Irish birds. A year later, his grandfather died and Russell was obliged to become a tutor at a school in County Leitrim. Russell had set his heart on entering Trinity College, Dublin, and studied hard for his examinations. He passed the exams, but failed to win a scholarship. At twenty-one he was still undecided about a future career until a cousin, John Russell, arrived in Ireland to cover the election as the special correspondent of *The Times*. John Russell realized that he could not cover the entire campaign on his own and organized a number of graduates capable of writing under his orders. He offered William '. . . one guinea a day and your hotel expenses'. William did not hesitate. Russell continued to contribute regularly to *The Times*, while studying for his law exams. The professionalism of young Russell did not go unnoticed and John T. Delane, the progressive editor of *The Times*, called him to London and suggested he take up residence and get a transfer to Cambridge to be ready for any brief that should need Russell's special knowledge of Ireland. He came with a glowing testimonial from his former schoolmaster, the Rev. Geoghegan, who wrote, 'I believe you to possess the very qualities requisite to form a good reporter'. As special journalism was as uncertain in its assignments as it was in its payments and Russell had no retainer from Delane, he took the position of a junior master at a school in Kensington. Instead of reading for his fellowship he spent his evenings making friends and exploring London with disastrous consequences. Russell at last concentrated on being called to the bar.

When he became redundant at his school, Russell took up freelance journalism but in 1842 Delane offered him a permanent post on the parliamentary staff of *The Times*. Over the course of the next few years he covered the Irish elections and unrest as well as the trial of Daniel O'Connell and his supporters. It was his report of the trial that should have been a 'first' for *The Times* and a feather in the cap for Russell; but being young and naïve, he failed to achieve either. Returning post-haste with the verdict of 'guilty', way ahead of every other newspaper, Russell arrived in London and took a cab to Printing House Square. At the door a seemingly idle bystander remarked that he was glad to hear that O'Connell was found guilty to which Russell obligingly replied, 'Oh yes! All guilty but on different counts.' There was some concern at *The Times*'s office the following morning when the *Morning Herald* reported the same news. Russell learned his first and most important lesson, that of keeping information to himself.

Russell continued his studies while writing for *The Times* in various capacities, including reports on the railways and from Parliament. In 1845, the *Daily News* appeared and made clear its intentions to crush all opposition. It offered good salaries to obtain the best men, causing an increase for all the reporters. Russell's talents had not gone unnoticed in the press world, and he was able to choose his paper. The *Morning Chronicle* paid nine guineas a week, two more than the *Daily News* and three more than *The Times*. Russell, as always short of money, had to switch his allegiance. After a session reporting Parliament, Russell returned to Ireland to get married and later reported for his new paper on the Irish land problems. In 1847, the *Morning Chronicle* reduced all salaries just at a time when Russell was ill. He found himself confronted with the ultimatum to get up and work or leave the paper. He chose the latter and, concealing this from his ailing wife, moved to

Crimean War: William Howard Russell of *The Times* (taken in the Crimea by Roger Fenton).

London. In depressing circumstances, without employment, Russell struggled as best he could with his illness while studying for his bar exams and writing the occasional article.

Relief came at last in the autumn of 1848, when Delane of *The Times* offered him a permanent post on the staff. He covered the State trials in Ireland in 1848. In 1850, Russell reported the Schleswig-Holstein War where he was slightly wounded and the following year covered the Great Exhibition of All Nations. In 1852 he was *The Times*'s reporter at the funeral of the Duke of Wellington. He was also called to the bar in this year but he went on to report numerous wars for *The Times* and later the *Daily Telegraph*. He was awarded five campaign medals and six foreign orders, before editing the *Army and Navy Gazette*. He was knighted in 1895, received the C.V.O. in 1902, and was an LL.D. of Trinity College, Dublin. He also held the post of Deputy-Lieutenant for the Tower Hamlets and was a Commander of the Legion d'Honneur. He died on 10 February 1907.

The Crimean War was fought for a variety of reasons, many of which concerned only politicians. The population looked for a more humane cause to champion: the quarrel between the Russians and Turks over the holy places and the Tsar's move towards the Danube with the publicized intention of protecting the thousands of Christians against the Islamic Turks inspired the nation. The newspapers were naturally the first to take sides and many, like *The Times*, were against any intervention. The cabinet was divided on the issue and even Queen Victoria was opposed to the war. There was no doubt that Turkey with its crumbling Empire was the 'sick man of Europe' and the Tsar had every intention of securing as much of the Balkans as he could. 'It will be a great misfortune,' he said, 'if one of these days Turkey should slip away from us . . . .' The British government feared that Russian territorial gain would menace the route to India and its borders, while France's grievance was more basic. But Napoleon III lost no time in siding with the British, with the intention of strengthening his position as Emperor and forcing the Tsar to treat him as an equal. On 5 October 1853, Turkey declared war on Russia and the following month defeated the Tsar's forces at Oltenitza, five days after the British fleet had entered the Bosphorus. At the end of November the Turkish fleet, advancing into the Black Sea, was destroyed and the so-called 'Massacre of Sinope' inflamed public opinion in France and Britain to such an extent that there could be no possible solution but war.

The mounting war fever was almost at breaking point as the population waited with bated breath for the politicians to make a move. On 14 February 1854 the first movements of troops were observed in London, and up and down the country scenes of troops preparing to embark were reported in the newspapers. Everywhere there was feverish activity amidst cheering crowds that gathered around the barrack gates. '... The whole multitude, military and civilian, patrician and plebians, proved that the heart of England was stung by the insulting bearing of the Tsar, and that the national spirit, goaded to war, met its prospects with unquailing energy.'

There was also feverish activity amongst the editors of the leading London newspapers as they appointed special correspondents or arranged with officers going to the seat of war to represent them. Delane immediately called Russell and informed him that an agreeable journey to Malta had been arranged and that excellent pay and allowances were to be given. Russell objected saying that he might lose his practice at the bar but Delane replied, 'There is not the least chance of that; you will be back at Easter, depend upon it, and you will have a pleasant trip.' Delane's forecast was far from what actually happened: to report on the war Russell spent nearly two years in the Crimea and the Near East.

On 19 February, Russell's friends gave him a farewell party and he journeyed down to Southampton on the 22nd to find that his troubles were about to start. His 'permission to sail' never arrived and he was calmly persuaded that the troop-ships were all crowded and he had best make his own way to Malta. Eventually, despite the hostile attitude of the authorities, Russell managed to get a passage to Malta. He soon realized that little preparation had been made to receive the troops who, '... left their floating prisons only to relinquish comforts to which they had the right, and to have to "rough it" on *terra firma* ... To speak the truth,' he continued, ' "somebody" is to blame for placing any of Her Majesty's forces in such a position that they had to endure some of the minor inconveniences of warfare before their time ...' They could get no candles, coal, or forage and painfully little accommodation. '... If the complaints to which I have alluded are well founded, serious blame rests in some quarter or other, and there is no use trying to evade it by shifting it from shoulder to shoulder ...'

War was declared on 28 March, Russell's thirty-fourth birthday, as British and French troops continued to pour into Malta. The declaration appeared in the *London Gazette.* 'It is with deep regret,' it started, 'that Her Majesty announces the failure of her anxious and protracted endeavours to preserve for her people and for Europe the blessings of peace.' The *Illustrated London News* of 1 April declared boldly:

> The Emperor of Russia, with a contemptuous insolence, unbecoming his position, though on all hands expected of him, has refused to return any answer to the demand made upon him by Great Britain and France to evacuate the Danubian principalities. . . . The struggle will immediately commence and the most ardent wish, the most sincere prayer of every honest man in the civilized world will be formed for the speedy downfall of the Imperial Barbarian . . .

Russell immediately started to make arrangements for a passage to Gallipoli and with difficulty secured a berth on the troop-ship *Golden Fleece.* To add to his troubles, however, as the ship sailed *The Times* correspondent found that the Maltese servant he had engaged and whose wages he had paid in advance had disappeared along with all his baggage.

When the British arrived at Gallipoli on 4 April, they found that the French forces had already landed and requisitioned all supplies along with the best accommodation. '. . . There was something depressing,' wrote Russell, 'in this silent reception of the first British army that ever landed on the shores of these Straits.' In Gallipoli, the preparations made by the French troops continued to show up the inadequacy and inefficiency of the British expeditionary force. Russell boldly denounced this inefficiency in his dispatch to *The Times:* 'The management is infamous,' he wrote, '. . . while these things go on, Sir George Brown only seems anxious about the men being clean shaved, their necks stiffened and their waist belts tight . . .' Russell's remarks, however, only made the authorities hostile towards him and the other correspondents:

> I run a good chance of starving . . . I have no tent nor can I get one without an order and even if I had one I doubt very much whether Sir George would allow me to pitch it within camp . . . I am now living in a pig-sty, without chair, table, stool or window glass . . . I live on eggs and brown bread, sour Tenedos wine, and onions and rice . . .

Crimean War: front page of *L'Illustration,* the French equivalent of the *Illustrated London News,* 21 July 1855. Note the duty stamps in the top right corner.

After a short stay Russell took the steamer to Constantinople and crossed to Scutari where the Guards were encamped. Russell's dispatches and Delane's hard-hitting leaders in *The Times* had not gone unnoticed in official circles and during June 1854 two minor 'victories' were achieved by *The Times*. On 9 June the government created the position of Secretary of State for War, the Duke of Newcastle becoming the first to hold the post. Russell's campaign against the soldiers' unsuitable uniform also came to fruition when tight neck stocks were abolished and he recorded that on the Queen's birthday, 'Her Majesty's Guards were actually commanded to parade WITHOUT STOCKS! . . . and never since they were formed did the regiments give three more ringing, thundering cheers.'

Russell was amazed at the rising cost of food and puzzled that, '. . . no Englishman had sufficient enterprise to go to Gallipoli with a stock of creature comforts . . .' Russell's tribulations and those of the other press correspondents were only just beginning. His companions included Thomas Chenery, *The Times*'s correspondent in Constantinople, Nicholas Woods of the *Morning Herald* and *Standard*,

43

*The birth of the modern war correspondent*

Crimean War: the Guard parading for the trenches (pencil sketch by H. J. W., 2 February 1855).

*The Guard parading for the Trenches*

J. A. Crowe and his fellow artists of the *Illustrated London News*. Any petty excuse to discourage these correspondents was employed by the authorities.

As the Russians moved into northern Bulgaria the allies decided to embark for Varna. The French and British newspapers now started to squabble over which nation could rightly claim the praise for the plans for landing. The Paris newspaper *Moniteur* attributed them to the genius of the Emperor himself while the *United Service Gazette* chose to lay this brilliant strategic move at the feet of Major-General MacIntosh, who advocated landing at Gallipoli, then Varna, and eventually south of Sebastopol in the Crimea. Early in June, however, preparations were made to embark for the new destination and Russell for one was glad to leave the stinking town of Scutari:

> . . . In the stagnant waters which ripple . . . on the shore there float all forms of nastiness and corruption . . . The smell from the shore was noisome . . . the fringe of buoyant cats, dogs, birds, straw, sticks, in fact all sorts of abominable flotsam and jetsam, bob about on the pebbles.

The slaughter-houses for the cattle which provided meat for the troops did nothing to improve matters as they were erected on the shore and the offal was thrown into the water.

Delane had now realized Russell's almost untenable position and used his influence and that of *The Times* at Horse Guards to obtain permission for his correspondents to draw rations as required and to accompany the army. The officers in the field, although bowing to superior command, were none too pleased, having already had a taste of Russell's pen when copies of *The Times* arrived in camp.

At Varna, however, the organization was even more confused and Russell wrote to Delane that:

> I have just been informed on good authority that Lord Raglan has determined not to recognize the Press in any way, or to give them rations or assistance and worse of all, it is probable that he will forbid our accompanying the troops.

Varna was probably more unhygienic than Scutari with more slaughter-houses and plagues of red ants and terrible 'maneating flies'. The management of the British army grew worse and Russell continued to denounce as hard as he could what he considered to be crass in-efficiency. He wrote in a dispatch, 'Where is the English Post Office? No one knows. Where does the English General live? No one knows. Where is the hospital to carry a sick soldier? No one knows . . .' But Russell was not the only correspondent to see the flaws in the army widening into large cracks. Nicholas Woods of the London *Morning Herald* and *Standard* described the poor quality of the shells issued to the Black Sea fleet. Some he alleged were over twenty-five years old and some were manufactured even before the Battle of Waterloo and 'not ten per cent of which exploded'.

The disease which was to threaten the armies of the expedition was poised to strike. Russell noted, 'Diarrhoea broke out in the camp soon after my arrival and continued to haunt us all during the summer.' But worse was to come. By July cholera had broken out in the French camp and it was not long before this fatal disease invaded the British lines. On 20 July Russell wrote, 'Up to this time there had been no case of cholera in the Light Division but early on Sunday morning, 23rd, it broke out with the same extraordinary violence and fatal effects . . .' Russell visited the hospital and recoiled at the primitive arrangements which allowed men with fever and other disorders to be put in with men who had cholera. It was not, Russell noted, due to the poor efforts on the part of the medical personnel, but to the fact that there were too few of them.

Of all the correspondents, Russell presented the most motley picture when it came to dress. He wore a commissariat officer's cap with gold lace band, a rifleman's patrol jacket, cord breeches, boots and spurs and in these clothes he was often being mistaken by the French for a British officer. Like the brilliant editor that he was Delane had made thorough arrangements to cover the war. Thomas Chenery, later to succeed Delane as editor but never to achieve his brilliance, was in Constantinople while a young officer of the East India Company's army, Charles Nasmyth, was already in Silistria. When at last news came that the army would invade the Crimea, William Henry Stowe, later to act as almoner for *The Times*'s fund, would move to Varna. Other newspapers had made similar postings to give their readers as wide a view as possible of the war both in the East and the Baltic.

By August, slackness and boredom, disease, death, and large-scale drunkenness were prevalent in the army. On 10 August, a great fire broke out in Varna destroying nearly a quarter of the town. While it might have been a blessing in disguise, as it destroyed many of the cholera-plagued houses, it was disastrous for the British army. The loss

Crimean War: the Russian attack on the heights above Sebastopol, 26 October 1854 (water-colour by J. A. Crowe)

Crimean War: group of the 47th Regiment in winter dress (photograph by Roger Fenton).

of 19,000 pairs of boots was soon to be regretted. The fleet too now suffered from cholera and the admirals put out to sea in an effort to escape the ravages of the disease. Too late it was discovered that what had appeared to be an adequate camp site was already known to the Turks as the Valley of Death:

> The . . . meadows nurtured the fever [wrote Russell], the ague, dysentery and pestilence in their bosom — the lake and the stream exhaled death, and at night fat unctuous vapours rose . . . from the valley and crept in the dark and stole into the tent of the sleeper and wrapped him in their deadly embrace.

The army was visibly weakened, a fact that the correspondents stressed in their dispatches. The situation was epitomized by the Guards, the élite troops, who were unable to carry their own packs. In the harbour, '. . . dead bodies rose from the bottom . . . and bobbed grimly around in the water . . . or drifted past the sickened gazers on board the ships — all buoyant, bolt upright and hideous in the sun'.

It can be seen that Russell was not afraid to write about what he saw and this new style of reporting had the wholehearted backing of Delane and *The Times*. Originally *The Times* had been against the fever of war and had even been accused of being the 'Russian organ of Printing House Square'. But once the war was declared, *The Times* was pressing for a successful conclusion. Even before a shot had been fired, Russell and other correspondents felt ostracized by the authorities who tended to view all newspapermen in the same light even though perhaps only Nicholas Woods of the *Morning Herald* and *Standard* approached anything like Russell's level of journalism. Mr. Duncan, 'the well known correspondent of a London Paper' at Turkish headquarters during 1854 had not found any hostility towards the press, but then the Turkish army was oblivious to any adverse comment by foreigners.

Eventually the army moved from Varna and landed in the Crimea at Kalamita Bay and even here the usual inefficiency and lack of preparedness was still evident. Russell observed the landing from on board the *City of London*. He saw the staff and skirmishers land and witnessed the first shots fired by the Russian Cossack cavalry. Once on shore Russell found the scene of confusion amongst the British 'curious, exciting but not exhilarating'. French newspapers too followed the movements of the Imperial army avidly and landed with the

Crimean War: J. A. Crowe inspecting the field after the battle of Inkerman.

troops at Kalamita Bay, but they found much tighter restrictions on their reporting and strict censorship of their dispatches. *L'Illustration Journal Universel*, equivalent to the *Illustrated London News*, had a number of artists and correspondents in the field, the two foremost being A. Dulong and Durand-Brager. Other newspapermen included F. Quesnoy and a correspondent named Roussel. Much of the French material which appeared in the press was usually taken from dispatches, received, edited, censored, and then handed out by the *'Ministre de la Marine'* or the *'Ministre de la Guerre'*. Even when reporting the landings the French correspondents were smugly proud of their army's and navy's efficiency when compared with their allies. *'Les Francais vont que leur marine est plus expedative que la marine des Anglais.'* [The French can see that their navy is more efficient than that of the English.]

Russell spent the first night on shore, being unable to get back on board ship, and he found conditions dreadful. The British were without tents, whereas the French and Turks had thoughtfully brought and pitched theirs. Even the highest-ranking officers suffered the same privation as their men. Sir George Brown slept under a wagon and the Duke of Cambridge made himself as comfortable as possible under a gun carriage.

> Few of those who were with the expedition [wrote Russell],
> will forget the night of the 14th September. Seldom or never
> were 27,000 Englishmen more miserable . . . No tents had
> been sent on shore . . . the showers increased about midnight
> and early in the morning dew in drenching sheets . . .
> pierced through the blankets and great coats.

This vivid style of journalism was to be the hallmark of all Russell's
war correspondence. His dispatches were read eagerly at home with
a sense of despair: the army which had gone to war amidst such
gaiety was now suffering untold hardships because of a totally archaic
and outdated military system. The detailed descriptive passages of
correspondents such as Russell and Woods inflamed popular opinion
against the government who, deny as hard as it liked, could not ignore
the obvious truth. While Russell was the first of 'modern' war correspondents to see that inefficiency and suffering were as newsworthy
as splendid victories, he was also the first to realize that his profession
wielded immense power. He felt duty bound to place blame where
blame was due and to report the facts and not what the authorities
wanted known to the British public. '. . . Amidst the filth and starvation, and deadly stagnation of the camp,' he declared, 'I did not go
about "babbling of green fields".'

On 17 September, the allied armies attempted to sort themselves
out and marched towards the River Alma where 15,000 Russian troops
were reported to have assembled. The march towards the river was
handled little better than the rest of the campaign to date. At first it
progressed well, the regiments marching to their bands with colours
flying, but soon a strange and eerie silence fell on the troops and
'. . . many sick men fell out and were carried to the rear. It was a pitiful
sight — a sad contrast to the magnificent appearance of the army in
front'. An officer of the 20th related that, 'Many of our men fell down
in the ranks, attacked by cholera . . . or from becoming faint and
exhausted for want of water . . .' Suddenly the Russians were sighted
and their artillery opened fire with a 'spirt of white smoke' which 'rose
out of a gap and round shot pitched close to my horse', wrote Russell,
'and covered me with dirt, tore over the column of our cavalry behind
and rolled away between the ranks of riflemen in the rear . . .' That
night, the army camped and Russell 'was lucky enough to get lodging
on the ground beside a kindly colonel, who was fortunate enough to
have . . . a bit of bread and biscuit to spare . . .'

The following morning the troops rose exhausted for the most part but some never rose at all. Russell, and the other newsmen were in a quandary as to where to place themselves best to observe the events and also doubted whether they would be allowed near the front line:

> I never was in a more unpleasant position. Everyone else on
> the field had some *raison d'être*, I had none. They were
> on recognized business. It could scarcely be a recognized or
> legitimate business for any man to ride in front of an army
> that he might be able to write an account of a battle for a
> newspaper.

Russell attached himself to the large group of staff and other officers that followed Lord Raglan. 'Mr. Russell, *The Times*'s correspondent, and other literary gentlemen of note [this included the Crimean historian Kinglake],' wrote Nolan in his *History of the War against Russia* (1857), 'also shared the dangers of the field, as military amateurs, or in the performance of their duty as correspondents to the Press.'

The 'duty', however, of the war correspondents was more difficult than can be imagined. It was just not enough to have a good turn of phrase or to write what one saw as this was bound to be a limited view of the general action. After the troops had crossed the Alma at great loss and had driven off the Russians, Russell was faced with this problem:

> How was I to describe what I had not seen? Where learn the
> facts for which they were waiting at home? My eyes swam as
> I tried to make notes of what I heard. I was worn out with
> excitement, fatigue and want of food. I had been more than
> ten hours in the saddle . . . My head throbbed, my heart beat
> as though it would burst. I suppose I was unnerved by want
> of food and rest, but I was so much overcome by what I
> saw that I could not remain where the fight had been closest
> and deadliest. I longed to get away from it . . . It was now
> that the weight of the task I had accepted fell on my soul
> like lead.

Russell was in no state to write his account and slept badly that night in an overcrowded and stuffy tent. The following morning, in spite of personal fatigue and exhaustion, a dispatch had to be written and Russell sat on a parapet and began his narrative. Some Engineer officers, seeing his discomfort, made a makeshift table from a plank

Crimean War: the battle of Inkerman, 20 October 1854 (watercolour by J. A. Crowe).

Crimean War: interior of the Malakoff, 9 September 1855 (watercolour by J. A. Crowe).

and barrels and, using the yellow pages of a Russian account book which someone had picked up, Russell set down his impressions. The first account of the battle never reached *The Times* and Russell was probably thankful for it, as later in the day he set out to inspect the battlefield and acquired a lot of new information. As a good correspondent, Russell included in his second narrative the ideal ingredients for a war reporter's dispatch: a brief and detailed description of the terrain and a flowing narrative of the principal events. The aftermath of the battle was what affected Russell most as he witnessed:

> ... The litters borne in from all quarters hour after hour — to watch the working parties as they wandered about the plain turning down the blankets which had been stretched over the wounded, to behold if they were yet alive, or were food for the worms ... Our men were sent to the sea three miles distant on jolting arabas or tedious litters. The French had well-appointed covered hospital vans ...

The wounded and dead were found for days after and on 22 September Russell recorded that he:

> ... found a corpse of a Russian outside the tent ... It was not there when we retired, so the poor wretched creature, who had probably been wandering about without food upon the hills ever since the battle, must have crawled down towards our fires and there expired ...

Russell and other correspondents noted grimly that cholera was still with the army when it marched on 23 September on the famous 'flank march' around Sebastopol to the small port of Balaclava.

The British and French installed themselves before the fortress of Sebastopol and took possession of Balaclava as their port of supply which Russell described as more like a '... little pond, closely compressed by the sides of high rocky mountains ...' While the Allied generals bickered amongst themselves as to the best plan of attack, assault or siege, the armies waited and suffered on the bleak heights above the port.

Public indignation had been roused at home not only by Russell's descriptive dispatches but even more by Thomas Chenery's descriptions of the hospital at Scutari and the arrival of the hospital ships bringing the wounded, the sick and the dying from Alma. Besides the surgeons, who were painfully few, the only orderlies were Chelsea pensioners organized into the Hospital Conveyance Corps.

Whether it was a scheme for saving money by utilizing the poor old men [complained Chenery] or shortening the duration of their lives and pensions it is difficult to say but they have been found in practice rather to require nurses themselves than to be able to nurse others . . . A few of the wounded [he continued scathingly] were well enough to walk and crept along, supported by a comrade . . . On many the marks of approaching death were set . . .

Chenery inspected the hospital wards and recoiled at the inadequate arrangements:

It is with feelings of surprise and anger that the public will learn that no sufficient preparations have been made for the care of the wounded. Not only are there not sufficient surgeons . . . no dressers and nurses . . . but what will be said when it is known that there is not even linen to make bandages . . . Not only are the men kept, in some cases, for a week without the hand of a medical man coming near their wounds — not only are they left to expire in agony . . . but now they are placed in the spacious building (removed from the hospital ships), it is found that the commonest appliances of a workhouse sick ward are wanting and that men must die through the medical staff of the British army having forgotten that old rags are necessary for dressing wounds . . .

At home Delane and other editors supported the attacks in their leaders denouncing those who sat by their firesides reading the paper and considering the war at a distance as an amusing spectacle. Delane's leading articles of the beginning of October demanded action from a country for the most part smug and complacent in its attitudes. Delane suggested that a fund might be set up and that a few thousand pounds would go far to alleviate the suffering and misery caused by an incompetent administration. The response was overwhelming and the famous *Times* Fund collected well over £20,000 during the last three months of 1854. There was also a more lasting result of *The Times*'s campaign. The Minister at War (as opposed to the Minister for War), Sidney Herbert, accepted the offer of a female nurse to organize a staff for the hospitals. Her name was Florence Nightingale. She was appointed 'Superintendent of the Female Nursing Establishment of the English General Hospitals in Turkey', a grandiose title which unfortunately existed on paper only. She sailed with thirty-eight companions for Scutari on 21 October. Another offer came from Soyer, the famous chef of the Reform Club, who went to the Crimea to improve the cooking of the army's rations.

Four days previously, the Allied bombardment of the Russian fortress of Sebastopol had started, witnessed by the army and the press. Russell's notes, later developed into a forceful dispatch in his usual style, gave a running commentary of events. At 8.40 a French magazine exploded, followed by another at 1.25 much to Russian delight; but at 1.40 a huge explosion rocked the centre of Sebastopol and at 2.25 the powder magazine in the Russian Redan fort was hit with disastrous results. At 3.30 loose powder in a Royal Navy battery was ignited by a Russian shell but five minutes later a British shell exploded the magazine inside the Russian Round fort. By dusk the fire had petered out and when night fell all was silent. The British and French had lost about 300 men, killed or wounded, and a number of guns, while the Russian loss, according to Russell who had the information from a deserter, was over 3,000 with the town and defences in a dreadful state. The Russian *St. Petersburg Journal*, however, commenting on Prince Menschikoff's dispatch, stated that only a few Russian guns were lost and that not only were the French silenced completely but the British had only two guns in position capable of firing.

The bombardment continued for the following two days and the correspondents tried in their own differing ways to write an individual account of the rather boring action. The *Morning Chronicle* man wrote that the men '. . . looked upon the whole firing as a spectacle got up for the special amusement, and expressed their approbation or disapproval according to the merits of the case'. The *Morning Post* correspondent, a young officer in the Commissariat, described by Russell as 'a purveyor's clerk named Henty', noted the reconnoitring of the Engineer officers who he considered far too '*cock-hatty*' when compared with the French who in the disguise of Zouaves, hopelessly drunk, staggered towards the town. When fired at they immediately fled with their sketches and information. 'The correspondents of our London morning papers,' wrote E. Nolan in his history of the war, 'not only communicated intelligence which but for them had never reached the British public but gave opinions in reference to military facts and probabilities . . .' It was above all the latter statement that the government and Lord Raglan were trying to discourage. The *Morning Herald* correspondent, Nicholas Woods, 'who had obtained a just celebrity for his accuracy', fully described Sir Colin Campbell's precautions against a Russian night attack, much to the annoyance of the staff.

Crimean War: a siege train at Camp Sebastopol. Covering gun wheels with sheepskin to prevent noise, in preparation to go to the trenches (watercolour by J. A. Crowe, war artist for the *Illustrated London News*).

On 25 October, the whole front came alive as the Russians sallied forth to engage the Allies. The immortal battle of Balaclava had commenced under the watchful eyes of the generals and war correspondents alike. The Russian onslaught caught the Allies by surprise and the redoubts manned by the Turks fell to the advancing hordes. There seemed nothing between the Russians and Balaclava now but the 92nd Highlanders.

> The Cavalry which have been pursuing the Turks on the right [Russell wrote afterwards] are coming up to the ridge beneath us . . . The Heavy Brigade in advance is drawn up in two lines . . . The Light Brigade is on their left in two lines also.
>
> The silence is oppressive; between the cannon bursts one can hear the champing of bits and the clink of sabres in the valley below.

The Russians on their left draw breath for a moment, and
then in one grand line dash at the Highlanders. The ground flies
beneath their horses' feet; gathering speed at every stride, they
dash on towards that thin red streak topped with a line of steel.

After a deadly volley the Russians were repulsed according to Russell,
although Woods's account states that the Russian cavalry did not even
close up enough on the Highlanders for their volley to be effective,
but the day was far from over and other actions were to attract the
attention of the reporters.

Too much has been written about the charge of the Heavy and Light
Brigade on this fateful day to repeat it here and the reports of the
correspondents must only add to the valour and glory of the most
useless cavalry charge in the history of the British army. About the
charge of the Light Brigade, Russell wrote pathetically that, 'The
whole action had taken less than half an hour — a little ground was
won, a little was lost.' The *Morning Chronicle* correspondent described
the aftermath:

> The disaster, of which the mere shadow darkened so many a
> household among us, is not much less than the annihilation
> of the light cavalry brigade. Had there been the smallest use
> in the movement . . . or part of any plan whatever, we should
> endeavour to bear this sad loss . . . Even accident would have
> made it more tolerable. But it was a mere mistake . . .

In the early morning mists of 5 November the Russians attacked
again and took the Allies by surprise on the Inkerman ridge. The battle
was one of isolated combats, neither group of men or regiment
knowing where its neighbour was or what it was doing. 'No one,'
wrote Russell on that evening, 'however placed, could have witnessed
even a small portion of the doings of this eventful day, for vapours,
fog and drizzling mist obscured the ground where the struggle took
place . . .' However, Russell was more fortunate than some other newspapermen as *The Times* had dispatched an additional correspondent to
help him, Colonel Eber, a Hungarian emigré who had already represented *The Times* in Turkey at the outbreak of the war and later in
Eupatoria.

Winter was fast drawing in and the state of the army was worsening
by the day as the mud deepened and mismanagement increased. Russell
and other newsmen described the terrible conditions under which the

troops survived and the awful state of their uniforms which had now become mere tattered and patched rags. During November the rain fell incessantly, turning the camp and the road to Balaclava into a sea of mud. A hurricane devastated the Allied camp, and sank a number of ships containing much needed clothing and supplies. Russell and other correspondents, especially the '. . . gentlemen of candour and ability' of the *Daily News* and Nicholas Woods of the *Morning Herald* blamed Lord Raglan for the tattered state of the army. On 8 November Russell had confided in Delane that:

> I am convinced from what I see that Lord Raglan is utterly incompetent to lead an army through any arduous task . . . But the most serious disadvantage under which he labours is that he does not go amongst the troops. He does not visit the camp, he does not cheer them and speak to them . . .

But *The Times* did not confine its attacks to Lord Raglan and Delane 'opened fire' on the Aberdeen ministry and the archaic military system. 'There was,' wrote an army chaplain, 'great dissatisfaction about the Commander . . . there is a severe storm brewing for him. S. G. Osborne is going to lay it bare in *The Times*.' The Rev. Sidney Godolphine Osborne was not only one of Florence Nightingale's most ardent supporters but also a *Times* special commissioner. At first Lord Raglan remained indifferent to the newspaper's attacks but later the same writer recorded that 'Lord Raglan has felt the article in *The Times*, but the officers say it is not severe'. The result of the campaign waged by the greater London daily newspapers was the eventual downfall of the Aberdeen administration and a shake-up in the organization of the army. Even the Duke of Newcastle when he visited the Crimea in 1855 remarked to Russell, 'It was you who turned out the government, Mr. Russell'.

Journalists with this measure of popular appeal and power even over governments were bound to come under attack for their behaviour, and their reports. Lord Raglan had referred to the Duke of Newcastle on 13 November 1854 the information contained in a *Times* dispatch. The Duke of Newcastle immediately wrote to Delane informing him that:

> . . . Many complaints have reached me from the army of the advantage conferred upon the enemy by the publication of intelligence from the Seat of War, not only letters from correspondents of the English newspapers, but in letters

written by officers to their friends at home in the spirit of
confidential intimacy, and which those friends send to
newspapers . . . without consideration of the evil consequences
to the army, and the public interest.

Newcastle appealed to Delane's patriotism to ensure a 'rigid supervision
of such letters and an endeavour to prevent the mischief of which
Lord Raglan so reasonably complains'.

Lord Raglan had commented on the leakage of information to the
Russians through the press reports:

. . . the enemy need spend nothing under the heading Secret
Service as I am doubtful whether a British army can long be
maintained in presence of a powerful enemy, that enemy
having at its command through the English press and from
London to his Headquarters by telegraph, every detail that
can be required of its number, conditions and equipment
of his opponent's force.

He urged the Deputy Adjutant-General to call a meeting of all the press
correspondents and inform them of '. . . the inconvenience of their
writings and the need for greater prudence in the future'.

Russell had on more than one occasion offered his dispatches for
censorship at headquarters but his offer was never accepted. He was
later to refute the charges of giving away information through his
dispatches and even the Russians after the war admitted that they did
not learn anything from the London papers that they did not already
know. The Tsar was meant to have remarked that he had no need of
spies, '. . . We have *The Times*', adding that, 'the best means of communicating the outcome of events from Sebastopol to Moscow was via
London', which seems to indicate the slowness of communication in
Russia at the time.

Even so, there was often open hostility to Russell and the other
newsmen. 'That blackguard Mr. Russell ought to be hung,' wrote an
officer of the 7th Fusiliers; 'I trust the army will lynch the *Times* correspondent when they read his letter of yesterday,' wrote Sidney Herbert.

I don't know how it is [ wrote Colonel Somerset Clathorpe ]
but the reporters of the English journals have made themselves
very unpopular. They appear to try and find fault wherever
they can, and throw as much blame and contempt on the
English authorities as if their object was to bring the British
army into disrepute with our allies.

Captain Clifford described Russell as:

> . . . a vulgar low Irishman . . . but he has the gift of the gab,
> uses his pen as well as his tongue, sings a good song, drinks
> anyone's brandy and water, and smokes as many cigars as
> foolish young officers will let him, and he is looked upon by
> most in camp as a Jolly Good Fellow. He is just the sort to
> get information, particularly out of the youngsters. And
> I assure you more than one 'Nob' has thought best to give
> him a shake of the hand rather than the cold shoulder *en
> passant*, for [he] is rather an awkward gentleman to be on
> bad terms with . . .

Information given in the newspapers which arrived in camp often gave
rise to a certain hostility towards the correspondents: a Fusilier officer
remarked that the Russians had ceased shooting at his camp until
Russell wrote that the cannon balls were reaching the tents; he
sarcastically added that Russell takes, '. . . precious care to live about
a mile out of range'. But the papers also had their uses as in other
campaigns. An officer noted that, 'The interiors of our huts were
usually papered with pages of *Punch* and the *Illustrated London News*,
which served to double purpose of excluding the wind which whistled
through the crevices of the boards, and of giving a more cheerful look
to the apartment.'

The attacks on organization in the army and Lord Raglan in particular continued but sometimes Russell was on the receiving end. He
complained to Delane that one newspaper had printed that he fled

Crimean War: 'The Welcome Arrival' (oil painting by Luard). The illustration shows the
officers' hut papered with pages from *Punch* and the *Illustrated London News*.

Crimean War: the ruins of Sebastopol (part of a panoramic photograph by James Robertson).

from Devna on the outbreak of cholera. Russell had written to the editor of the offending paper that, 'I will trounce his lying correspondent within an inch of his life if I ever catch him . . .'

The war dragged on through the severe winter of 1854-5 which caused so much hardship, death, and pain. Sebastopol was still not taken and resisted the bombardments. In May 1856 Russell accompanied the expedition to Kertch where he witnessed wanton destruction by the troops. W. H. Stowe, an almoner of *The Times* Fund, took over the job of sending dispatches during his absence. In June, Russell returned to find Stowe dying of cholera in a hut, having been refused admission to the military hospital for which *The Times* Fund had done so much. He was moved to Balaclava but too late. Russell, in a frenzy of despair, wrote to Delane and *The Times* announced this martyrdom to its readers adding that it would not risk another life where 'British inhumanity is to be encountered'.

The eventual end of the Crimean War or perhaps its slow fizzling out is well known history. In December 1855, Russell was allowed home to England for a while and was replaced by F. Hardman who found little but the inactivity of the camp to write about. Russell returned to the Crimea for the last time to watch and write about the withdrawal of the troops, his last words being from Alma: 'And so I take leave of this little river, which shall henceforth be celebrated in history to the end of time.'

It is easy to forget the other newspaper correspondents who covered the war, both military and civilian, as Russell's name has ever since been associated with the Crimea. His name is best remembered not only because of the quality of his writings and his talent as a skilled journalist but also due to the powerful influence of his newspaper, *The Times.* S. T. Sheppard, in an article in the *United Service Magazine* of March 1907, summed up Russell when he said that '...his work is not to be measured by quantity, but by quality — and it was the best'. His press colleagues were certainly, perhaps with the exception of Nicholas Woods, less energetic and certainly less observant than Russell and he did not entertain a very high opinion of most of them and their seeming indifference to their job. More than once he had written to Delane about them:

> The *Morning Post* 'correspondent' lives on board the *Caradoc* and comes on shore now and then after a battle to view the ground. The *Daily News* correspondent lives on board another ship and never I believe comes on shore at all . . . The *Daily News* man lives on board ship, or did so till lately and the *Chronicle* man I know not. The *Morning Advertiser* is represented, I understand, by a Mr. Keane, who chiefly passes his time in preparing cooling drinks.

It was hardly an encouraging opinion of what would not be considered an essential profession to accompany any army in action, but Russell had established a precedent for reporting which would be followed by many others during the years that followed. The Prince Consort had stooped to describe Russell as a 'miserable scribbler' but no newspaper reader could or would be allowed to forget the Crimea now that the modern war correspondent had come into being . . .

# 2

# The 'newly invented curse to armies'

## (1857–70)

*. . . sent out when a war begins to minister to the blind brutal British public's bestial thirst for blood. They have no arenas now, but they must have special correspondents.*
Rudyard Kipling

The army hardly had time to carry out its reforms and the country still remembered the horrors of the Crimean War, which had claimed tens of thousands of lives for the most part from disease and neglect, when in June 1857 reports filtered through to the London newspapers of the mutiny of the native regiments of the Bengal army at Meerut. There had been unrest in the Bengal army since February when the new Enfield rifle was issued with its greased cartridges. Rumours were spread in the bazaars and brothels that the British intended to destroy the caste system and convert the sepoys to Christianity and had greased the new cartridges with a mixture of pig and cow fat. These cartridges had to be bitten before being poured down the muzzle of the rifle. The cow was sacred to the Hindus and the pig unclean to the Muslims and so those who listened to the prophecy that the British rule would last for a hundred years after the battle of Plassey in 1757 were able to spread alarm among sepoys of both faiths. The mutiny of the 19th Native Infantry in February and the disbandment of the regiment the following month did little to stir the authorities who considered this to be a totally isolated incident. In London, the complacent Victorians, if a little shattered by the events of the Crimean War, either looked

Indian Mutiny: the hanging of mutineers (photograph by Felice Beato who, with James Robertson, broadened the use of war photography).

Indian Mutiny: blowing mutinous sepoys from the guns.

upon the omens with disbelief or ignored them. Even the news of the massacre and mutiny at Meerut was treated with seemingly unruffled concern by the newspapers: the *Illustrated London News* blamed the incident, which they were sure was over, on Russian intervention as it was common knowledge that the Tsar had been plotting the destruction of British India for many years. *The Times*, however, dismissed the idea of a Russian plot and stated that the unrest lay solely with the army. They thought the remedy was to disband all native troops and to rule the sub-continent with the Queen's soldiers.

But even as the newspapers thundered away with their own explanations and points of view, events in India had gone too far to stop. Delhi was already in the hands of the mutineers and every day rebellious sepoys marched to join their comrades. British officers and civilians, women and children had been slaughtered and even if some of the sepoys had so wished it, no-one could just forget what had happened. The editors of the London papers soon anticipated the likely turn of events and made arrangements for full coverage. Most of them possessed correspondents in Calcutta and Bombay who were busy sending news as and when they could get any information from the outlying stations, but special correspondents would have to be sent or other arrangements made. Delane of *The Times* naturally chose William Russell, who, ten days after his return from the Crimea, had left to cover the coronation of Tsar Alexander II. On his return he had conducted a successful lecture tour. In November he was ordered to India but managed to delay his departure until 26 December 1857. While the newspapers made their arrangement and commented on stale news, Lucknow was besieged by the rebels and the British troops had encamped and begun siege operations against Delhi. Conjecture was the main ingredient for the leader writer because news and letters took so long to arrive in London. *The Times* of 31 August 1857 could only report news dispatched up to 30 July from Bombay and up to 20 July from Calcutta. The same edition reported on page six the massacre of the civilians at Cawnpore, the 'intelligence being furnished by [the] Government'.

While the dreadful news affected many people, the English were still divided as to the cause of the rebellion. Newspapers took their stands and amplified their views in the leader articles. 'We have not won the reverence due to ourselves as a nobler race', commented *The Times* while the *Illustrated London News* denounced the British rule as being too soft. 'India is not our colony but our conquest, and as a conquest we must treat it, if we hope to retain it.' Confidently *The Times* announced on 31 August 1857, '... the van of the avenging host has appeared. Two thousand British bayonets — the first wave of that approaching tide which is to roll over these devoted plains — have at length flashed in the faces of the murderers ...'

Russell's terms of reference, like those of other special correspondents leaving England, were to inquire into and report on the atrocities and the progress of the various field forces in stamping out the mutiny. Troops too were leaving England for India with remarkable rapidity, the government not wishing an early repeat of the Crimean disaster. On board ship Russell noted in his diary the differing opinions of his companions about the Indians and the solution to the problem. Prophetically he wrote:

> It would seem then if these views are right, that the Anglo-Saxons ... in India must either abate their strong *natural* feelings against the coloured race ... or look forward to the day, not far distant, when indulgence of their passions will render the Government of India too costly a luxury for the English people.

The press correspondents found that, except among certain generals and higher-ranking officers, they were still as unpopular as they had been during the Crimea. 'Sundry camp scribblers', was how Lieutenant de Bois Lukis of the 64th Regiment described them in a letter to the *Illustrated London News* while some officers ordered their men not to have any conversations at all with 'representatives of the press' on whatever subject.

On landing, Russell met Lord Canning, the Governor-General, who furnished him with a letter to Sir Colin Campbell at Cawnpore. Sir Colin, in his brisk Scottish manner, immediately made clear to Russell the conduct he expected of the press:

> Now Mr. Russell, I'll be candid with you [he said]. We shall make a compact. You shall know everything that is going on. You shall know all my reports and get any information that I have myself, on the condition that you do not mention it in camp or let it be known in any way, except in your letters to England.

Russell agreed. Sir Colin's 'helpfulness' was by no means a benevolent gesture, as it was common knowledge that the tough Scot was anxious

Indian Mutiny: William Russell, in checked coat, looking on at the sacking of the Kaiser Bagh, March 1858.

Indian Mutiny: the relief of Lucknow and triumphant meeting of Havelock, Outram and Sir Colin Campbell (key to the painting by T. Johns Barker from sketches made on the spot by Egron Lundgreen).

Indian Mutiny: the action at Bareilly (pen and ink drawing by Major Crealock, a frequent contributor to the *Illustrated London News*).

to 'stand well with public opinion at home, and not at all anxious to fall out with the press,' now more than ever a powerful political and social instrument.

It was naturally impossible for any one correspondent to see even a single action in its entirety and the nature of the Indian Mutiny was such that the general action was not even confined to one area. At home the London editors did not lack information and strove to present a coherent account of what was happening by using not only the reports of their special correspondents but also letters from combatants and civil servants in India, combined with the official dispatches released to the press as well as local Indian papers.

Other newspapers too had their correspondents or had made suitable arrangements for the receipt of information. The *Illustrated London News* did not at first have a special correspondent on hand and had to rely for their 'Mutiny in India' column on private letters, extracts from the local Indian papers such as the *Calcutta Englishman*, *Lahore Chronicle*, *Friend of India*, and *Bombay Telegraph* and *Courier* as well as official telegrams to the War and India Offices, '. . . placed at the disposal of the press'. Many officers sent back sketches to the *Illustrated London News*, one of the most prolific being John H. Sylvester, a medical officer of Probyn's Horse. During the siege of Delhi, Ingram secured the services of an officer of the 9th Lancers, 'who, wounded by round shot' the newspaper boasted, 'and unable to hunt "Pandies", employed himself with sketching'. (Mutineers were often referred to as 'pandies' after Mangle Pande, a sepoy of the 34th Native Infantry at Barrackpore who, half-demented with drugs, killed two British officers while the rest of the regiment stood silently watching. Mangle Pande was hanged on 8 April 1857 and from then on mutineers were often referred to by the British as 'pandies'.)

One lesson learned by the authorities during the Crimea, that of not under-estimating the power and influence of the press, was applied in India. In 1857 five Indian newspapers, amongst them the *Hurkaru*, the oldest Calcutta newspaper, were suppressed. The *Friend of India*, '. . . the first', as it announced, 'to feel the iron heel of despotic and irresponsible authority' had its licence restored after six days.

Russell followed the campaign before Lucknow and in April set out with the force under Sir Colin Campbell to reconquer Rohilkand.

> I can compare a column on the march to nothing handy to mind [wrote Russell] except a block of omnibuses in Fleet Street, when the footpaths are thronged with foot passengers, and the interstices of the larger vehicles gouted in with Hansoms and cabs. The column is but a small, compact, orderly body; but on each side of it, and behind it miles back, are elephants, camels and horses enough for a grand army.

Russell must have indeed felt pleased with his efforts when he received letters from Delane and MacDonald of *The Times*. Delane congratulated him:

... on the perfect success with which you have sustained your fame. I feel myself, and hear everybody saying, that we are at last beginning to learn something about India ...

MacDonald assured Russell that:

> ... your work has given entire satisfaction here, and that we consider you have amply sustained your old supremacy over all competitors. Some of the electric letters [this referred to telegraphed dispatches] were astonishingly vivid; and so far from joining in the outcry against the wire as unfavourable to literary effect, my decided conviction now is that in competent hands it may be made to yield the most brilliant results.

Commenting on the expense of telegrams, MacDonald continued that '... it would never have done for us to have been content with moving neck and neck with the penny papers'.

The dispatches sent by Russell and other correspondents not only detailed the events blow by blow but gave the average reader in England an account of life in India and opened up to them a completely new world which had hitherto been merely a name. Russell explained the caste system and the organization of the numerous camp followers and their respective duties. Although the sultry sweltering heat of the sun could melt a patent leather head-dress peak in minutes, there were few of the discomforts which Russell had experienced in the Crimea. The vast entourage of camp followers saw to every need, pitched tents, struck camp, and generally ministered to the well-being of troops and correspondents alike. In his letter to *The Times*, published 6 May 1858, Russell described the extraordinary riches encountered on entering the Kaiser Bagh after Lucknow and the looting and pillaging of the troops. 'It was a great drawback to have a conscience under such circumstances,' reported Russell, '... a greater not to have a penny in one's pocket.' Delane replied to Russell and added in his letter, 'Pray draw £10 on my account and carry it all in gold about you when you next accompany a storming party. To think that you got nothing out of the Kaiser Bagh for the want of a few rupees...'

At the end of April 1858 Russell with Sir Colin Campbell's force crossed the Ganges into Rohilkand, where he was seriously injured as a result of being kicked by a horse. He was in such pain that he had to be carried in a litter and witnessed and wrote his dispatch on the Battle of Bareilly on 5 May from this strange conveyance. After

Indian Mutiny: 'How we carried on the correspondence of the Indian Horse Guards' (pen and ink drawing by Major Crealock).

the Battle of Mohamdi on 24 May resistance was at an end and Russell made arrangements to convalesce in a more suitable area. On 3 June he journeyed to Delhi, where he saw the palace and the sick and aged king, before leaving to travel to Simla. For most of the rebels the Mutiny was over and for Russell his task was near its end. Except for a few dispatches of a generally descriptive nature, his war correspondence was ended.

While Russell was often openly critical so were other correspondents. One, who wrote under the title 'Disabled Officer', was notorious for his attacks on Sir Colin Campbell. But at the same time they were fervent patriots who, like other Victorians of this period, were stirred by the martial splendour of the British army and navy. 'The bright scarlet of the Bays shines brightly in the sun . . .,' wrote Russell. 'There go the Rifles — the dear old brigade . . .' Delane attributed to the influence of Russell's pen, the stopping of indiscriminate execution of mutineers and other Indians and the mild reconciliation policies of the post-Mutiny period advocated by the Viceroy 'Clemency' Canning.

Indian Mutiny: the Secundra Bagh after the slaughter of 2,000 mutineers by the Highlanders who surrounded them (photograph by Felice Beato).

Russell saw the Mutiny as '... a war of religion, a war of race, and a war of revenge ... to shake off the yoke of a stranger, and to re-establish the full power of the native chiefs, and the full sway of the native religion'.

While other newspapers had focused their readers' attention on the outrages committed by the sepoys, dreadful as they were, Russell also commented on acts occasionally committed by British troops. 'These were the acts of barbarous savages,' he said about the sepoy outrages. 'Were our acts those of civilised Christians?' But the generals had received orders and Canning advised General Anson to make '. . . a terrible example. No amount of severity can be too great.'

Even as the Mutiny was being put down, there was minor trouble in China. In all the sixty-four years of Queen Victoria's long reign, there would not be one when British or Imperial forces would not be engaged in either protecting or expanding the British Empire. As the size of the Empire grew, the number of war correspondents increased to cater for the ever-growing demand for stories of adventure, narrow escape, glorious victory and heroism, but there were few to equal Russell's descriptive style. Many of the new journalists followed a stereotyped formula in their dispatches, catering for the changing public taste which now found heroic fiction but watered-down reality more palatable than sordid and bloody fact. The entire nation wanted to read of the glorious deeds of its army, but there was no market for writings about suffering.

The Third China War broke out in 1858. It is often called the Arrow War after the name of the boat on whose pretext Britain and France went to war. Although the ship was Chinese and the authorities were in their right to board and arrest some of the sailors, it was once registered in Hong Kong and this 'insult', which perpetrated the myth that a British ship had been boarded, led to war. Conveniently, the French discovered that a French missionary had been murdered some time previously and they sided with the British. Most newspapers had representatives in or around China and they were summoned to cover the progress of the troops. Wingrove Cook and a Mr. Bowlby reported for *The Times*, the *Daily News* dispatched their Shanghai correspondent, and the *Illustrated London News* their artist and correspondent from Hong Kong. The entire campaign, which lasted some three years, was a simple and well-conducted advance from the mouth of the Pai Ho River to Peking where 'just retribution' was claimed, by burning down the Summer Palace, which to the annoyance of the British had already been looted by the French.

It was the first war fought by the British using the new Armstrong breech-loading field-gun and it was about this gun that a minor scandal broke in the press. To close the breech end, the system relied on a 'vent block' slipped into a recess which, once tightened up, sealed the breech. These 'vent blocks' were very unreliable. The *Examiner* of 2 November 1861, amongst other newspapers including *The Times*, was still complaining about the scandal.

Second China War: entrance of the Taku Forts (photograph by Felice Beato).

> Mr. Russell [wrote the *Examiner* leader] has made one great
> exposure of the effects of mismanagement; that gentleman
> scotched the snake, but he did not kill it . . . Who ever heard
> of the partial failure of the field-pieces sent to China? Not a
> soul saving her Majesty's Minister at War. We knew, indeed,
> that the French preferred their own guns to ours, but never
> were told the cause. Unhappily the *Times'* able correspondent,
> Mr. Bowlby, was foully murdered, and the truth was left to
> official pens, Pallmall [The War Office] alone received the
> true impression . . . What a sum of money the death of poor
> Mr. Bowlby has cost this country! For assuredly we
> Englishmen should have known through his pen that which
> Frenchmen did know . . .

The breech-loading system was eventually abandoned and a return
made to muzzle-loading guns.

It was not, however, only the wars, campaigns, and expeditions
which were waged in Queen Victoria's name that thrilled the public.
The pervading demand for adventure at second-hand made any war
between any opponents equally newsworthy. In 1861, after a period

of some tension in America, a civil war broke out between the Northern and breakaway Southern states. Details of British campaigns were not forgotten as the North-West Frontier of India was a constant and seemingly inexhaustible source of news about punitive expeditions against the Pathan hill tribes.

The American Civil War was perhaps the first to receive the onslaught of the press in vast numbers. Besides the veritable 'army' of Northern war correspondents (it was said that at one estimation they numbered 500), there were also the representatives of the London and foreign press. While the number of correspondents used by even a single newspaper was greater than anything previously experienced, they were also properly organized for the first time into an army of news-seekers. The Brady photograph of the headquarters of the *New York Herald* in the field shows seven 'intrepid' correspondents with their well-pitched tent, presumably near telegraph lines, and their mobile H.Q. carriage, a far cry from Russell's working conditions and experiences in the Crimea only six years previously.

American Civil War: war correspondents of the *New York Herald* with their mobile headquarters.

The war was also unique in being the first between conventional armies extensively covered by war photographers. True, there had been others before Matthew Brady. There were photographs taken in India in the late 1840s and also in Mexico, but these and the work of Roger Fenton and James Robertson, who had photographed in the Crimea, had not shown the horrors or suffering of war but set groups and views. The first photographer to produce convincing photographs of human suffering in war was Felice Beato. A Venetian by birth, later a naturalized British subject, he travelled and took photographs in the Near and Middle East with James Robertson and produced some remarkable pictures showing the destruction and desolation caused by the Indian Mutiny. He later continued on his own to record the Second China War in 1860 with vivid photographs which showed amidst havoc and death the true face of war.

Brady and his twenty-two teams of photographers and assistants again tarnished the romantic image of war as Russell had done in the Crimea. His numerous photographs showed the aftermath of battle with the hundreds of dead and dying. Brady himself died in a poor ward on 15 January 1896 after having been forced to sell many of his negatives to pay his debts, so little was the interest shown in his work after the Civil War. Fifteen days after his death, an exhibition of his Civil War photographs opened in New York. In selecting his views, it was said, Brady once remarked that dead men do not move, very useful when the plate had to be exposed for several minutes. Some of Brady's men became famous in their own right. Alexander Gardener, for instance, was sent to cover the war in the South, argued with Brady and went his own way, producing in 1866 two volumes of photographs entitled *Photographic Sketch Book of the War*. Timothy H. O'Sullivan was also a 'Brady' man and went South as Gardener's assistant but later produced remarkable work on his own account. George N. Barnard accompanied General Sherman in his historic march through Georgia. As the government's official photographer he had a brief to take plates of bridges, railways, and other military installations. Unfortunately none of the illustrated newspapers such as the American *Frank Leslie's Illustrated Newspaper* and *Harper's Weekly* and the *Illustrated London News* could reproduce Brady's photographs and the world would have to wait until the perfection of the halftone process for printing photographs before appreciating the work of the pioneer war photographer.

American Civil War: Frank Vizetelly, artist and correspondent for the *Illustrated London News.*

Travelling with the correspondents there was inevitably a gathering of artists illustrating the progress of the war with their sketches. The drawings of Edwin Forbes, and those of the brothers Alfred and Winslow Homer and Henry Lovie, turned up as wood-block pictures in *Leslie's* and *Harper's.* Printed in the *Illustrated London News* were reports and drawings by the debonair and heavily moustached Frank Vizetelly, the former wood engraver and one of the brothers who had helped Ingram to found his newspaper. The *Daily Telegraph*, the first great penny daily newspaper which in the 1860s boasted the largest circulation in the world, even surpassing *The Times*, relied for its reports on George Augustus Sala, a vivid, lucid writer and one of the most professional of journalists. *The Times* sent Russell to America before the war broke out and he visited both the Southern and Northern states. While in the North, Mr. Davis, *The Times*'s New York correspondent, continued to cover the preparations of the Federal troops and politicians. Davis was replaced in February 1862 by a Mr. MacKay. 'Davis's proclivities were entirely Northern,' wrote Delane to Russell, 'and he gave them expression to the exclusion of all others.'

The London and foreign newspapers naturally took sides and the majority of the London press supported the Southern cause with the notable exception of the *Daily News*, the *Spectator*, and the *Manchester Examiner*. The chosen policy of a newspaper or editor was not, of course, the decision of the correspondent in the field, certain of whom found difficulty and indifference shown to them by the Northern authorities, if, for example, their newspaper favoured the Confederate cause. After reporting the rout of the Federal troops at the first battle of Bull Run in 1861 and the general offensive action of the South, Russell, like others, found that permission was denied them to accompany the Northern armies in any further engagements.

General Sherman had an intense dislike of war correspondents and did not hide his animosity towards them. 'Reporters print their limited and tainted observations as their history of events they neither see nor comprehend,' he wrote. He also considered that all war correspondents ought to be summarily hanged, and would have been happy to perform the task himself. Southern generals considered enemy newspapers a useful source of intelligence as they usually reached the Confederate War Department on the day following publication. President Lincoln was not averse to consulting war correspondents because they were, '. . . often behind the scenes at the front and I am able to get ideas from you which no one else will give'.

Northern newspapers on occasion had to be careful of what they printed, especially in their leader articles, as those that were not whole-heartedly behind Lincoln and the Abolitionist policy found themselves closed down and on occasion the editors were insulted or shot at and their offices destroyed. Mr. Bollymeyer, editor of the Dayton *Empire*, was murdered by an Abolitionist and the assassin was acquitted of the crime. General Burnside, waging a political campaign, caused the Chicago *Times* to be closed and forbade the distribution of the New York *World* in the areas under his control. The Southern press did not have the same problem, not because the newspapers were for the most part behind their cause, but because the result of the Northern blockade of the coastline had made supplies and especially paper scarce. There are examples of Southern newspapers printed on wallpaper because of this shortage.

The American Civil War inspired progress in a great number of fields. Not only was it the first war to see the widespread use of

American Civil War: the death of General Lyon, 10 August 1861 (pencil drawing by Henry Lovie for Frank Leslie's *Illustrated Newspaper*). Leslie issued all his artists with drawing pads containing preprinted copyright notices, 'An actual sketch made on the spot by one of the Special Artists of Frank Leslie's *Illustrated Newspaper*. Mr. Leslie holds the copyright and reserves the exclusive right of publication'.

breech-loading, repeating small arms, and the introduction of the machine-gun capable of rapid and devastating fire, but it also saw the first clash between ironclad ships. For communication, portable field telegraphs were widely used by the military and press alike. The first-ever combat photographs were taken during the war and newspapers were used for propaganda purposes.

The social, political, and military implications of this first modern war were stupendous and opened the eyes of some, unfortunately not the majority, to what future wars would be like. Railways established their importance as a fast method of supply and of moving troops, although the enemy ripped up lines and destroyed bridges and tunnels. The use of balloons as a means of reconnaissance was avidly noted by some European powers, who viewed the conflict with interest. Military communications, although never perfect, showed an immense improvement on the conditions under which the military and press laboured in the Crimea only six years before. Despite the new equipment, the tactics of inexperienced generals and the use of outdated forms of attack and defence failed to prevent vast casualty lists. It was soon realized that modern weapons and ancient tactics did not go together.

The press on both sides, as well as foreign representatives, suffered hardships and dangers, while the proprietors, such as the famous Horace Greeley of the powerful *New York Tribune* and that of *Harper's Weekly*, used their columns for propaganda purposes. In *Harper's* issue of 17 August 1861, a fictitious engraving represented Confederate soldiers bayonetting wounded Union men. Designed to inflame hatred of the South, the caption read '. . . the savages who fought under the Confederate Flag systematically butchered the wounded, and this not only in obedience to their own fiendish instincts, but by order of their officers'. It was the first of the many so-called major atrocity stories of the war. Hatred was nourished by the press as the war lengthened from months into years and usually anything reported was believed.

American Civil War: the signal telegraph as used at the battle of Fredericksburg (drawing by  A. R. Waud).

Russell of *The Times*, who had reported the battle of Bull Run, found himself the victim of vitriolic attacks from disbelievers and the majority of the Northern press, the *New York Times* being his only notable champion. President Lincoln remarked when he met Russell, 'The London *Times* is one of the greatest powers in the world; in fact, I don't know anything which has more power, except perhaps the Mississippi.' But that did not help Russell. A general officer remarked to him, 'Of course you will never remain when once all the Press are down upon you. I would not take a million dollars to be in your place.'

Other correspondents found that the passes issued by various commanders were considered worthless by front-line troops, and they were often turned back or openly menaced. The foreign press, especially the English, who were mainly supporters of the Southern cause, suffered greatly, while the correspondents of the powerful pro-Lincoln newspapers were welcome in camp and able to pitch their mobile vans near the military telegraph wagon.

There was a new danger for correspondents and artists. Bullets, wounds, and even death were accepted and usually handsomely compensated for, but now spies were used by both the North and South. Often arrested on suspicion, journalists found that passes issued by army headquarters were little help and they were held and confined until they could be checked, which meant the loss of news for their papers. The Union government had first employed the services of Allan Pinkerton, later to found the famous Pinkerton Detective Agency, but after faulty and over-exaggerated intelligence had caused serious embarrassment to General McClellan, a military intelligence department was set up. Civilians who travelled near troops, or in the vicinity of defences, or army headquarters, were viewed with suspicion and any attempt to pass through the lines in search of news usually ended in capture or even being shot on sight.

A number of war correspondents from northern newspapers were held in Confederate prison camps, notorious for their overcrowding, bad construction, and insanitary conditions. Albert D. Richardson and Junius Henri Brown, star war correspondents of the *New York Tribune*, were captured and, despite their credentials, imprisoned in the 'Rat Hell Cellar' of Libby Prison in Richmond, Virginia. For attempting to escape, and after being proved to be non-combatants, they were transferred to a prison at Salisbury in North Carolina, where they were later joined by W. T. Davies, the war correspondent of the *Cincinnati Gazette.* Attempts to escape by soldiers were frequent but usually unsuccessful. After ten months together in the prison, where they were assigned to work in the hospital, they decided to make a bid for freedom, despite the fact that of the seventy-five men who had attempted to escape, only five had reached Northern lines.

On the night of 17 December 1864, all three were on duty in the hospital. While Davies and Brown held passes to allow them into the dispensary for supplies, Richardson was not so privileged. By swopping passes, which the guards rarely asked to see knowing the two men so well, the three were able to walk out and into open country. Here they split up, for in front of them lay 340 miles to safety.

On 14 January 1865, the *New York Tribune* printed the following short and poignant dispatch from their long-lost correspondent.

> Knoxville, Tenn., January 13, 1865.
> *Out of the jaws of death; out of the mouth of hell.*
> Albert D. Richardson.

The details of their escape and their adventures in reaching the Northern lines were later amplified. Luckily press passes bore no photographs at this time, although they did in the late 1860s and 1870s.

The progress of all military operations in the war was followed by a vast public in Europe and England where the population had already taken sides, arguing the politics and the principles of every phase of the war. The *Pall Mall Gazette* pointed out on 14 October 1865, 'The street boys of London have decided in favour of "John Browne's Body" against "My Maryland" and "Bonnie Blue Flag".' All war songs were immensely popular at this time. According to F. G. de Fontaine, a celebrated Southern war correspondent, the favourite songs of the Southern troops were 'Old Folks at Home' and 'My Kentucky Home', although 'When Johnny Comes Marching Home Again', 'Dixie', and the famous 'Battle Hymn of the Republic' became national tunes.

The American Civil War, in all its bloodiness, set the pattern for the total and absolute war that the world would experience in 1914. Its lessons were not fully appreciated by some military powers, especially those on campaigns against natives, but for the soldier and correspondent it had been a new experience. One young Confederate private,

American Civil War: defeat of the army of General Pope on the old Bull Run battleground, 30 August 1862 (pencil and Chinese white drawing by A. R. Waud).

who was captured and switched to the Northern cause, would never forget it. His name was Henry Morton Stanley who later wrote that while a soldier he had been employed '...for American journals — though very young — and witnessed several stirring scenes in our Civil War...' Another young soldier who had fought for the Southern cause, although not an American, was twice sentenced to death but managed to dodge the firing squad and later became a famous war correspondent, Bennet Burleigh.

One of the major inconveniences for the war correspondents was the lack of transport and the excessive price of both food and transport. War, in whatever continent, even the sandy wastes of the Sudan, would always have this effect on commerce. Food and essential supplies doubled in price overnight, while horses and carriages were at a premium. William Howard Russell noted in his diary that at first

American Civil War: battle of Munfordville, Kentucky, 14 September 1862 (pencil sketch by Henri Lovie). Note the artist's instructions to the wood block engraver top right, 'Put as much fallen timber and dead limbs between figures as you can'.

the price of a horse was $1,000. When Russell complained, the owner remarked, 'If you want to see this fight a thousand dollars is cheap.' Russell demurred but found the following day that the price was now $1,100 because as the owner said: 'I don't want my animals to be ripped up by them cannon and them musketry . . .'

Foreign correspondents found it difficult to get passes or permission to accompany troops. In a letter to Mowbray Morris of *The Times*, Russell explained:

> In a few days I shall learn whether I can get away with the army or not . . . I have applied to:— General M'Clellan . . .
> No answer. Genl. Marcy . . . Not satisfactory.
> Genl. M'Dowell . . . Cannot without Genl. M'C's orders.
> Genl. Van Vliet . . . Will help if he can. Secy. of State . . .
> No answer. Secy. of War . . . Has refused the Press and
> does not think he can help me, but will see.'

American Civil War: stone wall at foot of Marye's Heights, Fredericksburg, 3 May 1863, twenty minutes after the storming party had passed up the hill (photograph by Captain A. J. Russell).

Concerning the American Civil War and the attitude of the British, Russell wrote in 1863:

> ... I really believe the great John Bull has lost his head, and is distracted by jealousy to such an extent that he has not only forgotten to be just and generous, but to be moderately reasonable.

The American Civil War was perhaps the first in which newspaper correspondents reported their own adventures and exploits as well as news of the fighting that they were sent to cover. Russell in the Crimea had, it is true, included accounts of his own tribulations in dispatches to *The Times* but these were intended as extra ammunition in the attack on an incompetent administration. The war also saw the start of professionalism among war correspondents and the race to get the news home first and numerous feats were accomplished by members of the Northern press corps. War correspondents had been accepted in America in the late 1840s when such journalists as George Wilkins Kendall of the

*New Orleans Picayune* and James Forrester of the *Delta* braved the heat and dust of Mexico to report the campaigns between the United States and Mexican troops on the Rio Grande between 1846–7. Even in these early days of war reporting, swiftness in relaying and publishing news was all important to newspapers and the legendary James Gordon Bennet, the founder of the *New York Herald*, repeatedly scooped his rivals. By using a special courier service he managed to beat even the official dispatches and mail services by several days.

During the war between the Northern and Southern states the race for 'hot news' was fierce and competitive and journalists employed every means to get the news home first or to hinder their rivals. Sometimes in their haste to be first on the streets with the news, correspondents anticipated the outcome of a battle with unfortunate results. At the first battle of Bull Run, witnessed by William Russell of *The Times* and twenty-five other correspondents, Henry Raymond of the *New York Times*, confident from what he had seen that a Union victory was inevitable, left the battlefield to telegraph the news of victory. In fact it was a disaster for the Union army.

To enable the newspapers to print as wide a view as possible on the war, the proprietors put a large number of men in the field, the *New York Herald* boasting forty correspondents, as many as the famous London *Times* would send to South Africa nearly forty years later.

At Fredericksburg in 1862 Henry Villard accomplished a most spectacular feat in getting news home first for the *New York Tribune*. Realizing the plight of the Northern army, Villard rode all night in pouring rain to get his dispatch to the *Tribune*, but on arrival at Acquia Creek he was informed that no correspondents would be allowed to proceed to the capital. Kicking his heels waiting, Villard knew he was still ahead of his rivals but this impression changed when Charles Carlton Coffin of the *Boston Journal* rode into the camp. Determined to beat his rival, Villard waited until Coffin was asleep before he decided on his course of action. Paying a negro boatman ten dollars to row him to a waiting ship, he climbed on board and told the captain he had urgent dispatches for Washington and promised a substantial reward. The ship sailed and the correspondent reached his offices soon after eight in the evening. There it was confirmed that he was first with the news, but that the government-controlled telegraph lines would not transmit it. While recovering from his epic journey, Villard encountered a senator whom he persuaded that Lincoln must be informed. The correspondent was bundled into a cab and taken to the President, where the situation was explained to Lincoln. On his return to the office, the editor queried his expenses of ten dollars to a boatman and fifty dollars to the ship's captain, whereupon an argument developed in which blows were exchanged. Eventually calm was restored, but the story was never published in its original form. It was suitably toned down before being printed.

The Battle of Gettysburg in July 1863 at last provided Northern war correspondents such as Sam Wilkeson of the *New York Times*, Charles Carlton Coffin of the *Boston Journal*, Frank Long of the *New York Tribune* and Homer Bynington, also of the *Tribune*, with the first convincing Union victory. The race to get this welcome news home first assumed monumental importance. Coffin left the battlefield early, intent on beating his rivals, but he was unable to beat Bynington of the *Tribune*. Homer Bynington, having witnessed the battle, hastily scrawled his dispatches and headed for the telegraph line. The lines had been cut by the enemy, so the *Tribune* correspondent quickly climbed the telegraph pole and effected a temporary repair to enable his dispatch to be sent. The previous year, after the Seven Days' Battle, George Townsend of the *New York Herald* achieved a remarkable scoop over other newspapers and especially over the arch rival, the *Tribune*. The correspondent, stricken with fever, set out for the nearest telegraph station at Washington, a seven-hour journey by steamer. He was not the only correspondent aboard, but knew that a scoop was what Bennet, the proprietor, demanded of all his men. When the boat reached the shore, he tied his dispatch in a bundle, tucked a five dollar bill in the binding and threw it to a cab driver while the steamer was twenty feet from the pier, giving instructions to get it to the train as fast as possible. As soon as the ship was tied up, Townsend jumped ashore and in another cab raced after the first, which he managed to overtake at the depot just as the train was leaving. Grabbing his dispatch he leaped aboard and late that night arrived at the offices of his newspaper with enough material to fill over forty columns. His ingenuity was rewarded by a large bonus from James Gordon Bennet.

George Townsend was also the first war correspondent to report from a balloon, but after fainting when fired on by the Confederates and having to be revived on landing rather unceremoniously with a bucket of water, he never again tried the experience. Townsend was not alone in the use of ingenious devices to beat his rivals. Frank Long of the *New York Tribune* accomplished a scoop by what would have been described by English correspondents as ungentlemanly conduct. Having swum the Rappahannock River with his dispatches to catch the train for Washington, he was questioned by a man whom he recognized as a *New York Herald* correspondent. Pretending to be a supply officer, Long confessed that '. . . all hell had broken loose' on the front, whereupon the *Herald* man offered one hundred dollars for an exclusive story which Long hastily fabricated. The *Herald* man paid up and the next day the false news was published and denounced by the rival *Tribune*, much to the embarrassment of newspaper and correspondent. Davidson, the shamed correspondent, determined to get his own back and in May 1864 he boarded a steamer with Henry Wing of the rival *Tribune*. Both men were intent on getting a first, but Davidson also wanted to put the hated *Herald* in an embarrassing position. While Wing was reposing in a cabin, found for him by his rival, he noted through the porthole that Davidson was about to board another steamer which was on the point of departure. Wing hastened on deck and shouted to the captain of the steamer, 'Do you know this disreputable-looking individual? He claims to be a correspondent. Take my advice, he should be put under surveillance and not allowed to go ashore until he has been indentified.' The fuming Davidson was kept under lock and key for several days before being released. Another frequent ruse was for rival correspondents to accuse each other of being Confederate spies.

Uriah Painter of the *Philadelphia Enquirer* scored a spectacular feat with his escapade. Having been captured by the Confederates, he overheard the men talking about a raid on Maryland. Managing to escape from his captors, he regained the Union lines, where he gave his story only to be told that it was impossible as all information pointed to the Confederates marching on Washington. Painter immediately wired his editor, who had men on hand when Stuart made his famous sweep through Maryland, resulting in a scoop for the newspaper.

Other correspondents got scoops either by luck or by having the right connections. George Smalley of the *New York Tribune* was one of the numerous correspondents waiting to get to the front, but barred by order of the Secretary of State for War. Smalley, using some influence, managed to get himself appointed an aide to General Sedwick and had a scoop on the Battle of Antietam. He left the battlefield at nine in the evening and rode thirty miles to Fredericksburg in six hours, reaching the town at four the following morning. He had to wait until seven o'clock before the telegraph office opened but his troubles were only starting. In his book, *Anglo-American Memories*, Smalley related that he asked the clerk to get a message through for him. 'After some demur he promised to get a short one through,' wrote Smalley; 'I sat down on a log by the door and began to write using sheet after sheet until a column or more had gone, as I supposed, to New York. The *Tribune* had been notified that a message was coming. But neither my private notice to the *Tribune* nor my story of the battle was sent to New York. It was sent to the War Office at Washington, and such was the disorder there prevailing that it was the first news, or perhaps only the first coherent account of the battle which reached the War Office and the President. They kept it to themselves during all that day. At night and in time for the next morning's paper, it was released, wired on and duly appeared in Saturday's *Tribune*.' Smalley was, however, a professional and, leaving the telegraph office, he made his way by train to New York, writing his follow-up story as he travelled. He arrived at dawn the following day and hurried to his offices where '. . . compositors were waiting, and at six o'clock the worst piece of manuscript the oldest of them had ever seen was put in their hands'. During the Franco Prussian War, Smalley ran the *Tribune*'s London office.

Perhaps the most spectacular and exciting episode in war reporting was accomplished by Henry Wing of the *New York Tribune*. After the Battle of the Wilderness in 1864, Wing disguised himself as a rustic and headed towards Washington, hoping to pass through the Confederate lines. He was unfortunately caught by some Confederate cavalry, who interrogated him. Posing as a Confederate spy he confessed convincingly that he was on his way to Washington. The troopers accompanied him to a tavern, where the owner recognized him as a 'Yankee' journalist. Spurring his horse, Wing dashed for the river and crossed it to escape his pursuers. Hiding for over an hour in the dense woods, Wing eventually continued his journey, only to be caught again by Confederate cavalrymen. They locked him up but during the day, as the soldiers dozed, he climbed the fence and escaped. As dusk fell, he was within Union lines but unable to get to Washington. A telegraph message was sent to the War Office for permission for the correspondent to proceed but the reply only demanded, 'Who are you and what is your story?' Wing replied that he was a *Tribune* correspondent. 'Send your news immediately otherwise I will have you arrested as a spy,' came the answer. Wing refused to reveal his information until the *Tribune* office had been informed and for over an hour the telegraph keys chattered carrying and receiving messages. After an hour of tense silence the keys started again and the following message came off the wires: 'Will you give me your news? We are anxious here in Washington. A. Lincoln.'

Wing insisted that the story must go to the *Tribune* first and the President agreed. Wing knew that if the story went now it would arrive for the Saturday edition, and, as the *Tribune* did not appear on Sunday, any delay would destroy his lead. On the President's promise, Wing dictated his report to the operator, who tapped out the dispatch to the President. True to his word, Lincoln passed the news to the *Tribune* in time for the Saturday edition. He also sent a carriage to bring Wing to the White House where he was thanked and was able to tell Lincoln the full story of the battle.

While there were many exciting stories, there were also numerous casualties among the correspondents. It was the first war in which they died in the service of their newspapers.

The cost of the war in lives and money was staggering. The Federal government between 1861 and 1865 had spent $6·19 billion dollars, 1·34 billion of that being in pay alone. In May and June 1864, the Northern armies of the Potomac and the James lost 77,452 men, a greater number than the Southern General had in his entire army. The Confederates lost 260,000 while the Union lost 100,000 more, although only 94,000 Confederates were killed in action against the Union's 110,000. The rest died from wounds and disease.

War reporting had become firmly established as a national necessity. Oliver Wendell Holmes wrote, 'We must have something to eat, and the papers to read. Everything else we can do without . . . Only bread and newspapers we must have.'

While the American Civil War, because of its violence and consequences, had tended to receive the greatest attention, British troops had in the meantime been engaged in fighting numerous native uprisings including the Ashantis in Africa in 1863—4, and the Maoris in New Zealand. In 1866, however, editors turned their attention to Europe where rivalry between Austria and Prussia had broken into open conflict. Russell hesitated in accepting the commission from Delane, but eventually went to the war with a young artillery officer to help him, Captain H. Charles Brackenbury, later one of the celebrated 'Wolseley ring' and a member of Military Intelligence. Brackenbury's interest was not entirely literary and he used his position to study the tactics and fighting qualities of the two great European nations. Other newspapers were quick to dispatch correspondents. The *Pall Mall Gazette*, the evening newspaper 'written by gentlemen for gentlemen', sent Henry Mayers Hyndman, while the *Standard* used a new correspondent who already had some experience in this type of journalism from the Crimea, George Alfred Henty, an ex-army officer who had decided to become a full-time journalist. European campaigning had its advantages as the telegraph wires which now spread over most countries were readily accessible to the correspondents. A new style of short concise telegraphed dispatches began slowly to oust the rather verbose reports written by Russell and Woods.

The British public did not have to wait long before an Imperial campaign occupied the press. The Emperor of Abyssinia had written to the Queen in 1863, requesting permission to send a delegation to England to explain the oppression of Christians by his Islamic neighbours. The Emperor did not receive a reply and, feeling slighted, he sought suitable retribution by locking up the British Consul, Charles Cameron, and having him tortured and flogged. Eventually in 1866 a letter, dated May 1864, was delivered by a Turkish explorer to the Emperor Theodore requesting the release of the Consul. Theodore refused the request and imprisoned the Turk as well. In September 1867 a final ultimatum was given to Theodore and in November the advance force of the expedition landed at Zoulla on the Red Sea.

The expedition was an extremely well-organized affair and Napier, its commander, took infinite care over the preparations, dealing with problems of transport and supply. Special equipment, including a newly designed pack harness for mules, was prepared at the Royal Arsenal, Woolwich. Many of the troops were armed with a breech-loading rifle and some were dressed in a rudimentary form of khaki uniform. The only currency universally accepted in Abyssinia was at this time the Austrian Maria Theresa thaler of 1780 and the British government ordered half a million from the Austrian mint. Newspaper editors also took care to order sufficient for the needs of their correspondents.

According to Henry Morton Stanley, the correspondent of the *New York Herald:*

> The English Press was very ably represented . . . and the
> correspondents consisted of some remarkable literary lights . . .
> They all messed together; and though there were contrasting
> elements in their natures, yet they seldom disagreed . . . I give
> them the credit of being the most sociable mess in the army,
> as well as the most lovable and good-tempered.

The English correspondents included Dr. Charles Austin of *The*

*Times*, W. Owen Whiteside of the *Morning Post*, Alex Shepherd of the *Daily News*, Mr. Adare of the *Daily Telegraph*; William Simpson, the artist who had covered the Crimea for Colnaghi's, the print specialists, represented the *Illustrated London News* and George Alfred Henty wrote for the *Standard*.

George Alfred Henty, the eldest son of a wealthy stockbroking mine-owner, was born in Trumpington near Cambridge on 8 December 1832. No one who knew him in his youth could ever believe that the huge, jovial, barrel-chested and bearded writer was once a frail and sickly child. Until the age of fourteen he was almost a permanent invalid who had spent much of his years in bed due to rheumatic fever. He was sent to Westminster School where he was incessantly bullied for writing poetry until he took up boxing. He left school and went to Caius College, Cambridge, but left university before attaining a degree to go to the Crimea, commissioned in the Purveyor's Department of the army. In the Crimea, he represented the *Morning Advertiser* and later the *Morning Post* before catching a fever and being invalided to England. Promoted to the rank of Purveyor, he was sent out to the Crimea with the Italian Legion, foreign mercenaries paid by England, at the end of the war. He was later in charge of the Belfast and Portsmouth districts in the capacity of Purveyor but eventually resigned his commission out of boredom. For some time, he was engaged in mining operations in Italy but in 1866 he decided to become a full-time journalist. He gave up the active life of a special war correspondent for the *Standard* in 1876 to devote himself to writing adventure books for boys. He was often described as the most Imperialist of the Imperialists, and his typical Victorian attitude to natives, 'the negro is an inferior animal and a lower grade in creation than the white man', was reflected in his eighty or so books for boys. Always intent, as he once said, to 'foster the imperial spirit', his vast output of adventure stories made use of much of the material he amassed while he was a correspondent. Like the correspondents of the 1870s he followed the essential recipe of heroic Tommy Atkins, the British soldier, the noble savage, and the faithful and often comic native servant. His stories, which were so popular among young people, consisted of fictitious episodes set against a factual background and included all the necessary ingredients that so besotted the late Victorians: perilous situations, narrow escapes, and heroic deeds. Henty also edited a boy's adventure newspaper, on the lines of the famous *Boy's Own Paper*, entitled the *Union Jack*. He died

*The 'newly invented curse to armies'*

in November 1902, having witnessed the greatest Imperial conflict, the Boer War, and a large part of his Imperial dream was shattered by its results.

Travelling with the Abyssinian expeditionary force was an interpreter who not only had considerable knowledge of the country and language but also had been Vice-Consul to Cameron. Theodore gave him the title of 'Basha Felecca', the Speedy Commander. Captain Charles Speedy was the prototype of the Victorian eccentric, and after leaving the Emperor Theodore's service went 'roving in search of fresh adventure, like another Quixote'. He embarked for New Zealand where as a captain of militia he fought in the Maori Wars. Henty described this strange eccentric:

> His appearance, although no doubt very imposing to the native mind, is yet extremely comic to a European eye. Imagine a gentleman six feet and a half high, wearing a red handkerchief over his head and round his neck the fur collar and tails of a chief's insignia; over his shoulders is the native white cloth wrappings with red ends. Below this is a long coloured silk garment; and below all this the British trousers and boots.

Speedy's last mission at the end of the campaign was to escort King Theodore's queen and son to safety. He then vanished and nobody has ever discovered what happened to him.

The expeditionary force pushed inland towards Theodore's fortress capital of Magdala, and by the beginning of March the troops were more than half-way towards their ultimate destination. One of the greatest hindrances to general and correspondent alike, H. M. Stanley reported, was that:

> All Abyssinians are the most stupendous liars, and everything related of the country ahead was certain to be found false as we journeyed along . . . I am not singular in these opinions.

All the correspondents remarked on the same peculiarities. Theodore was not a particularly dangerous enemy, but the force moved at a ponderous pace. The authorities in London had been all in favour of a lightning dash by a flying force but had luckily been dissuaded from this course by Napier, who advised a careful but sure advance. Even Charles Austin, *The Times*'s special correspondent, considered that a squadron of cavalry dashing off to the Emperor's camp could finish the expedition in under a month. 'Sir Robert was too patient a man to be flustered,' wrote Stanley. By all accounts, Theodore was now almost insane, slaying large numbers of friend and foe alike. An attempted *coup d'état* by the King of Shoa had failed and Theodore was said to be fortifying Magdala. The *Illustrated London News* printed that 'Letters received from an officer at headquarters state that Theodore has thirteen guns at Magdala, and that he is storing the place with provisions . . . The British officers and men were anxious to storm the fortress.'

The army moved slowly towards the capital, its pace hampered by the mountainous terrain. Elephants had been brought from India but on steep marches, as Stanley wrote, they:

> . . . toiled up laboriously with their ponderous burdens, and the other baggage animals invariably passed them; but on moderate roads these gigantic animals with their 1,800 pound loads were masters of the situation and made excellent time . . . They were invaluable on the campaign.

The march, although highly organized in comparison with previous wars and expeditions, was by no means easy. Stanley describes the journey from his point of view:

> The hardships of those whose business it was to keep up a lengthy correspondence after arrival at camp were but now commencing. After being in the saddle close to our baggage, to protect and escort it, for twelve or fifteen hours, . . . it was no light task to sit down and hammer away at a letter, jotting down the incidents of the route, and raking up latest political intelligence. Then to snatch a sleep of three hours, hastily swallow a cup of sugarless tea and dry azinous bread, and mount saddle again at five o'clock in the morning to undergo the same experience, was no joyous picknicking . . .

The pace was particularly slow in mountainous country when the force could only move in single file and in this way 5,000 men and 10,000 animals could cover only about ten miles in a day.

Still no enemy had been engaged and the 'specials' filled their letters with descriptions of the scenery and camp gossip, tinged occasionally with political and local information as friendly natives and chiefs came to treat with General Napier. By 20 March the army and the correspondents found themselves within striking distance of Magdala and orders were issued not to allow any excess baggage to go to the front. Every available animal went to commissary stores and officers were allowed '. . . a greatcoat, blanket, and an indiarubber sheet'. Stanley noted sarcastically that 'Sugar, rum, coffee, tea, potatoes, onions and such luxuries, must be left behind, as "a forced march is to be made upon Magdala"!'

'The higher we ascend, the grander the scene!' wrote Stanley, and the other correspondents including Henty were equally awed by the magnificence of their surroundings. Owen Whiteside of the *Morning Post* noted the ruggedness yet simple beauty of the terrain while Alex Shepherd of the *Daily News* seemed more preoccupied with the discomfort of his saddle and the scarcity of grain and fodder. Correspondents and army alike would soon be glad of the thalers they carried. H. M. Stanley wrote that it was:

> ... an omnipotent genius; it causes water to flow from solid rocks; it brings forth food in abundance for 20,000 men and 60,000 animals ... it causes the inhabitants to pull down their houses and give their rafters to the Commissariat Department ...

The food supply amazed Stanley and especially Henty, who had been a Purveyor in the British Commissariat in the Crimea; it was already cooked when delivered, the troops having only to eat it, a far cry as Henty noted from conditions in the Crimea where even the coffee beans were issued green! But it was also a question of supply and demand when it came to price. Stanley noted that the correspondents' expenses '... including Commissariat bills, since leaving Antalo, averaged seven dollars *per diem*'. (The Maria Theresa thaler was worth U.S. $1.08.)

For the first time a photographic unit accompanied the British force in an official capacity, although in the spring of 1855 two specially trained officers had been sent as photographers to the Crimea. They were, however, nothing to do with the press and their function was to produce photographic copies of maps. In March 1856, the government, impressed with the results of Fenton's and Robertson's photography in the Crimea, ordered that four non-commissioned officers should be sent to a certain Mr. Thurston Thompson to learn the art of photography. In September 1867, a sergeant and six photographers were attached to a company of Royal Engineers on the expedition. Besides the maps, they also recorded scenes during the force's advance to Magdala but none were available to the press.

As the army pushed forward, weighed down by its supply train, food grew scarcer by the day. Stanley recorded that 'We were living on the toughest of beef — one pound per day, sugarless tea, ten ounces of flour, four ounces of rice, and half an ounce of rock salt, while our servants got but half of the soldier's ration...' The prospect for the following days was worse: 'Two days at the furthest would consume all our stores.' The force moved on slowly and encountered Theodore's old camp, Bet Hor:

> ...so often heard of in the newspapers... Around the camp [wrote Stanley] was the blackness of desolation, which invariably follows in the train of a ruthless war. There were still to be seen the booths... which served as tents for the soldiers. The bleached bones of sheep and oxen covered the ground. Here and there scattered pieces of native blankets... A significant sign to us of the cruelty with which Theodore governed his people was a human arm in the last stage of corruption, and a skull with a great hack across it...

On Good Friday, 10 April 1868, the army struck camp and moved on only to be stopped by the news that Theodore and his troops were close at hand. At 10 a.m. the correspondents who had stayed behind to enjoy a leisurely breakfast and to '...smoke the very last of our cheroots' had their tents struck and rolled up. Stanley described the ensuing scene as the news was received: 'The English Commander-in-Chief mounted his charger, the Staff sprang nimbly to saddle, the "specials" *en masse* order their horses up, and booted and spurred, mount also.' Despite all this urgency and alarm, there were still those who thought that Theodore would not fight, many officers were of the opinion that the Emperor had left Magdala and had fled. At 3.30 p.m. the enemy appeared, and opened fire on the army. 'Still the group of English gentlemen did nothing but stare,' wrote Stanley in admiration, 'even when they saw the six cannon which they had counted were being got ready.' There appeared for a moment nothing to avert a certain disaster as the main body of the force was still half a mile to the rear.

The scene was indeed ominous as Stanley took up the story:

> Onward, still onward they came, horsemen and foot soldiers vying with each other. They flung their flowing symas, their besans and many flung their loin clouts away, and with lances and shields in rest they bore down the hill, reached the plateau, and inundated it with their dusky bodies. A clear open plain was before them, over which they rolled like a huge wave. Where was the opposing force to sunder and dash this furious wave backwards?... Acisis stared the General in the face.

*The 'newly
invented curse
to armies'*

Abyssinian Campaign: Kafir-Bar gate, Magdala, 1867.

The correspondents must have gaped with awe as they tried to jot down the quick passing of events. The Abyssinians drew closer and, as Henty wrote, 'we expected that at any minute their rain of spears would fall devastatingly among us'. But in the true tradition of the later Henty novels and adventure stories, help was at hand. The Naval Brigade arrived and without a pause responded to the order 'Action front' and '. . . hardly had the words died away from their lips before sailors had unstrapped rocket tubes and carriages, and had them arrayed on the knolls'.

> 'Fire!' and, even in the act of launching their spears, a stream of fire darted along the enemy's ranks, ploughing its fiery way through their swaying masses. Another and another rushed

through them; and cheer after cheer issued from the lips of the sailors and marines.

The battle had begun. The rockets, which were quite unknown to Abyssinians, stopped the enemy and paralysed them with astonishment. The Abyssinians broke and under the continued hail of fire retreated as best they could. Some of Theodore's chiefs managed to rally their men and once more they flung themselves towards the British.

The correspondents, with the staff, had an admirable view of the action as the mountain artillery battery came into action lobbing their shells amongst the advancing hordes. Once again they stopped and the infantry with breech-loading Snider-Enfield rifles were ordered to open fire on the main body. The baggage train lumbering behind the column was also menaced and the two companies guarding it were ordered into action.

> . . . along the line of soldiers . . . there ran a rattle of musketry [wrote Stanley in admiration]; a clicking of triggers; and a roar of sharp musketry; — steady, deep-toned, like the thunder rush of an express train through a tunnel. Practised men were at work with the Snider rifle . . . — one could tell the difference by the mere sound; there was no break, no pause, no hesitation in it; it was continuously rolling.

Charles Austin, *The Times* correspondent who had witnessed the fight, wrote in his dispatch that:

> To describe the fight after the Snider came into play would be only to describe a battue. Its short cracks following each other in breathless succession were the death-knell of the Abyssinian cause. The unfortunate foe had no longer even the shadow of a chance, but went down like grass before the scythe . . .

As night fell the retreat was sounded by the British, as there was '. . . nothing more to be gained by useless butchery'. The army rested that night but had to wait until midnight before rations came up for the famished troops. During the night Stanley and others lay awake listening to '. . . jackals and hyaenas [who] had come to devour the abundant feast spread out by the ruthless hand of war'.

The following day, the field of battle presented a horrific sight, with the corpses torn by jackals and other animals. The dead were counted and buried and the seventy-five wounded enemy who had survived the night's ordeal were taken to the field hospital along with the British casualties.

Alex Shepherd of the *Daily News* recorded that:

> At seven in the morning a tremendous hurrah drew all loiterers
> first to the entrance of the camp, and then collected them in a
> group around Sir Robert's [Napier] tent. Mr. Flad and
> Mr. Prideaux had come to us riding on Abyssinian ponies . . .
> Then for the first time we learned the completeness of the
> effect caused by our weapons. Two days before the action
> Theodore had butchered 318 native political prisoners, cutting
> the throats of and shooting some, and throwing about half
> down a precipice . . . After nightfall the Abyssinian warriors
> returned, overwhelmed by the events of the day. At twelve
> Theodore admitted that he had been beaten, that the battle
> of the previous evening had ruined him; that half his army
> had gone, and all his bravest killed.

Napier demanded an unconditional surrender but Theodore hedged
and tried to obtain terms:

> Great was the delight of all [continued Shepherd], when it
> was announced that in a few minutes all the captives would
> be in camp. About eight they arrived — a motley crew as far
> as dress was concerned — some in uniform some in old-
> fashioned Abyssinian costume.

There was no further resistance although the *Illustrated London News*
believed that if the Abyssinian army had remained in place:

> . . . and defended it with the spirit it showed in the battle of
> the previous Friday, there might have been a heavy loss in
> forcing the steep, narrow pass leading up to a strong gateway.
> But before the actual siege came on the Emperor's force had
> become a rabble . . . The end was that Magdala was taken
> with no loss on our side, and with but little on that of the
> enemy.

During the final advance, Adare of the *Daily Telegraph* showed
Stanley where the bodies of the murdered prisoners had been flung.
'. . . If you can conceive 308 dead people,' wrote Stanley, 'piled one
upon another, stripped naked, in a state of corruption, with gyves and
fetters round their limbs, you will save me the unpleasant task of describing the scene!' The fortress town was captured and prisoners taken
but the Emperor had committed suicide by shooting himself in the
mouth with a revolver which Queen Victoria had presented to him in
1854. The troops on entering gave three mighty cheers and '. . . the
National Anthem of England . . . was never played or sung with greater

effect or vigour than when the hoary crags of Magdala responded to its notes in an overwhelming chorus of echoes'.

The inevitable search for loot was undertaken by soldiers and correspondents alike, but on Easter Monday Magdala was destroyed. Alex Shepherd of the *Daily News* wrote:

> The work of devastating Magdala — blowing up the gates, the magazine and burning the buildings — was entrusted to the Royal Engineers. The sulphur and saltpetre in the magazine were scarcely more combustible than the houses themselves; everything burned like tinder, and the flames were rapidly spread by a steady breeze from the eastward. It was intended to have left the church standing as a testimony to the heathen; but a pyramid of fire laid hold upon it and licked it up, leaving the church bell alone standing to proclaim by its silence the terrible fate of the tyrant who lies beneath those ruins, and who neither feared God nor regarded man. When twilight was beginning to spread over the hills, and the glow of the conflagration was brightest against the evening sky, the northern gateway was blown to fragments, and a last cheer proclaimed the work of mercy and vengeance fully accomplished. There was not in Magdala one living thing, nor one stone upon another.

In every way the object of the expedition had been accomplished.

> In the instance of the war which has just been brought to so successful a conclusion [said the *Illustrated London News*], there remain no regrets or self-reproaches which usually allay the satisfaction of victory. Our object was in every sense a righteous one — to deliver from the hands of a semi-barbarous potentate those of our countrymen whom he had snatched from their peaceful and benevolent pursuits and laden with fetters; and, above all, to assert and vindicate the inviolability of the Queen's representative while engaged on her behalf . . . A sense of national obligation was the sole impelling cause of this military expedition — not ambition, not greed, not glory — . . . England desires only . . . to leave Abyssinia as nearly as possible as she found it.

After the war, H. M. Stanley resented his not receiving the Abysinian war medal awarded to the expedition. The question of whether to award campaign medals to war correspondents and artists was a difficult one. True, Russell and others had received the Crimean medal, and the Mutiny medal, but the War Office made it plain that this had not established a precedent. Stanley complained that he had helped

Captain Speedy obtain large supplies of fodder and grain and he had therefore been in government service without receiving any recompense. In his book *Commassie and Magdala* (1874) he referred to the expedition for food:

> This was a very important service which I assisted Speedy to perform for the British Government. Yet I regret to say the magnanimous British Government has never even thanked me for it, least of all have they given me a medal such as all Abyssinian heroes obtained, which I consider to be a strange oversight . . . and deserving of the gravest reproof . . .

Stanley had to content himself with a newspaper scoop which would alter his career. It was after the capture of Magdala that Stanley showed the British journalists what he was capable of. Although he had written that the English press corps was most sociable, lovable and good-tempered, inwardly he knew that they looked down on him.

> I was made to feel [he wrote] that, though a journalist like themselves, an American journalist was not of such fine clay as a Briton of the same profession . . . There was no great harm that a number of English pressmen should make merry at my expense, but had an English correspondent visited an American press tent, the American who should have ventured to ridicule England and her institutions would have been shamed to silence.

While the English correspondents were making their way in a leisurely fashion towards the coast, Stanley, after buying a few souvenirs, made a dash for the coast to catch the first ship up the Red Sea towards Suez and the telegraph line. Before his arrival in Abyssinia, Stanley had taken the precaution of calling at the Suez telegraph office and greasing the palm of the head telegraphist to make sure that his future dispatches would take precedence. With Stanley on the ship was Colonel Millward, who had been entrusted with the official dispatches by Napier, and the possibility of a world-wide scoop seemed remote. He might beat his rivals, but the newspapers would print the government announcement. However, luck was with Stanley. Because of an outbreak of cholera on board, the ship was placed in quarantine but the resourceful Stanley smuggled his report ashore with a note to the head telegraphist. The telegram was duly sent to London and then relayed to New York where the *Herald* immediately published it. The news caused considerable confusion in government circles as Napier's dispatches were still held up by the five-day quarantine at Suez. When the passengers were allowed ashore, Millward and Stanley hurried to the telegraph office, the former with his official dispatches and the latter with a follow-up story written on board. Although the official dispatches *should* have taken precedence, it was Stanley's report that was put on the wire first. By some coincidence, as the last word of Stanley's dispatch was tapped out by the operator, the submarine cable between Alexandria and Malta broke, depriving Millward and the other correspondents who had now caught up from getting their news to London. Millward and his colleagues were forced to travel to Malta by ship before they could telegraph their dispatches. When the official news finally arrived and the rival newspapers were able to print the dispatches of their special correspondents, the accusations against the *New York Herald* of fabricating news suddenly ceased. As a result, Stanley received a roving commission from his newspaper. He spent some time in Europe where he reported the revolution in Spain and was instructed in 1869 by James Gordon Bennett, proprietor of the *New York Herald*, to find Dr. Livingstone. In May 1872, he returned having accomplished the most spectacular mission of his career.

In the future the war correspondent would have less freedom of movement than he had previously enjoyed and the authorities would no longer feel obliged to aid in any way the 'gentlemen of the press'. They were looked on as a hindrance and an encumbrance, but such was their influence that they could not be excluded. They could however be deterred. In 1869, Garnet Wolseley published his controversial *Soldier's Pocket Book* and if any correspondent had cared to study it he would have found himself and his colleagues described as follows:

> These gentlemen, pandering to the public taste for news, render concealment most difficult, but this very ardour for information a General can turn to account by spreading fake news among the gentlemen of the press and thus use them as a medium by which to deceive the enemy.

Wolseley went on to describe the press as, 'Those newly invented curse to armies, who eat the rations of fighting men and do not work at all'.

In the next three decades, the war correspondents would have to contend with two high-ranking officers who were notorious for their hatred of journalists: one was Garnet Wolseley and the other, Horatio Kitchener, at this time still a cadet at the Royal Military Academy, Woolwich.

# 3

# The telegraphic correspondent

## (1870–8)

*. . . a man who combines the skill of a first class steeple chaser
with the skill of a first class writer*
Lord Salisbury

In 1870 Europe again became involved in the politics and the brutalities
of war. Not since Waterloo had Britain been so close to a conflict which
involved highly trained 'civilized' armies. Since the Crimea, Britain's
army had undertaken numerous wars but always against natives. She
wanted no part in this Franco-Prussian War, and, for her own good,
chose to assume an indifferent neutrality. But Queen Victoria and
her children were attacked by the *Pall Mall Gazette* (23 February
1871) for a breach of neutrality through their communication with the
King and the Crown Prince of Prussia. The press viewed the impending
war quite differently. Two great powers clashing on the battlefields
of Europe was far more newsworthy than the slaughter of poorly
armed savages, even though Imperial troops were not involved. The
human need to enjoy without involvement the misfortunes of others
was fully grasped by the newspapers. A 'modern' war between adver-
saries armed with the latest in breech-loading guns and rifles, when the
French would employ their *mitrailleuse* machine-gun, was too big an
event to rate a small paragraph or even a single column. War was news,
news sold newspapers, and the proprietors made their fortunes, in
spite of the comments of a naïve young second-lieutenant of the 4th

Hussars, Winston Churchill, who wrote in 1897: 'Exciting times cost newspapers much more in telegrams, correspondents etc., than they gained in increased circulation.' Admittedly the cost was high but the return was even greater: the newspaper 'barons' who were to emerge at the end of the century proved the value of news and the advantages of expert coverage. Newspapers paid well for their news, but they were able to sell it at great profit.

The Franco-Prussian War of 1870-1 was the most formidable conflict in Europe since the war against Napoleon and, whereas they had taken years to topple the Emperor, this new war disposed of his nephew's régime within a year. France had opposed, for her own safety, the increasing Prussian dominance over the Germanic states especially after her victory over the Austrians in 1866. Bismarck in his attempt to form a united Germany out-manoeuvred the French Emperor, Napoleon III, who was over-confident of his army's material and numerical strength. War became inevitable. The French were optimistically relying on Italy and Austria being allies, and thinking that the southern Germanic states would remain out of the conflict, they declared war on the Prussians. None of their hopes came true: the Italians and Austrians adopted the British policy of neutrality and the Germanic states united in one concerted effort.

The French were soon shattered as the Prussians inflicted three humiliating defeats. The army of the Rhine was beaten and besieged at Metz in August while the relieving army led by the Emperor was halted at Sedan and surrounded. Archibald Forbes, an ex-cavalry trooper, now the *Daily News* correspondent with the Prussians, witnessed the heroic but futile charge of the French *Chasseurs* at Sedan. Against modern weapons, cavalry charges were fast becoming outmoded:

> At a gallop through the ragged intervals in the confused masses of the infantry came dashing the *Chasseurs d'Afrique*. The squadrons halted, fronted, and then wheeled into line, at a pace and with regularity which would have done them credit in the *Champ de Mars*, and did them double credit executed as was the evolution under a warm fire . . . Not a needle gun gave fire as the splendid horsemen crashed down the gentle slope with the velocity of an avalanche.
>
> I have seen not a few cavalry charges, but I never saw a finer one, whether from a spectator's or an adjutant's point of view, than this one of the *Chasseurs d'Afrique* . . . Like thunder

claps sounding over the din of a hurricane rose the measured crash of the battery guns, and the cloud of white smoke drifted away towards the *Chasseurs* enveloping them for the moment from one's sight. When it blew away . . . only a handful of all the gallant show of five minutes before were galloping backward up the slope . . .

In the following month the army of the Loire was smashed and Paris was wide open to the Prussians. The civilians of Paris who had watched the army going to war with cries of 'A *Berline!*' and had rejoiced in the 'false' news that the Prussians had been beaten and 25,000 prisoners taken, were soon faced with an advancing force of Prussians and painfully few means of defence. The old fortified city of Paris had fallen into decay and hurried efforts were made to repair the ramparts. The people braced themselves for a fight to the finish. The Louvre was converted into an armaments workshop, the Gare d'Orleans became a balloon factory and the Gare de Lyon was an arsenal and munitions factory. Napoleon III surrendered to the Prussians on 2 September. He was at Sedan with over 80,000 men, and three days later, the Government of National Defence was proclaimed in Paris. The newspapermen who had covered these events could hardly keep up with the swiftly changing situations. For the first time in living memory, a country in Europe had to endure the siege of its capital accompanied by the menace of a bloody civil war. The Prussian victory would not be complete without Paris, but the Parisians had no intention of giving in. The hastily formed troops included regular units and volunteers were taught defensive action. General Trochu, the commanding officer, knew that he did not possess the strength to counter-attack but the Prussians were wary of entering the city and becoming involved in street fighting. The only logical outcome was bombardment and siege. Although the Emperor had surrendered at Sedan, Metz still held out until the following month but Paris was going to endure 217 days of siege.

The newspapers had been busy. Russell, the indefatigable correspondent of *The Times*, was sent to Berlin where during a meeting with Bismarck he was told, 'You shall go. We make a general rule against newspaper correspondents going with our army but you shall be an exception . . .' Russell was not the only exception as J. E. Hilary Skinner, a talented linguist from the *Daily News*, and the long-sighted artist, Mr. Landells of the *Illustrated London News*, also joined the staff of the Crown Prince. John Merry Le Sage of the *Daily Telegraph* accompanied the Prussian army, and later reported for his newspaper from Paris. Napoleon III had refused to allow any British correspondents to cross his lines although he was unable to stop men such as James O'Kelly who, while serving with the French army, was acting as the correspondent for the *Daily News*. The leading London papers usually had a few correspondents in various areas of Europe. The *Daily News* correspondents, however, seemed to be everywhere and the information which this paper obtained from an unknown thirty-two-year-old Scottish ex-trooper of the Royal Dragoons, Archibald Forbes, daunted even *The Times*. Their proud claim to press supremacy was shattered by Forbes's knack of always getting the news home before any of his rivals. News was now international and the American and German newspapers all had their representatives, swelling the press corps and making the rivalry for news highly competitive.

According to S. T. Sheppard, Archibald Forbes was not the 'inventor' of the swift telegraphic dispatch. Forbes had written out in long-hand his dispatch about the capitulation of Metz and posted it on 28 October, and must have been as astonished as all the *Daily News* readers to see on the morning of the 30 October a two-column story about it. S. T. Sheppard explained:

> It has been sent by a young surgeon, a German-American named Muller, who had arranged in London to do what journalistic work he could find time for. He had seen the capitulation, ridden northwards forty miles to the Luxembourg frontier, and, from a little village named Esch, had sent off his telegram. Then this pioneer utterly vanished: *stat nominis umbra*. This achievement taught the war correspondent a great deal, it opened up new fields for him to conquer. It made Mr. Forbes, who profited so much in after years by the example, write: 'In modern war correspondence the race is emphatically to the swift, the battle to the strong. The best organiser of the means for expediting his intelligence, he it is who is the most successful man — not your deliberate manufacturer of telling phrases, your piler-up of coruscating adjectives.'

The invention of the telegraph revolutionized communications. Previously messages had been sent by semaphore towers spaced at intervals, but this was neither practical nor international. Ever since William

Cooke and Charles Wheatstone had sent signals between Euston and Campden Town railway stations in 1837, and Samuel F.B. Morse had telegraphed a message to Washington and Baltimore in 1844, governments, railway companies and newspapers appreciated this new means of communication.

A network of wires connected relay stations and towns of importance as the system employed a battery, a transmitting and receiving instrument, and the insulated wires, which formed a circuit. The sending apparatus or key made or broke the circuit as the operator tapped out the message. Once the written message was received by the operator he transcribed this on to the 'wires' with the aid of a key, using a system of short and long taps to represent each letter of the alphabet. This was called Morse code, which took Morse a number of years to perfect.

By the 1850s, a large number of private companies had obtained contracts to set up telegraphic networks and offered their services at a shilling for twenty words. Countries were soon linked up and continents used submarine cables or an elaborate system of overland cables running through various countries. Telegraph lines were not as dependable as might be imagined. Wires broke, posts were blown down, dissident tribesmen or superstitious natives cut the wires, peasants looted it for their own domestic purposes or used the insulators for target practice. A breakdown in the 'wire' involved many hours and often many days of work in checking the position of the damage and repairing it, especially if it ran through desolate country. Damage to a submarine cable took months of work to repair or re-lay. In the early days of the Dover to Calais cable, French fishermen were constantly hauling the cable on board and then hacking it, mistaking it for a particularly tough type of seaweed.

The telegraph was not infallible, being at the mercy of the two operators at the ends of the line, which resulted in many garbled or misunderstood telegrams conveying meaningless or inaccurate messages. Security was an important factor, especially when governments used the telegraph and for war correspondents intent on a scoop. To ensure secrecy the British authorities maintained a system of 'red routes', telegraph lines that ran through only British territory or submarine cables that were laid at the bottom of the ocean and free from tampering. In 1902, an Imperial committee reported:

From an imperial point of view and from a supreme right of self preservation, intercommunication between the scattered units which form in their aggregate the British Empire, should as far as possible be in British hands, and should not be dependent upon the friendship or the caprice of other nations.

During wars and campaigns, armies laid field telegraph lines for use by the military when the country did not have its own domestic system. Although primarily intended for military use, these were open to war correspondents. During the American Civil War, for example, the Union military telegraph corps laid over 15,000 miles of wire which carried some 1·8 million messages and reports.

By the end of the nineteenth century, various independent companies were taken over by postal authorities: the Atlantic Telegraph Company founded in 1845; the Indian Junction Telegraph Company founded in 1857; the Red Sea and India Telegraph Association formed in 1858; and the Eastern Telegraph Company, formed in 1870, which laid a cable from London to Bombay via Lisbon, Gibraltar, Malta, Alexandria, Suez, and Aden. There were over 51,000 nautical miles of cable to be tended to and in 1919 at the height of its popularity, the Post Office boasted that it handled 82 million telegrams that year.

By the beginning of the twentieth century, international telephone systems were widely used and the telegram declined, although even today it is in its various forms still a useful and speedy means of communication. The single-wire system first developed by Morse developed rapidly to allow more than one message to travel on the wires at the same time and in 1872 Stearn patented his duplex system, followed two years later by Edison's quadruplex system. The basic concept has been developed further to include what today are considered essential communication systems. Photographs can be sent 'over the wire', handwriting can be transmitted, and even instant conversations can be conducted using the modern Telex system.

The telegraph was a great help and also caused a change in the style of journalism, making the race for news an exhausting and competitive business. Bennet Burleigh said, 'it is an age of hurry, and the war correspondents are in the running'. Most of the press had their vans or carriages, their servants and tents, and Russell of *The Times* proudly boasted his family crest painted on the side, while his

Franco-Prussian War: military dispatch rider, 1870

assistant, Colonel 'Kit' Pemperton, later killed at Sedan, had his name and rank painted in large characters on the van. This caused some comment and suspicion from the Prussians, the rank colonel not figuring in their military system but only in that of the French! After Sedan, Russell and Skinner had both ridden for the coast, boarding the boat at Ostend and bringing their news to London on 5 September to find that they had been beaten by over two days by the telegraph. During the Franco-Prussian War the supremacy of the telegraph was finally established and its use perfected by Archibald Forbes, whom Rudyard Kipling described as 'the chiefest, as he was the hugest of the war correspondents . . . and his experience dated from the birth of the needle gun . . .'

The *Standard* and *Globe* had as one of their correspondents, Arthur Williams A'Becket, a journalist of little talent, who later became editor of the *Sunday Times* (1891-5) and assistant editor of *Punch* and editor of the *Naval and Military Magazine* (1896). The *Illustrated London News* employed the talented war artist William Simpson, while a Mr. Edwards and a Mr. Kelly worked under Russell for *The Times* and the *Standard* had the able correspondents, George A. Henty and Alfred Austin. There were, of course, numerous others, all striving to get the news home first. For the first time, the *Manchester Guardian*, a provincial newspaper, thought it worth its while to be personally represented rather than rely on the reports of Reuter and the London dailies. While it possessed correspondents in the European capitals it did not as yet have any war correspondents. C. B. Marriot sent out an erratic correspondence from besieged Paris while Lieutenant R. H. Armit, R.N. 'navigated by pocket compass and the light of his cigar' to report from Prussian headquarters. D. Eaton, another *Guardian* man, was with the Prussians at the siege of Strasbourg while on the French side the newspaper had Arthur Ory and C. T. Robinson. Armit did not really take to his new occupation, writing in one of his early reports, 'I am heartily sick of war and carnage; I have never before seen it as a looker-on, and the feeling is very different in this case to that where you are yourself actively engaged.' Ory, oversleeping in Vendôme with the French Army of the Loire, awoke to find himself a prisoner of the Prussians but he was later released while Robinson enjoyed the position of being the only English correspondent in Metz during the siege. With the help of a French officer he organized a field post and balloon factory but only a few, brief dispatches ever reached the *Guardian*. The

*Manchester Guardian* also used the services of an official German correspondent, a Dr. Horn. However, the *Manchester Guardian* was more than pleased with its efforts which, according to James Grant in *History of the Newspaper Press* (1872), was carried on '. . . regardless of expense'. The *Manchester Guardian* correspondents:

> . . . distinguished themselves by the earliness, the accuracy and the fullness of the information they furnished to the paper they represented. In fact, the *Manchester Guardian* proved itself, on repeated occasions, more than a successful competitor with some of our metropolitan daily journals.

At the end of September, *The Times* became concerned by the speed with which the *Daily News* received its dispatches and Mowbray Morris urged Russell to make free use of the telegraph rather than send written dispatches by the *Feld Post* (Prussian Field Post Office) which '. . . linger from seven to ten days on the road . . .' *The Times* set up a service of couriers between the front and London in an effort to 'scoop' the news and even arranged a special train in which Russell dictated his report to Kelly; but their rival newspaper still continued to get on the streets first.

The advancing Prussian armies closed on Paris; on 18 September the last mail train left the city and the following day the only remaining telegraph lines were cut. Correspondents had to get their dispatches out of the besieged capital by 'Balloon Post'. The Post Office was still accepting letters but as Henry Labouchere, the correspondent of the *Daily News* who signed himself 'A besieged Resident', noted no-one knew how they were to be delivered. Labouchere saw a postal van loaded with mail one morning, driver in place, ready to leave at the correct hour but there were no horses! Twenty-eight postmen tried a breakthrough on foot on 21 September but only one was successful. He made four other journeys but was eventually caught and shot by the Prussians.

The 'Balloon Post' was organized under the command of that intrepid showman, balloonist extraordinary, and photographer, Felix Tournachon. The 'Balloon Post' continued to function remarkably well under the circumstances even though a few fell into the hands of the Prussians. In Paris, the food shortage worried the population more than the Prussians. The enemy had encircled the capital and were installing their heavy siege equipment but as yet not a shell had fallen.

Franco-Prussian War: 'The Besieged Resident',
Henry Labouchere, war correspondent of the
*Daily News,* during the siege of Paris, 1871.

Early sorties by the French army had met with indifferent success and Parisians and the correspondents settled down to weeks of boredom. The newspapermen were Captain John Augustas O'Shea of the *Standard*; Henry Labouchere, later proprietor and editor of *Truth* and M.P. for Northampton and described as 'witty and intrepid', of the *Daily News*. James O'Kelly was also in Paris for the *Daily News* and Henry Richard Vizetelly, one of the two brothers who helped start the *Illustrated London News*, was there with his son. Ernest Alfred Vizetelly, at the time only eighteen, represented not only the *Illustrated London News* but also the *Pall Mall Gazette* and the *Daily News* and later claimed to be the youngest war correspondent on record. The *Daily Telegraph* was represented by John Merry Le Sage among others. Le Sage had followed the events with the Prussian army and then entered Paris where he remained during the siege.

The correspondents described life in Paris, commented on the food shortage, the ever-changing political scene, and the confidence of the soldiers and civilians. On 15 October, the *Illustrated London News* published a dispatch from Vizetelly:

> The last few days have had their full share of those bizarre and novel incidents which have characterised the later stages of the war. Paris, though closely invested, can still communicate with the outer world. The service of the *post aerostatique* is conducted with some pretence at regularity, and the escape of Mr. Gambetta from Paris was effected by the same agency . . . In Paris every voice is still for war. The German siege guns have not yet opened fire though their batteries already crown the heights behind Sevres, St. Cloud and Bougival . . . The bombardment it is expected will be directed in the first place against the forts. For the moment, however, the food question is uppermost in the minds of the inhabitants. Meat is already getting scarce, and nondescript scraps of dubious origin are set before guests at restaurants formerly of high repute . . . Already 300 of our own country people, who, from poverty or failure of remittances, were unable to leave Paris in time, are being fed from a daily soup kitchen at the Embassy. Unless the garrison can compel the enemy to raise the siege . . . the fall of Paris, like that of Strasbourg, is simply reduced to a matter of arithmetical calculation.

On 26 October a party of British and American civilians gave a farewell dinner before leaving the capital with Prussian permission. (The British were, however, turned back.) Henry Labouchere explained:

'. . . there is neither soup nor vegetables, that the only *entree* is a sardine, the only *hors d'oevre* a pickled onion, and that for dessert they throw you a cigar.' In this state, money was short and everything and anything was for sale, the shops, especially food ones, having run out of much of their stock. Even Prussian helmets, allegedly picked up on the battlefield, were sold although later their manufacturer, a wily Parisian, was arrested. The kerbs of the streets were lined with hawkers selling every conceivable article, including caricatures and photographs which one correspondent noted were '. . . frequently of a most indecent description'. News could also be sent into Paris as Gambetta had taken pigeons with him when he fled from the capital. These birds carried messages into the besieged city while the balloons carried messages and the pigeons out. In order to get more news of the war into the city, dispatches and messages were photographed and printed in reduced form and thus one pigeon could carry some 225 messages. The messages were enlarged and then delivered to the recipients in the same way as a telegram. Over 60,000 messages were sent into Paris during the siege in this way, in spite of the Prussians' measures to stop them by using a large number of hawks imported from Saxony.

Being a war correspondent was dangerous at any time, but there were great hidden dangers in being a correspondent in a campaign fought between 'civilized' nations. To a native enemy, whites were equal targets whether they represented the Queen or *The Times* and the risks were clear, but in wars such as the Austro-Prussian and the Franco-Prussian, correspondents could not have freedom of movement. Correspondents had to carry an identity card with their credentials and wear a *brassard* to distinguish them, but even so, men accredited to one side would hardly ever venture over to the other where they might be mistaken for spies or, worse, be considered as pro the enemy cause. Journalists also had to ensure that their dispatches did not offend the army to which they were attached or the country they were reporting from; and anyone breaking these 'unwritten' rules usually had his permission withdrawn and his editor was requested to remove him. Even for a correspondent's newspaper to profess support for the enemy was dangerous. Henry Labouchere of the *Daily News* was denounced by a passer-by in Paris as a suspicious character and only saved himself by jumping on to a café table and extolling the virtues of France and the French. As the newspapers from London were received by both sides, extra caution had to be exercised.

Franco-Prussian War: an intrepid photographer at work in the ruins of the Hôtel de Ville, Paris, after it had been set on fire by members of the Commune, 1871.

Russell complained to Delane about putting 'From our Military Correspondent' after the dispatches of Captain Brackenbury who had reinforced *The Times* team in December 1870, as it caused the Prussians to view him with suspicion. Delane replied to Russell that 'Men whose business is killing and who are paid to be killed cannot be *aux petits soins* with every curious neutral who comes to see how he likes it . . .'

While the correspondents outside continued to write dispatches about Prussian supremacy and the universal collapse of the French, those inside wrote about worsening conditions and the shortage of food. The animals in the zoo were killed one by one and the meat sold. In the new year, the Prussians at last opened fire on the capital, destroying buildings and part of the fortifications, although during the previous month they had contented themselves with aiming only at the encircling military forts. The bombardment of civilians provoked an outcry in the press and Parisians thought for an instant that world opinion might force the Prussians to stop and withdraw. *The Times*, who had condoned the bombardment of the fortresses and been pro-Prussia, skilfully kept out of trouble when news of the French civilian casualties arrived. 'Much as we may feel disposed,' stated the leader article, 'to denounce the Bombardment of Paris as an outrage upon humanity, we think the Prussians who resorted to it may share the blame with the French who provoked it . . .'

As Vizetelly had written some months before, capitulation was only a matter of time. Russell obtained a scoop for *The Times*, but not before he had witnessed the King of Prussia being proclaimed Emperor of Germany at Versailles, which was perhaps the most far-reaching and significant event of the entire war. The emergence of United Germany as a first-rate power became more and more certain and the *Saturday Review* of 11 September 1896 was to declare that:

> In the Transvaal, at the Cape, in Central Africa, in India and
> the East, in the islands of the Southern Seas and in the far
> Northwest . . . the German and Englishman are struggling
> to be first. A million petty disputes build up the greatest
> cause of war the world has ever seen.

On 23 January, Russell heard from a friend that Jules Favre, the Government of Paris representative, was in Versailles where he had been sent secretly to see what terms Bismarck would offer. Russell, being the good journalist that he was, had the news confirmed by Prussian head-quarters and then sent a telegram to Delane. Mowbray Morris replied to Russell in an exalted mood after *The Times* had published the news on the 24th, 'You have achieved great success . . . We have beaten everybody.' Paris surrendered on the 29th and German troops marched into the city, in a triumphal procession, on 1 March. But Paris was far from peaceful and on 3 March when the Germans marched out, signs of revolution were in evidence. On 15 March, the *Illustrated London News* correspondent announced:

> When we wrote a short time ago, that the departure of the
> Germans from the neighbourhood of Paris would probably be
> a signal for revolutionary demonstrations, we willingly admit
> that we did not anticipate a complete overthrow of order and
> authority . . . The mob is master of Paris. The Government has
> fled to Versailles. Numbers of the National Guard have become
> rebels and numbers of the regular troops have become
> traitors . . . The Hôtel de Ville, the Place Vendôme and all the
> other points, the possession of which means control of the
> capital, are in the hands of the revolters.

On 1 April the same newspaper reported the creation of the Commune, and during April and May, a bloody civil war was enacted. At last, unable to maintain their hold, the Communards fired public buildings in the city and shot hostages. The government troops for their part were without mercy and over 20,000 insurgents and innocents were massacred during the slow reoccupation of Paris. The German occupation in France lasted up to September 1873.

The means of communicating news had clearly speeded-up during this war, the foremost instigator being Archibald Forbes, who despite every effort on the part of other papers, managed with uncanny regularity to get his reports to London first. Russell at one moment thought that he had discovered his method but he was wrong. He considered that a courier armed with Red Cross credentials and able to pass through French and Prussian lines could beat the *Feld Post* easily, but this theory was shattered when the noon edition of the *Daily News* on the morning of the bombardment of St. Denis carried a full and comprehensive story of the affair: a complete dispatch written, transmitted, and type-set in less than three hours! Forbes wrote to Russell in 1899, and explained how he had accomplished his journalistic feat. It seems that he was on excellent terms with the Crown Prince of Saxony who was:

> ... frank and open about details, both of the present and
> future, if they believed in one's honesty ... It was arranged
> that I might send home in advance of both bombardments
> full details ... making the editor bound not to print details
> until I should give the word. When the first gun was fired
> against Avron, I galloped twenty miles to Mayence and
> promptly wired 'Go ahead'.

Forbes repeated the same method for the bombardment of St. Denis
with the magic telegram 'Go ahead'.

> Full details of the position [he continued], ... and
> complements of the artillery appeared in the noon edition of
> the *Daily News*, the same morning, the matter being already
> in Type, but carefully guarded until the moment came.

Archibald Forbes was perhaps the epitome of the late Victorian war
correspondent. Intense and notoriously bad-tempered, he was born in
1838, the eldest son of the Rev. I. W. Forbes, and educated at the
local Scottish parish school before entering Aberdeen University. He
left the University without a degree and in 1859 enlisted in the Royal
Dragoons as a trooper. He served until 1864 when he paid £20 to be
discharged at his own request. The Franco-Prussian War was his first
experience of war reporting and the undoubted success of his campaign
and his predominance over others during the next nine years established
him as one of the foremost war correspondents of his time. While
Russell was considered the 'father of modern war correspondents' or
the 'parent of a luckless tribe' as he once said, Forbes was looked upon
by the public as the unbeatable champion who could easily have
stepped straight from the pages of his own dispatches. There were never
any ill feelings towards him among the other correspondents who all
had the highest respect for the tall, tough and ugly Scotsman. Forbes,
describing himself perhaps, wrote, 'Correspondents had to be...big
and ugly enough to impress the conviction that it would be highly
unwise to take liberties with.' Kipling, whose admiration for Forbes
was almost unlimited, wrote, 'There was no man mightier in his craft
than he. He always opened a conversation with news that there would
be trouble in the Balkans in the spring.' Melton Prior, artist for the
*Illustrated London News*, described Forbes as 'That brilliant Military
Correspondent'. Forbes gave up the active life of a 'special' after the
Zulu War of 1879 and devoted himself to writing biographies of famous

men and a number of books on his reminiscences while lecturing on his experiences as a war correspondent. On 30 March 1900 he died in a delirium in the arms of his editor. With starting eyes he uttered, 'Those guns, man, don't you see those guns. I tell you, the brave fellows will be mowed down like grass . . .' A dramatic ending to one of the most dramatic of correspondents who brought in a new dimension to the profession, the importance not of writing the news but of getting it home first.

When Russell learned of his death, he wrote sadly, 'That incomparable Archibald, he has left no one to equal him.' In nine years Forbes had maintained his supremacy even over the veteran Russell. What perhaps rankled *The Times* most about Forbes was that in 1870 he had offered his services to them but they had refused him.

Kipling wrote that correspondents did not just have to be good observers and writers but needed '. . . the constitution of a bullock, the digestion of an ostrich and an infinite adaptability to all circumstances'.


The significance of a powerful and united Germany was not yet appreciated in Britain when, in 1873, news reached London of trouble on the west coast of Africa. The Ashanti nation, a proud and war-like people who had already skirmished with the British, had invaded the East African British Protectorate in June, causing great desolation. Britain was at first reluctant to begin an expensive, punitive expedition in an area which was the most unprofitable of all her colonies. At first, the government thought that perhaps the local troops, a few Royal Marines, and the 2nd Battalion the West India Regiment plus the friendly Fanti tribe could control the invaders but many of the Marines were sick and the natives cowardly, which left painfully few men to stem the advance, let alone subdue the Ashantis. In August, the government selected the youngest major-general in the army to be Commander-in-Chief and the notorious press-hater, Garnet Wolseley, barely thirty-eight, sailed for Africa in September with thirty-five specially selected officers who were known as the 'Wolseley ring'. Nearly all were later to attain high rank and all, although young, were renowned for their forward military thinking, devotion to their profession, and disregard of traditional military precedents. On the voyage out they devoted their time to thoroughly acquainting themselves with

Ashanti War: Sir Garnet Wolseley, in khaki uniform worn during the campaign.

the area of operations, reading every scrap of available literature and poring over the latest maps. They were perhaps the first generation of truly professional officers: and the correspondents who accompanied them were equally professional in their trade.

The west coast of Africa was still a very unhealthy place for white men. Wolseley was determined then to achieve immediate success and had asked for two battalions of British infantry to be equipped for the climate and to be on stand-by in England should the local troops prove inadequate. To him, the added encumbrance of war correspondents was insufferable. The 'race of drones' as he described them descended with the advancing forces. The Commander-in-Chief made certain members of his staff correspondents for the more influential London papers and by this means he hoped not only to prevent bad publicity but also to make known only news which was to his and his staff officers' advantage. The professional members of the press did not take kindly to this intrusion and Stanley, a force to be reckoned with in Africa, explains that:

> He seems to be animated with a desire to compete with the
> natural purveyors of news, with us the special correspondents.
> I do not blame him, . . . but it is none the less novel and
> singular . . . We of course cannot compete with him if he
> refuses us the same facilities he employs himself . . . As
> Sir Garnet may be priding himself upon a successful 'beat'
> over four special correspondents, I may as well record the
> feat in his favour with a good grace.

Stanley had already sensed this exclusion of the specials when on board ship, the *East Africa*, he inquired who composed Sir Garnet Wolseley's staff. The first two names given were enough to convince him of the difficulties that lay ahead. The tall and ugly Captain Brackenbury for one was an established *Times* man while Lieutenant Maurice, the winner of the 'Wellington Prize Essay', was another. Stanley noted that Brackenbury was '. . . an indefatigable caterer for the Press . . .' and that Maurice (later a major-general) '. . . writes for one if not two newspapers'. 'I will take it for granted,' Stanley continued, 'that they [Wolseley's staff] are mostly all newspaper writers in military clothes.'

While the steps taken by Wolseley gave him a monopoly on the news to a certain extent, the London papers still preferred to send their own men. Winwood Reade, an ex-medical student with an explorer's mentality, represented *The Times*, F. Boyle wrote for the *Daily Telegraph*, the inimitable George Alfred Henty, the doyen of adventure writers, informed and entertained the *Standard* readers, while Melton Prior, on his first of many campaigns, reported and drew for the *Illustrated London News*. The *Daily News* adopted the established precedent of having two officers write for them, '... whose names the unwritten laws of military etiquette forbid us to record ...' The *Western Morning News*, the *Scotsman* and *Manchester Guardian* were also represented. Reuter's, now an established news agency, appointed a coastal trader to send them telegraphic dispatches.

The *Graphic* did not have an artist on hand at the beginning of the Ashanti War and presented their own idea of Sir Garnet's arrival at Cape Coast Fort, much to the mirth of the other newspapers:

> Some surprise and a good deal of amusement have been
> caused by a cartoon which appeared in the *Graphic* of the
> 1st of November, and which professes to be a 'fancy sketch'
> of Sir Garnet Wolseley's landing at Cape Coast. Besides many
> other remarkable features in it, such as a mounted Arab —
> both Arabs and horses being wholly unknown on the Gold
> Coast — an ill-looking, overdressed negro is represented in it
> as ceremoniously saluting Sir Garnet Wolseley, and the
> readers of the *Graphic* are informed 'that this is the half-caste
> Colonial Secretary, a very fine gentleman dressed in the
> height of Parisian costume.' The post of Colonial Secretary
> at Cape Coast has for some time past been filled by
> Mr. Goldsworthy, an English gentleman, late an officer in
> the 17th Lancers. When Sir Garnet Wolseley landed at Cape
> Coast the post of Colonial Secretary was filled by
> Captain Lanyon, of the 2nd West India Regiment, a native
> of the north of Ireland ... It will doubtless cause great
> surprise to both of these gentlemen as it has caused to their
> friends to learn they are 'half-castes', and scarcely less to
> find that they dress 'in the height of Parisian costume'.

Wolseley's first move was to order the friendly Fanti chiefs to assemble all their fighting men, but his demand met with little success and out of a possible 60,000 he obtained 1,200 men. Wolseley's orders were met with excuses such as, 'I have small-pox today but will come tomorrow'. The Commander-in-Chief had no alternative but to ask for three regular battalions from England. On 14 October, with a force of 158 marines, 29 sailors, 205 of the 2nd West India Regiment, 126 local Hussars, 40 armed natives, and 270 bearers, Wolseley moved against the

Ashanti War: Henry Morton Stanley, war correspondent of the *New York Herald*.

Ashanti War: George Alfred Henty, war correspondent of the *Standard*.

insubordinate tribes, the nearest village being Essaman. Using the advice he gave in the *Soldier's Pocket Book*, he made it known that he was about to march eastwards, but his attack on Essaman lay to the west. Stanley probably spoke for all the specials when he complained that he failed:

> ... to see anything commendable in it. Sir Garnet is now engaged in an expedition against savages on the West Coast of Africa, far removed from the influence or the enterprise of the public press, and any intelligence he would care to impart could not injure his mission whatever, but rather benefit him. It takes twenty-one or twenty-two days for a letter to reach England, it will take as many days for the newspaper publishing it to reach Cape Coast Castle, I therefore fail to see any plausible reason for Sir Garnet's reluctance to speak of his intentions...

Stanley was no doubt peeved, as was Reade, at Wolseley's references to that dreadful creature, 'One Who Knows' and those twin brothers, 'The Man on the Spot' and 'The Man who has been There'. Both of them qualified, the one as the man who found Livingstone and considered himself the official correspondent's authority on Africa and the other who had passed some time in West Africa as an explorer.

F. Boyle of the *Daily Telegraph* witnessed the entry into Essaman. After one volley from the natives, it was found to be deserted. The column rested, then moved to the next village, Amquana, and shortly encountered the Ashantis.

> The din was deafening [wrote Boyle in his dispatch]. Not one in ten took aim, and half the muskets were fired in the air; in fact, so that they fired, they did not seem to care in the slightest in which direction the rifles were directed, and often as I have been under fire, I do not know that I ever felt more uncomfortable than I did here for a few minutes. At length the efforts of Sir Garnet Wolseley and the whole of the officers put a stop to this reckless waste of ammunition. The wood on the left was now attacked ... The main body of the column continued to push forward and without any further opposition being encountered the village of Amquana, down on the sea beach, was reached after two hours' further march. It was found to have been abandoned and was destroyed.

Reinforcements were put ashore from the ship *Decoy* together with

'. . . a case of claret for the thirsty Marines . . .' 'Those who say,' continued Boyle, 'the British soldier will not drink claret should have seen the pleasure with which those men drank their allowance.'

Very little could be done with the available troops and Sir Garnet waited until the New Year for the three regular battalions from England to arrive. Small probing expeditions were mounted and the Ashantis, in their withdrawal to Pra, found that they had surrounded a force of sailors, Marines, and native troops whom Wolseley was about to recall. Winwood Reade of *The Times* and F. Boyle of the *Daily Telegraph* had made their own way to Abakrampa, where the first serious fighting of the campaign broke out. Wolseley had considered Abakrampa unimportant and had ordered the return of the sailors and marines when the attack came.

> When I reached the church roof [wrote Boyle] the volleys of
> our men had been stopped, but the Ashanti muskets alone,
> booming and full voiced as small artillery, made a deafening
> fusillade . . . Columns of smoke arose amongst the trees as
> volley after volley was fired by the thousands of savages
> congregated in one spot or another. They were evidently
> working down towards the valley lying along our left flank.
> Suddenly . . . a myriad voices struck up the Ashanti war
> song. Very fine and very stirring it is, sounding quite unlike
> any savage music I had heard hitherto. With a thousand
> voices chanting in chorus . . . no wonder Fantee hearts fail
> them at the sound. Scores of horns, modulated in tone,
> played a wild accompaniment, and even the tom-toms came
> in harmoniously. When the song was finished, the fusillade
> recommenced more furiously than ever . . . They were met,
> however, by a fire too crushing for savages to stand . . . I could
> not have believed that troops armed with muzzle-loaders,
> for the most part, could have kept up such a thundering roar.
> The sunny landscape was so draped in smoke, lurid and yellow
> in the declining rays, that we [Boyle and Reade] could not see
> a foot distant from the church top. Through the dense cloud,
> now and again a line of leaping flame close to the ground told
> that our troops were firing. At longer intervals the Sniders made
> angry crackle borne above the din . . . On the port side [after
> all it was the Royal Navy and Marines] issued a sheet of flame
> that stilled the uproar for a moment . . . Every Marine stood
> at the 'ready' by window and loophole . . . Towards 5 p.m.
> after an hour and a half of hideous uproar, the enemy's fire
> began to slacken, and a rocket from the church, well directed,

reduced them to silence . . . everyone is astonished at the boldness and persistence of the attack . . .

The following day the Ashanti threw themselves once again to the attack but at about 6 p.m. Sir Garnet Wolseley arrived with about 100 Hussars and natives. Reade recorded that he, rifle in hand, emerged from the church and had great satisfaction in returning the fire of an Ashanti sniper whom he later found dead.

> It was dreary waiting at Cape Coast Castle for news [wrote
> Stanley at the end of November] and expecting the arrival of
> the white troops . . . who are said to be coming to destroy
> Coomassie [Kumasi] . . . Many like myself, found it hard work
> to live week after week in a Fantee hut, stationed in a
> malarious valley, doing nothing but smelling the abominations
> around us . . . If one went in a desperate state straight to
> headquarters seeking news, it was ever the same answer
> 'Nothing new'.

The Wolseley attitude towards newspapermen had filtered through to his officers and they were short with inquiries from correspondents.

> Meet any of them [remarked Stanley] without the face of
> inquisitiveness and the nose of a news-gatherer, and the eye of
> an itinerant newspaper man, and you will find them as genial
> souls as any who ever called themselves English gentlemen.

To break this boredom and to have something to write about, Stanley proposed to Henty a trip to the mouth of the Volta river in the *New York Herald* launch to see the supporting expedition of Captain Glover, charged with subduing the tribes of the Volta and mounting an attack to the east of Kumasi. Henty was nearly drowned on this little adventure which was suitably elaborated in his dispatches but they both brought back plenty of information, extolling Glover's drive and efficiency.

Concerning this little expedition, Henty later wrote:

> No doubt it does seem a stupid sort of thing to do, if it had
> been an Englishman I would draw back; but if Stanley can
> do it, I can; and I am not going to let any Yankee say he was
> ready to do a thing, but an Englishman funked going with him.

Stanley wrote in his account of the campaign that he offered to take any correspondents on the trip with him who wished to go, adding that 'I would not venture in such a tiny boat on the Atlantic for a thousand pounds'.

On New Year's Day, the extra battalions arrived. Little time was lost in organizing the new troops and an advance was made towards Kumasi. The new troops were cosseted, each man being dosed with quinine every day and given a list of 'do's and don'ts' for the tropics. Such was the efficiency and forethought of Sir Garnet Wolseley that the expression 'All Sir Garnet', meaning everything in tip-top condition, crept into the English language. By 24 January, the main force was some thirty miles from the Ashanti capital, with various supporting forces, including Glover's, closing on their objective. King Coffee of the Ashantis, a name which the correspondents and leader writers made great play with, sent various notes to Wolseley offering reparation but Wolseley's demands were impossible to meet. Sir Garnet had no doubt imposed these terms, as later Bartle Frere, Governor of the Cape and High Commissioner for South Africa, did on King Cetewayo of the Zulus in 1879, for his own glorious ends. A campaign ending in overwhelming victory was far more use to a young and ambitious general than a political compromise.

To advertise his intentions and his success in liberating some white prisoners, Sir Garnet telegraphed to the coast where the news was put aboard a ship, the *Samaritan*, with immediate orders to sail for Gibraltar. The ship, with neither passengers or freight, carried nothing but '. . . a good news telegram of less than fifty words'. 'This excessive desire which Sir Garnet had manifested to inform Parliament of his progress will cost the British people the little sum of £7,000', wrote Stanley. One of the most expensive telegrams ever! The news correspondents were perhaps a little annoyed, not by Wolseley's usual trick of keeping the news to himself but because he had sent an empty ship with a useless piece of information to the extremity of the telegraph line. They rightly thought that they could have sent some of their own dispatches on the same vessel.

But even as the ship was on the high seas, '. . . all diplomatic negotiations with the Ashanti had fallen through', Melton Prior of the *Illustrated London News* remembered, '. . . there was nothing else left for us but to fight'. On 31 January the main force pushing towards the village of Amoaful came into contact with the enemy. The 42nd, the Black Watch, were sent forward, much to the delight of the

Ashanti War: Sir Garnet Wolseley and army giving three cheers for the Queen in Coomassie, 3 April 1874 (pencil sketch for the *Illustrated London News* by Melton Prior).

correspondents, who always seemed to find Highland troops in action a good dispatch filler. The British tried to fight in a square, a hopeless formation in broken terrain, and the Ashantis in their traditional 'horseshoe' formation enveloped the flanks, and invaded the disintegrating formation, in which units lost complete contact with each other. The enemy swarmed on the headquarters and staff in the centre and bullets seemed to be falling everywhere. Melton Prior remembered that he and Henty, being unable to find cover, headed for the Highland lines. 'It was difficult and perilous work,' he wrote, 'but we arrived there at last and I succeeded in making a rough sketch of the "42nd hard at it".' Correspondents in this type of war were usually armed to the teeth just like the troops and Prior noted that he had a double-barrelled shotgun loaded with 'Swan shot' with which he neatly blasted two of the enemy.

The British force encountered the enemy again on 4 February and that afternoon the troops entered a deserted Kumasi. Prior celebrated the 'victory' by calling to his bearers to bring up his 'drawing material'. He, Henty, and Stanley then sat and drank a glassful of champagne which '. . . much revived the three of us'.

F. Boyle of the *Daily Telegraph* described the empty city:

> . . . A town over which the smell of death hangs everywhere, and pulsates on each sickly breath of wind — a town where, here and there, a vulture hops at one's very feet, too gorged to join the filthy flock preening itself on the gaunt dead trunks that line the road; where blood is plastered, like a pitch coating over trees and floors and stools . . .

Stanley described the scene in much the same way:

> We saw thirty or forty decapitated bodies in the last stage of corruption and countless skulls which lay piled in heaps . . . The stoutest heart and the most stoical mind might have been appalled.

Wolseley had issued strict orders against looting and even summoned all the correspondents to ask them '. . . on your honour not to take anything . . .'. Melton Prior was unable to resist the temptation of two gold buckles which '. . . would make a very handsome brooch for my wife . . .' and he admitted, 'I must own to filling my pockets with the smallest things I could find . . .' On the return march, Wolseley had ordered that no loot should be taken over the river Pra and set sentries to search everyone. Prior neatly bundled his loot into his hammock, climbed in, covered himself up and pretended to be ill, and so escaped the search.

The capital was fired by the order of Sir Garnet, and the King's palace was blown up by the Engineers. That morning Wolseley sent an officer to England with dispatches and gladly let him carry Prior's sketches for the *Illustrated London News*. Peace was signed on 13 February and the correspondents gathered at Cape Coast Castle. They were offered a passage in the government steamer *Dromedary* which they gladly accepted.

These men took the hardships and heat in their stride, '. . . if I am stupid enough to follow Tommy Atkins, I must share his luck. It is not all beer and skittles', wrote Prior who on account of his bald head and high-pitched laugh was known amongst his press colleagues as the 'screeching billiard ball'. Although the correspondents paid for Commissariat rations, they also had their own well-stuffed baggage. Prior had a fifty-pound case of preserved meat, rice, and biscuits plus, amongst other things, a sixty-pound case of claret and whisky. All had their tents, wagons, servants, and porters, but campaigning was still hard. The main problem in the tropics was health and Prior boldly announced that he owed his good health to the fact that '. . . when I drank water, with or without a stimulant, I always put a teaspoonful or half a teaspoonful of Pyretic Saline in it.' Pyretic Saline was as indispensable to globetrotters as cod-liver oil was to the Victorian nursery. 'Wherever the Union Jack rears aloft its benificent influence,' said the advertisement, 'wherever English is spoken — from Pole to Pole — have dwellers borne testimony to the *Life Preserving* qualities of Lamplough's Pyretic Saline.'

While the newspapermen were ready to face the dangers and hardships of campaigning to satisfy their editors, to produce enough stories of high adventure to earn their bonuses, they were also keen to relate their own adventures in published books. After every campaign in the late Victorian era, a large number of correspondents published their own vivid, but on occasion inaccurate, account of the fighting. But the market for adventure stories was still open.

In 1873, the Carlist War had erupted in Spain but attracted very little attention, being, as Stanley described, 'ever enduring, . . . the most uninteresting campaign ever planned'. Newspapers still took some note of it, dispatched correspondents and made local connections. Among the journalists were the inimitable Melton Prior, Archibald Forbes, Meginal, Henry Lane, Irving Montague, and James Thomas.

José Lopez Dominguez, a local man, reported for *The Times* who also sent Colonel Frederick Gustavus Burnaby, better known as 'Battling Burnaby of the Blues'.

Frederick Burnaby was born in 1842 and after joining the Royal Horse Guards with the rank of cornet became widely known as a traveller, politician, journalist and balloonist. He was reputedly the strongest and tallest officer in the British army, standing some six feet four inches, and was once reputed to have bent a poker around the neck of the Prince of Wales. Two years after the Carlist War he explored Asiatic Russia accompanied by a Tartar dwarf servant. He wrote his adventures in a best-selling book, contested Birmingham as a Tory in 1880, and crossed the English Channel in a balloon in 1882. He had a 'rare time' fighting Dervishes in 1884, 'bagging Fuzzy Wuzzies', but was killed in this pursuit at the battle of Abu Klea in January 1884. On his death, the *Daily Telegraph* believed that his name would live for ever '. . . as long as valour and faithfulness unto death remain the watchwords of the sons of the Island Queen'.

The Serbian War lasted from July 1876 to the end of October and attracted the attention of the journalists, not because it was a large-scale campaign but because, as Archibald Forbes, still representing the *Daily News*, wrote:

> From the point of view of the war correspondent, the campaign, at least on the Serbian side, fairly bristled with adventure and with opportunities for enterprise. There were few days on which a man, keen for that species of pleasure, could not, somehow or other, find a fight in which to enjoy himself. If he stood well with the military authorities . . . he was impeded by no restrictions in regard to his outgoings and incomings.

Life, however, was '. . . without beef-steaks . . . and there was no champagne to be had'. Forbes was joined by other correspondents, Melton Prior, George Alfred Henty and a newcomer, Frederick Villiers, representing the *Illustrated London News*'s rival paper, the *Graphic*. Villiers teamed up with Forbes in this war, his first in a long career which would win him twelve English and foreign war medals and in which he would be the first, as he claimed, to use the 'cinematograph' and to introduce the bicycle as a means of transport for the war correspondent.

The Serbian War was one of many attempts by the Christian Serbs to be free from outside oppression. In this instance the oppressor was

Russo-Turkish War: 'Thorough' Archibald Forbes, war correspondent of the *Daily News,* as depicted by Spy in *Vanity Fair,* 5 January 1878. Note the distinguishing armband. Others caricatured in this magazine included Russell and Bennet Burleigh.

Turkey, and the Bosnian and Herzegovina Serbs were joined by those liberated from Serbia and Montenegro. Even though the Ottoman Empire was decaying rapidly, the Serbs could not stand up to the numerical and material superiority of the Sultan's troops.

> With flaming volleys [wrote Archibald Forbes], the Turks swept forward over the hedges and through the copses, with a confident steadfastness that boded ill for the militiamen waiting waveringly to confront them. As the Turks came on, I watched the Serbian line give a kind of shudder; then it broke . . .

At the attack on Alexinatz, Forbes recalled:

Of the detached incidents of this day I have no record. I wrote
as I rode, making short notes as events occurred, and tearing
the leaves out of my note-book and sending them into town
for despatch by post to my colleague at Belgrade, who
telegraphed from the Austrian side of Semlin everything
that reached him from the front. But no post went out that
night . . . since the officer who undertook to deliver my
letter . . . was killed by a shell.

*The telegraphic
correspondent*

Villiers was worn out and returned early to town to try to send away
some of his sketches. Forbes considered him, '. . . cool but without
being rash' and Villiers of the *Graphic* established a reputation equal to
that of Melton Prior for his objective drawings and short, pertinent
descriptions.

The inevitable collapse of the Serbians was only saved by the
intervention of the major European powers who forced Turkey to
reorganize the Balkans. Opposed as always to the nibbling away of
her frontiers, Turkey resisted, and in 1877 Russia declared war on
the Ottoman Empire. War correspondents seldom had any political
knowledge of the situations leading up to a war, nor did they bother
to clutter their dispatches with political argument; this they left to the
leader writer. Their prime concern was lively journalism whether from
the side of the just or the unjust, the loser or the winner.

The most skilful in this style was Archibald Forbes, who often gave
little attention to the events of the war being more concerned with
telling his own personal adventures, unless there was a chance of
getting a first. Evidently, the *Daily News* readers preferred this and
Forbes, the egoist, was only too glad to cater for popular demand.
The Russo-Turkish War of 1877 was no different from others in
the eyes of the press and the London editors dispatched their best
men, adequately armed with funds to get the reports back first.
The *Illustrated London News* sent a number of artists including
Irving Montague, Colonel E. Matthew Hale, later of the Post Office
Rifles, and their star artist, Melton Prior, who insisted on taking his
wife, although Ingram '. . . did not seem very pleased with the
suggestion, as he thought it would keep me from my work . . .'
*The Times*'s men included George Dobson, later to run the Petrograd
office of *The Times* during the Russian Revolution, and Mr. Coningsby.
Frederick Villiers, now on his second campaign, drew and reported for the *Graphic* while the *Daily News* sent their ace reporter

Archibald Forbes and also Francis Scudamore. Camille Barrere, later a French Ambassador, represented the French press while Boyle and Henty as usual wrote for the *Standard*, which was now boasting a circulation of some 200,000 copies per day. The *Sheffield Daily Telegraph* was represented by Mr. Dow and the London *Daily Telegraph* by Drew Gay, described by Melton Prior as a '. . . lively young correspondent'.

> The war correspondent who accompanied the Russian Army which crossed the Danube [wrote Forbes] . . . and who had the good fortune to be a welcome person, found his path of duty made exceedingly easy for him. And whether he was a welcome person or not depended almost entirely on himself. His newspaper might be held in obloquy, but the authorities ignored the hostility of the paper . . . and the correspondent was not held responsible for the tone of his journal, but only for the matter in it which he himself contributed . . .

The *Standard* was not considered pro-Russian but Boyle was readily accepted until one of his dispatches gave offence. '. . . Everybody ought to rejoice that this fate befell him,' wrote Forbes, as it resulted in an amusing book *The Diary of an Expelled Correspondent*. The *Daily Telegraph* was bitterly against Russia and when Drew Gay presented himself at the Russian Headquarters for his credentials, he was refused.

Correspondents had to wear a distinguishing badge on their arm, '. . . a dreadful brass plate such as street-corner messengers now wear . . .' and they carried a pass showing a photograph:

> . . . with a dab of red wax on his chest, on which was impressed the headquarters seal, while on the back were written certain cabalistic figures, which, . . . instructed all and sundry to whom 'these presents' might come to recognise the bearer and assist him . . .

Then they could go anywhere at their own risk. Dispatches and sketches were censored by both sides and Melton Prior related how the Turkish authorities held up a number of his drawings. Marching straight to the censor's office, Prior drew out from the red envelope, always used by the *Illustrated London News* correspondents, some sketches showing brutalities which Prior had seen. He threatened to forward these by fair means or foul unless his other sketches were released.

Russo-Turkish War: the perils of a war correspondent—Melton Prior of the *Illustrated London News* arrested by the Austrians in Ragusa as a spy.

Prior won. Correspondents often had difficulty in proving their identity because the soldiery of both sides were usually illiterate. While this proved an insurmountable problem in some cases where credentials were in order, it also allowed the bolder correspondents to bluff their way through outposts. Irving Montague, a freelance artist during the war, recounted two episodes of bluffing carried out by pressmen:

> One night I remember escaping durance vile through the ready wit of a fellow correspondent, who, pointing to 'I, Lord Granville,' &c., &c., &c., printed in large letters on his passport, assured the guard that he was himself that nobleman, and I his secretary . . .

On another occasion, a correspondent:

> . . . when required to show his papers, having no passport to produce, handed up his tailor's bill which he happened to have in his pocket, an awe-inspiring document upon which the medallioned heads of the several potentates whom the tailor numbered amongst his patrons were printed. This so overcame his interlocutor . . . he allowed him to go on his way.

The most notable occurrence of the war was the siege of Plevna witnessed by a number of correspondents of both sides including George Dobson, Archibald Forbes, Frederick Villiers, and J. A. MacGahan, whose report on Turkish atrocities in Bulgaria was described by Disraeli as 'Coffee House Babble'. Forbes, Villiers recounted, sat under heavy shell-fire on the top of the hill of Radishova writing a full account of the action. Villiers commented drily that, 'You might as well work as stand still and do nothing'. The siege lasted until December when the Turks capitulated from starvation. Forbes, in his usual professional style, had arranged a series of post horses ready and waiting. One day when the news was exciting he jumped into the saddle and rode non-stop over the Carpathians, covering 140 miles in thirty hours, to telegraph his dispatches and post Villiers's sketches. The following day, even before the news was known in the Russian capital, the *Daily News* alone carried the full account of a Russian assault on Plevna which failed the day after the event.

During any war in the later nineteenth century the increased use of the telegraph made it vitally necessary to be a good rider or to have a professional dispatch rider, as some correspondents did. This was the only way to send news quickly.

After the defeat of the Turks, the might and influence of Russia started to worry the other European powers. The Austrian army was mobilized on its frontiers and the British dispatched a fleet to the Dardenelles. Fortunately Tsar Alexander II yielded to pressure from Britain and Austria over the Balkans and a certain war was averted.

# 4

# The jingoistic journalist

## (1878–81)

*We don't want to fight but, by 'jingo' if we do,*
*We've got the men, we've got the ships, we've got the money too!*
From a music hall song of 1878 by G. W. Hunt

While the term 'jingoism' was only coined in 1878, what it stood for had been pervading Victorian society since the early 1870s. The country's preoccupation with wars and its Imperial patriotism was immediately seized on by the press and adventure writers. The correspondents now cast themselves as the supporting players and often the star of the campaigns they wrote about, exploiting the love of adventure to the full. The stereotyped and self-centred style of reporting of the war correspondents was encouraged by the Education Act of 1870 which established State-run schools and greatly increased the literacy of the population, especially the younger age-groups. To cater for this growing young market, eager for adventure stories, various magazines were produced; the *Boy's Own Paper*, perhaps the most famous of all, appeared first in 1879. It was soon followed by a host of others such as the *Union Jack*, edited by George Alfred Henty, one-time war correspondent of the *Standard*, *Sons of Britannia*, and the *Young Englishman*, all filled with heroic 'sun drenched, blood-stained prose'. This love of adventure at second hand pervaded all classes and all ages and helped to create the many preconceived ideas of the late Victorians and Edwardians with regard to Imperial right, and the attitude to foreigners, especially natives.

To the reader in England, the most urgent priority was that every battle and every adventure was described by an eye-witness and the fact that the writer brought more of his personal adventures into the dispatch than actual news was neither here nor there. During the First World War, the British love of eye-witness accounts was characterized by the German press (later reported in the *Illustrated War News* of 26 May 1915):

> I am writing this dispatch [the British 'eye witness' was supposed to be saying], with the roar of the big guns around. The enemy aircraft circle overhead. The British public will be interested to learn that my pet dog . . . can now distinguish a Taube [German fighter plane] from a British aeroplane. On seeing one, he gives three short barks as a signal to our anti-aircraft guns.
> [*Note:* After the retreat from Mons and the famous 'Amiens' dispatch of William Moore of *The Times*, war correspondents were refused permission to accompany the B.E.F. During this period (late 1914-15) an 'official' correspondent was appointed to feed news to the papers. He was Lt. Colonel Sir E. Swinton, R.E., who signed his material with the byline 'Eyewitness'.]

Needless to say the heavy German humour was not appreciated by the British, but its shows what store the public set by first-hand reporting.

The 'age of jingoism' was also the age of the African wars, the Afghan War being the only large-scale Indian operation during the years 1878-82. For the most part the wars were won, as the music hall song stated, only because '. . . we've got the men, we've got the ships, we've got the money too!' The cost in manpower and material was enormous and in many cases it was only sheer weight of numbers, and those armed with modern equipment, that defeated a native uprising, or an enemy such as the Boers who were considered '. . . shambling oafs who grinned vacuously and fell over their rifles'. While the British usually always won, severe defeats were inflicted and numerous blunders were committed, but the full impact of these was not always apparent from the newspaper accounts which now had lost much of the objective style of reporting of Russell and Woods in the days of the Crimea. The criterion now was not accuracy of reporting but the ability to excite.

In 1878, the revolt of some tribes in Kaffirland, headed by various chiefs including Tiny Macomo, called for military action. The 90th Regiment was ordered from England and Melton Prior of the *Illustrated London News* and his rival artist, Charles E. Fripp of the *Graphic*, managed to get passages with the troops on the S.S. *Nubian*.

The main complaint this time was voiced by Melton Prior, who had to '...rise at a most unreasonable hour, so as to attack...at the break of day'. The British forces captured a large number of Kaffir women and children and Prior wrote that this had a '...wonderful effect in bringing this wretched little war to a close'. For the correspondent, the Kaffir War offered little scope and many newspapers did not even bother to send out specials, the cost not justifying the results. There were more newsworthy events happening in India where the Afghans, as always resentful of the British Imperial meddling, refused to accept a British mission to Kabul and instead signed a treaty with Russia. British interest, it was thought, would best be protected in Afghanistan, a buffer between India and Russia, by offering a financial subsidy and demanding the presence of the resident who under armed escort was turned back at the Khyber Pass. The loss of face and the ever-present threat of Russia was enough to cause immediate mobilization of a field force which was to invade Afghanistan and impose the Imperial will on the tribesmen. The army assembled and divided into three field forces: the Peshawar Field Force under Lieutenant-General Sam Browne, the Kandahar Field Force under Major General Stewart, and the third under a Major Roberts who was given the local rank of Major-General. This third force, the smallest, was to bear the brunt of the fighting and to establish Roberts in the annals of British military history.

The defence of Imperial rights was far more important than a *battue* war in Kaffirland. The newspapers sent their best men to India to cover the invasion of Afghanistan. Suitably kitted out with tropical clothing, armed with the best London-made revolvers and rifles, equipped with portable baths, tents, stools, beds, furniture, and servants together with suitable provisions of whisky, claret, brandy, and tinned foods to fortify the inner man, the specials sallied forth. William Simpson represented the *Illustrated London News* (who also had a number of 'obliging military correspondents') as Melton Prior was still in Kaffirland, Hector Macpherson reported for the *Standard* and Archibald Forbes, clad in knitted hat and sheepskin coat, wrote for the *Daily News*; while Frederick Villiers, now fast becoming a veteran, drew for the *Graphic*, Howard Hensman reported for the *Pioneer* (Allahabad), and Drew Gay for the *Daily Telegraph*. Some newspapers had made arrangements with officers on the spot, which was the usual procedure when not personally represented. Letters written under this arrangement were usually worth between five and ten guineas to the correspondent depending on the newspaper. The *Daily Telegraph* was supposed to be mean, according to a comment by the editor of the *Pioneer* to a young officer, Winston Churchill, in 1896. Perhaps this was true for freelance correspondents but they were not to their own men.

The newspapermen who accompanied Roberts were fortunate as this officer considered:

> ... it due to the people of Great Britain that the press correspondents should have every opportunity for giving the fullest and most faithful accounts of what might happen while the army was in the field; and I took special pains from the first to hear the correspondents with confidence, and give them such information as it was in my power to afford. All I required from them in return was that the operations should be truthfully reported, and that any correspondent who did not confine himself to the recording of facts, and felt himself competent to criticise the conduct of the campaign, should be careful to acquaint himself with the many and varied reasons which a Commander must always have before deciding any line of action.

The correspondents felt that this was a refreshing attitude when compared with the restrictive and secretive exploits of Sir Garnet Wolseley.

To accompany the expedition, Lieutenant-General Donald Stewart asked for a complete photographic unit from the Royal Engineers but James Burke, a civilian photographer from Peshawar, agreed to supply all his own equipment and to accompany the force provided he was given a local commission and attached to the staff of Lieutenant-General Sir Sam Browne. Burke set off to join the force without waiting for confirmation of the arrangements which were later refused. He travelled with the force as far as Gandamak and then returned to Peshawar where he sold copies of the photographs he had taken to defray his costs.

As the British ultimatum was not answered, Roberts's force crossed into Afghan territory in the early morning of 21 November and moved along the Kurram valley towards the Afghan army situated at the Peiwar Kotal. The narrow well-defended pass they encountered seemed impossible to take, especially as it was overlooked by a strongly fortified

# THE ILLUSTRATED LONDON NEWS,

No. 2064.—Vol. LXXIV.　SATURDAY, JANUARY 4, 1879.　WITH TWO SUPPLEMENTS SIXPENCE.

Second Afghan War: special correspondents of the *Daily News, Illustrated London News* and *Daily Telegraph* sleeping on the battlefield the night before the attack on Ali Musjid (front page of the *Illustrated London News,* 4 January 1879).

mountain towering above it. Roberts waited in front of the pass for several days and amassed what information he could about enemy numbers and positions before deciding on a desperate plan. Giving the enemy every idea that he was to launch a frontal assault on the pass by building many gun positions, he marched at night around the left flank of the forbidding mountain and assaulted the Afghans who were taken completely by surprise. This rarely happened to them and they retreated immediately, leaving the way open. The *Illustrated London News*'s military correspondent Colonel J. J. H. Gordon supplied a sketch of the action at Peiwar Kotal.

After a suitable rest and having received large reinforcements of men and munitions, he pushed forward to the end of the Kurram valley securing all in his path and establishing a firm line of communication with field telegraph lines. Unfortunately cutting the telegraph lines was a favourite sport of the Afghan tribesmen and heliographs had to be arranged at suitable intervals as a second line of communication.

On 7 January an incident occurred in Roberts's camp which brought no credit to the war correspondents and caused Roberts to argue with one of the leading London newspapers. The enemy were discovered trying to creep into the camp and 'At the sound of the first shot, the prisoners all jumped to their feet, and calling each other to escape attempted to seize the rifles belonging to the Guard ...' After a due warning, and fearing for the safety of his men, the Native Officer gave the order to fire. Six prisoners were killed and thirteen wounded. In Parliament the incident was represented on the *Standard*'s authority as the slaughter of ninety prisoners tied together with ropes.

Roberts had already had to warn MacPherson of the *Standard* about his abuse of the favours and confidence Roberts had shown the press.

> Judging from his telegrams [wrote the General], which he brought to me to sign, the nerves of the Correspondent in question must have been somewhat shaken by the few and very distant shots fired at us on 28 November. These Telegrams being in many instances absolutely incorrect and of the most alarming nature, were not of course allowed to be despatched until they were revised in accordance with the truth ...

MacPherson evidently altered one of his telegrams after Roberts had countersigned it and, when hauled before the General, he promised

Second Afghan War: the victory of Kandahar, 1 September 1880 — the 9th Lancers charging the Afghans (painting by Stanley Berkeley).

never to do it again, although '. . . not apparently realising that he had done anything at all reprehensible'. MacPherson dispatched a telegram about the prisoner incident which was never shown to Roberts until he read it together with one of MacPherson's letters '. . . over which I have no control . . .' and 'most subversive of the truth' in copies of the *Standard* that arrived in Kurram.

> It was on receipt of these letters [wrote Roberts] that I felt it to be my duty to send the too imaginative author to the rear. What to my mind [he wrote strongly] was so reprehensible in the correspondent's conduct was the publication in time of war, and consequent excitement and anxiety at home, of incorrect and sensational statements, founded on information derived from irresponsible and uninformed sources . . .

The war was brought to a successful conclusion when Shere Ali fled to Russia and Yabub Khan, his son, became the new ruler. He was anxious that 'the friendship of this God-granted State with the illustrious British Government may remain constant and firm'. On 26 May the Treaty of Gandamak was signed, allowing a British envoy in Kabul, ceding territory to India, and establishing telegraph lines between the Afghan capital and the Indian frontier. Britain was to control Afghan foreign policy and in return promised protection from aggression. It seemed that the Russian threat to India had been minimized.

The money that newspapers were able and willing to spend to obtain a scoop was well known in government circles. Disraeli, the Prime Minister, confided to Lady Chesterfield on 11 May 1879:

> The Afghan news is very good and I credit it; but, strange to say, the Government has not yet received any telegram confirming it. But we cannot compete with the *Standard* newspaper which does not hesitate to expend £500 on a telegram!

Second Afghan War: 'Homeward Bound'. The staff descending the Kabul river (drawing by the war artist of the *Graphic*).

During the autumn of 1878, the British government had become more preoccupied with the worsening situation in South Africa and particularly with the conduct of the Zulus and Boers, and their own High Commissioner. South Africa had for some time been an area of rising tension. In 1877, the British annexed the Transvaal to prevent the Boers from infiltrating and occupying more of Zululand and to avert what was considered a certain disastrous war between Boer and Zulu. While Sir Bartle Frere saw his problems with the Boers as ones that could be settled by discussion, the increasing militance of the Zulus crowding on the Natal and Transvaal borders could only be resolved by force. The British government considered the problem of minor importance and was not willing to be engaged in yet another colonial war; but the Governor of the Cape and High Commissioner for South Africa, Sir Bartle Frere, and the new commander of the British forces in South Africa, General the Hon. F. A. Thesiger (later Lord Chelmsford), saw the situation in a different light. Requests for more troops for South Africa were refused, as it was the government's opinion that '. . . by the exercise of prudence, and by meeting the Zulus in a spirit of forbearance and reasonable compromise, it will be possible to avert the very serious evil of a war with Cetewayo'.

However, the letter from London with the express demand not to provoke a war arrived too late. Frere had summoned the Zulu chiefs to the frontier to give them the results of the boundary commission on the land disputed between Boer and Zulu. Although the commission found for the Zulus, to Frere's annoyance, he did not change his intentions. He took the opportunity to serve the Zulus with an ultimatum. Certain minor events provoked his action: the rumoured treatment of missionaries and Cetewayo's despotic and bloodthirsty attitude; the 'invasion' of Natal by the sons of a Zulu chief named Sirayo to drag back two adulterous wives, who were then killed, the penalty demanded by Zulu law. The ultimatum contained among its terms some that were impossible for Cetewayo to agree to, one being the disbandment of the Zulu army. As the structure of the Zulu nation was based precisely on military supremacy, this demand would make Cetewayo and his nation an impotent addition to the British territories in South Africa.

On 11 January 1879, as there was no reply to the ultimatum, the British army crossed into Zululand as the *Natal Times* notified its readers that morning:

... to exact from Cetewayo reparation for violations of British Territory committed by the sons of Sirayo ... and to enforce compliance with the promises made by Cetewayo at his coronation for the better government of his people.

The British Government has no quarrel with the Zulu people [continued the newspaper]. All Zulus who come in unarmed, or who lay down their arms will be provided for ...

When the war is finished, the British Government will make the best arrangements in its power for the future good government of the Zulus in their own country ...

The plan devised by Bartle Frere and Lord Chelmsford was typical of the tactics utilized in small colonial wars, namely a three-pronged thrust to the enemy capital. Lord Chelmsford, with Colonel Glyn in charge of the centre column, crossed the Buffalo river at Rorke's Drift mission station, which was used as a supply depot; while Colonel Charles Pearson and the left column crossed at Lower Drift and the right column, under Colonel Evelyn Wood, invaded Zululand at Utrecht.

With the central column rode Charles L. Norris-Newman, a retired army captain, known to his close friends as 'Noggs'. In the tradition of keen special correspondents, Norris-Newman was the first white man to splash across the river and set foot in Zululand. He represented the *Natal Times* and the London *Standard* and had attached himself to the staff of Commandant Lonsdale of the Natal Native Contingent and sported their badge, a twisted piece of red cloth tucked in the loose muslin band that encircled his sun helmet. As the N.N.C. were for the most part poorly armed natives with no uniform, the red cloth worn around the head served as a mark of identity.

The centre column brushed with the Zulus on 12 January and on 20 January camped at Isandhlwana. Norris-Newman recorded that on the night of 21 January '... Our mess had a jolly little dinner at which a few guests were present and afterwards many comrades looked in for a chat ...'. Norris-Newman had the advantage of being the only English newspaper correspondent in Natal, commissioned to act for the *Standard* by its shrewd editor William H. Mudford. The result of the war was thought so certain that none of the other London dailies, the most powerful and influential newspapers in Britain and the Empire, thought it worth their while to give any commission. In the early morning of 22 January, Norris-Newman rode out with a column under the command of Colonel Glyn, accompanied by Lord Chelmsford. They were to reinforce a forward party under Major Dartnell who had reported sighting a force of Zulus, and he hoped for some 'meaty' material for his dispatches. He left his native servant, tent, belongings, and spare horses at the camp having no need of them in what he thought was to be a short and swift skirmish with the Zulus.

What actually happened at Isandhlwana the morning of 22 January was one of the gravest military disasters of the late nineteenth century. The battling men, overwhelmed by the Zulu attack, fought to the last, few escaping the fatal thrust of the assegais in spite of their discipline and modern weapons. The blow-by-blow account of the action was never reported, nor were the numerous heroic incidents that occurred as the only journalist capable of reporting the event, Norris-Newman, was some twelve miles away. He might have cursed later that he had missed the scoop of the century, but he would probably not have been able to profit from his presence in the camp, lying with his stomach rent open by the spears of the enemy with the 1,329 other men who died that day.

Lord Chelmsford was not unaware of Zulu activity. At 9 a.m. at breakfast he received a message brought by a rider stating that the Zulus were advancing in force on the camp. The message was timed at 8.05 a.m. and went on to request the General to return at once. One of Chelmsford's A.D.C.s climbed to the top of the ridge and surveyed the camp through a telescope and reported that nothing appeared unusual except that the '. . . cattle had been driven into the camp close around the tents'. At 11 a.m. Chelmsford was still moving away from Isandhlwana towards the proposed new camp-site for the column; in the camp cooks were hard at work on the midday meal and the men not on duty were trying to escape the hot sultry sun stripped to the waist in their tents. At midday when Chelmsford stopped for lunch, the Battle of Isandhlwana was almost over. Chelmsford's force had heard cannon fire and men had been observed moving through the camp, but all had become quiet. If an attack had been launched, it had obviously been beaten off as the tents were still standing. (Tents were to be thrown down if the camp was threatened according to standing orders.)

The situation seems confused as the dispatches sent from the camp neither warned Chelmsford nor explained clearly enough the urgency of the situation.

At this juncture [wrote Norris-Newman] one of our mounted
natives came galloping down from the opposite ridge, whence
the camp could be seen, and reported to a staff officer that an
attack was being made on the camp . . . On this being reported
to Lord Chelmsford, he at once galloped up to the crest of the
hill, accompanied by his staff, and on arrival every field-glass
was levelled at the camp. The sun was shining brightly on the
white tents, which were plainly visible, but all seemed quiet.
No signs of firing nor of any engagement could be seen, and
although bodies of men moving about could be distinguished,
yet they were not unnaturally supposed to be our own troops.

Meanwhile part of the advance force, alerted by the message from the
camp, had turned about and were marching on Isandhlwana, At
3.15 p.m. the entire forward party had halted some four miles from
the camp when Captain Lonsdale of the N.N.C., who had turned back
some time previously to arrange supplies for his men, came galloping
back as fast as the diminutive pony would carry the large officer.
'The Zulus have the camp,' blurted Lonsdale. 'I shall never forget
the scene,' wrote Norris-Newman, 'the looks of amazement, grief and
horror . . .' Chelmsford had left a thousand men to guard the camp.
The advance column halted for the rest of the force to catch up and
it was not until 7.45 p.m. when night had fallen, that the men were
some half a mile from the camp. Advancing with fixed bayonets,
Norris-Newman recorded:

> We began to stumble over dead bodies in every direction, and
> in some places . . . the men were found lying thick and close,
> as though they had fought till their ammunition was exhausted,
> and then been surrounded and slaughtered.

They camped that night amongst the dead of the day and the debris
of the camp.

> But oh! how dreadful were those weary hours [wrote
> Norris-Newman in the columns of the *Standard*] . . . How that
> terrible night passed with us I fancy few would care to tell,
> even if they could recall it . . . During the night we noticed
> fires constantly burning on all the surrounding hills, and in
> particular one bright blaze riveted our attention throughout,
> as it seemed to be near Rorke's Drift, and we feared for the
> safety of those left in that small place, knowing how utterly
> powerless we were to aid them in any way before morning.

Zulu War: the Battle of Isandhlwana, 22 January 1879 (oil painting by
Charles E. Fripp, a war artist for the *Graphic*).

Zulu War: photograph of the battlefield of Isandhlwana showing the
abandoned wagons, skeletons and bones.

The blaze was in fact the thatched roof of the hospital at Rorke's Drift, as 141 men fought for their lives against an overwhelming number of Zulus. The bravery of the defence of Rorke's Drift under Lieutenants Chard and Bromhead, both officers in their early thirties who had failed to get promotion, heroic as it was, gaining eleven Victoria Crosses, seven to the 24th Foot (the largest number given to a single regiment in any one action), could not erase the shame of the massacre at Isandhlwana.

Chelmsford had no desire to linger at the camp longer than he had to, not even to bury the dead, and the column moved out towards Rorke's Drift in the early hours of the morning of 23 January. As dawn came up, the scene was even more horrific than they had imagined.

> The corpses of our poor soldiers [wrote Norris-Newman] white and natives, lay thick upon the ground in clusters together with the dead and mutilated horses, oxen and mules, shot and stabbed in every position and manner, and the whole intermingled with the fragments of our Commissariat wagons, broken and wrecked and rifled of their contents . . . The dead bodies of the men lay as they had fallen, but mostly with only their boots and shirts on, or perhaps a pair of trousers or a remnant of a coat . . . In many instances they lay with sixty or seventy empty cartridge cases surrounding them, thus showing they had fought to the very last . . . it was really wonderful that so small a force had been able to maintain such a desperate resistance for so long.

To Chelmsford's relief, he found Rorke's Drift still intact, but hurriedly moved the remnants of his column into Natal. The two other columns had not done much better; that under Pearson had been attacked on the same day as Isandhlwana at Inyezane and had fallen back on Eshowe while Wood's column, on hearing the news of 22 January, fortified itself at Kambula Hill.

Lord Chelmsford immediately dispatched a cable to the Prime Minister which was taken by rider to Pietermaritzburg, the nearest telegraph station, and relayed to Cape Town, where together with Norris-Newman's dispatch to the *Standard*, it was put aboard the *Dunrobin Castle* sailing for London. The Master called at the Cape Verde Islands, the southern extremity of the submarine cable, to send the dispatches which arrived in London on 11 February. The

*Illustrated London News* of 15 February published, later than others being a weekly paper, the headline of 'British Reverse' and said:

> Telegrams of Cape news to Jan. 27, received by way of
> St. Vincent, bring news of a terrible disaster to the British
> troops in Zululand. In the first brush with the enemy, which
> took place on Jan. 12, and lasted one hour, the Zulus fled,
> leaving forty of their number dead, besides many who were
> taken prisoners; our troops having two killed and fourteen
> wounded. But on Jan. 22 a force of 20,000 Zulus attacked
> a British column consisting of a portion of the 24th
> Regiment and 600 natives, with one battery, and killed
> 500 men and thirty officers. The Zulus are said to have lost
> 5000 in killed and wounded, and the British force is reported
> to have been annihilated. A valuable convoy of supplies,
> including ammunition and commissariat stores, was captured,
> and the colours of the 24th Regiment fell into the hands of the
> enemy. The English army has recrossed the border, and a
> steamer has been sent to Mauritius to ask for reinforcements,
> and an appeal for additional troops has been sent to England.
> The position of Natal, the telegrams say, is serious.

Except for the *Standard*, most newspapers then reprinted Lord Chelmsford's telegraphic dispatch which the War Office issued to the press, which began with the poignant sentence:

> I regret to have to report a very disastrous engagement which
> took place on January 22nd, between the Zulus and a portion
> of No.3 column left to guard the camp about ten miles in
> front of Rorke's Drift.

The first newspaper to carry the story and a detailed casualty list was the *Natal Times* who published an extra on 23 January giving details of Isandhlwana and the defence of Rorke's Drift.

The news was received in London with mixed feelings of incredulity and horror. The Cabinet immediately ordered reinforcements to sail for the Cape, while the newspaper editors frantically made arrangements to send correspondents and recalled their best men from other assignments. 'The power of Cetewayo must be broken,' declared *The Times*, 'swift and terrible retribution must be exacted.' Other newspapers such as the *Pall Mall Gazette* edited by W. T. Stead, the pioneer of the personal interview, and the *Daily News* criticized the deliberate starting of the war in which 'Death had prematurely visited hundreds of peaceful homes in England'.

Zulu War: Lord Chelmsford and staff looking for Ulundi, June 1879 (watercolour drawing by Melton Prior).

Large numbers of troops concentrated on Southampton and Portsmouth and with them the special correspondents and artists. Francis Francis, later fishing editor of the *Field*, represented *The Times*, the renowned Archibald Forbes the *Daily News*, Melton Prior as always the *Illustrated London News*, F. R. MacKenzie the *Standard*, Charles E. Fripp the *Graphic*, and from Paris *Le Figaro* sent a correspondent named Delage, not to study the war but mainly to report on the Prince Imperial, the son of the exiled Napoleon III who had gone to Zululand as a British officer. The smashing of the Zulu army was but a matter of time when faced with the overwhelming resources of Britain and the inevitable happened on 4 July at Ulundi, but not before the tragic death of the Prince Imperial had cast shame on a British officer and caused embarrassment between England and France.

Chelmsford's troops had visited Isandhlwana on 14 March and Norris-Newman, still in his enviable position as sole London newspaper correspondent, amplified the horrible scene of desolation but nothing was done to bury the dead. By the end of May both Bartle Frere and Lord Chelmsford had each been told to relinquish his duties to General Sir Garnet Wolseley, Frere only maintaining his position of Governor of Cape Colony. As Wolseley prepared to sail,

William Howard Russell, now editor of the *Army and Navy Gazette*, offered his services in his old capacity of war correspondent to *The Times*, but he was refused. Russell, now in his fifty-ninth year, was determined to get to Zululand and he approached Levy Lawson of the *Daily Telegraph* who, aware of the power of Russell's reputation with the public, offered him £200 per month. Lawson did not want Russell to compete with the other correspondents with regard to telegraphic dispatches but to write '. . . old world sort of correspondence with reminiscences and a general view of affairs . . .': in fact it was his name the *Daily Telegraph* wanted and not his capacity for newsgathering. Meanwhile Arthur Aylward, '. . . the clever but quite unbalanced editor of the *Natal Witness*', was keeping the *Daily Telegraph* readers informed of events.

Lord Chelmsford, for the sake of his own reputation, was determined to finish Cetewayo before the arrival of Wolseley. Chelmsford's brother had cabled him, 'For God's sake do something, Wolseley superseded you'. The state of the war was far from satisfactory. Eshowe had to be relieved and on 12 March an escort and wagons had been attacked at the Intombi river and had fallen back with heavy losses, the commander killed and the second-in-command later court-martialled for leaving his men when he galloped for aid. Wood and his column had taken a severe beating on 28 March at Inhlobana Mountain, but on the following day the Zulus were beaten off with heavy losses. On 1 April, a carefully prepared column, marching under Chelmsford to relieve Eshowe, defeated the Zulus at Gingihlovo.

A member of the besieged force wrote later in *Blackwood's Magazine* about the arrival of Chelmsford's force. 'On the afternoon of the 3rd April, the column . . . left the fort under General Pearson, to meet the relief column . . . A solitary horseman was seen towards 5 p.m. galloping up the new road to the fort. He had an officer's coat on, and we could see a sword dangling from his side. Who is he? . . . He proved to be the correspondent of the *Standard* . . . A second horseman appeared approaching the fort, his horse apparently much blown. Who is he? . . . The correspondent of the *Argus* (Cape Town). They had a race who would be first at Eshowe, the *Standard* winning by five minutes!'

Melton Prior was meant to be with the column marching on Eshowe but confessed to having a premonition of his impending death. He enlisted the services of Colonel Crealock and a private artist named Porter. At Gingihlovo Porter was one of the first killed.

On 20 May, a party accompanied by the war correspondents returned to Isandhlwana to bury the dead, except those of the 24th who by request were left until June when they were interred by their own regiment. Melton Prior, Archibald Forbes, Norris-Newman and others rode with the detachment and were able to give a first-hand account of the scene they witnessed:

> I found the whole site of the conflict overgrown with grass thickly intermingled with great and growing stalks of oats and mealies. [This was the grain spilt from the wagons during the fight.] Concealed amongst these, lay the corpses of our soldiers, in all postures and stages of decay [wrote Norris-Newman], . . . I had the melancholy satisfaction of discovering my own tent . . . and immediately behind it the skeletons of my horses with the bodies of my servants, just as I had left them piquetted on the 22 January . . . my papers, letters and books were lying torn up. I found and brought away with me some mementos, some of my wife's letters . . .

Melton Prior who had yet to see the field confessed:

> In all the campaigns I have been in I have not witnessed a scene more horrible. . . . Here I saw not the bodies, but the skeletons, of men whom I had seen in life and health and some of whom I had known well, mixed up with the skeletons of oxen and horses . . . all in the greatest confusion.

Prior and others picked up numerous letters and photographs from the field. Archibald Forbes gave much the same account of the scene:

> There was none of the stark, blood-curdling horror of a recent battle field; no pools of yet wet blood; no torn flesh still quivering . . . A strange dead calm reigned . . . So long in places had grown the grass that it mercifully shrouded the dead, who for four long months had been scandalously left unburied.

Wagons and other items were taken away and except for the 24th, the bodies buried. Forbes noticed that the vultures had stripped the horses and oxen but '. . . never touched the corpses of our ill-fated countrymen'.

On 1 June, the Prince Imperial was scouting with a small party which was suddenly put to flight. Being unable to mount his horse and thus left alone he was assegaied by the Zulus. The following day a search party, accompanied by Prior, Forbes, Francis, Mackenzie, and the Frenchman, Delage, went in search of the body. Forbes and Prior were the first to reach it and while the correspondent of *Le Figaro* placed a penny over the missing eye in 'hopes of closing it', Prior was avidly sketching. The account of Forbes contained what might be considered a suitable epitaph for a Prince, '. . . slain by savages in an obscure corner of a remote Continent . . . a miserable end truly for him who once was the Son of France'. Prior worked through the night and sent his sketches off at daylight to catch the post, enabling the *Illustrated London News* to be the only illustrated paper to give pictures of the event.

As the force moved carefully towards Ulundi finally to settle the Zulu problem, the main worry of the correspondents was transport and many teamed up together to get carriages and to save costs. Loose horses were seized and branded the property of the Post Office and Prior recalled that Francis Francis of *The Times*, '. . . had to ride about as though he had been enrolled into Her Majesty's Postal Service as a postman', the nine-inch broad arrow, crown, V.R., and P.O. proclaiming the rider's duties to all and sundry.

On the morning of 4 July, Archibald Forbes had wagered £100 that no battle would be fought that day but shortly after 8 a.m. he lost his bet and paid up as the Zulu *impis* threw themselves at the British square. Inside Forbes could be seen in his sun helmet strolling around making notes, while Melton Prior was busily drawing sketches which he hoped that evening to work up into a large impression of the action. At one point Prior lost the sketch book which he always kept in the holster of the saddle and '. . . in sheer despair I fell on the ground and burst into tears'. Sir William Gordon Cumming, later to be involved in a card scandal with the Prince of Wales, offered his own. After three quarters of an hour, the depleted *impis* wavered and broke under the murderous fire and were swiftly chased by the cavalry. After the battle, Prior was chatting with some men when Archibald Forbes announced that he was riding down to Durban with his dispatch and that he would take any drawings Prior had. Prior drew a detailed sketch of the action and gave it to Forbes, who was also carrying a telegraphic dispatch for Lord Chelmsford. As usual, Forbes was determined to maintain his reputation.

A hundred miles away lay the nearest telegraph station, at Landman's Drift, and Forbes with a single horse covered the 100 miles in just under twenty hours to file his dispatch and that of Lord Chelmsford.

He immediately remounted and rode on to Ladysmith where he obtained a buggy and horses and then pushed on to Pietermaritzburg, an additional 175 miles, a total journey of 300 miles in fifty hours. He travelled on by rail to Durban where he posted Prior's drawings, enabling the artist to get a 'first' as well as himself. On 24 July the *Daily News* published Forbes's telegraphic dispatch which covered just over a column and must have been enormously expensive, but then the *Daily News*'s policy since the Franco-Prussian War had been that whole dispatches were to be telegraphed, not just key news, at whatever the cost.

The news that Forbes had carried these dispatches in the 'Ride of Death', as the press headlined it, was greeted in Parliament with cheers from both sides yet he was not awarded the campaign medal. Like Stanley in Abyssinia, Forbes felt cheated and continued to harangue the War Office and to produce evidence of his claim to being an official dispatch rider for Lord Chelmsford. Whether or not the affair of the medal, which should have been a Victoria Cross according to George Augustus Sala, affected Forbes's attitude, one cannot tell, but it is significant that this was the last war he reported as a war correspondent.

Zulu War: Archibald Forbes after his historic 'ride of death' (oil painting by Sir Hubert von Herkomer).

Zulu War: 'The art of Politeness' (cartoon from *Fun,* illustrating the dispute between Sir Garnet Wolseley and William Russell).
*Sir Garnet Wolseley* 'Pardon me, my dear doctor, if I say that you have been hoaxed by gross exaggerations and transparent untruths.'
*Dr Russell* 'Forgive me, my dazzling young general, for mentioning that you are a pig-headed ignoramus, and don't know what you are talking about.'

A friend of Archibald Forbes wrote to the authorities about his claim for the Zulu war medal, having been on 'official business' as a dispatch rider, and received the following reply. 'As the Secretary of State for War considers that civilians who attach themselves to an army ought not to be deemed eligible for war medals, the adverse decision with regard to Mr. Forbes must remain untouched.' Correspondents were therefore wary of carrying any dispatches but their own or those of their colleagues unless they were officially recognized and thus able to claim the war medal, a prize among certain newspapermen. During the Arabi Revolt in Egypt in 1882, Melton Prior was riding towards Ismalia with his drawings when a general asked him to carry a message to Lord Wolseley. Prior respectfully declined but added that '. . . if on the other hand, however, you turn me into a soldier for the time being and order me to carry it I will do so with pleasure'. Prior later explained that:

What I meant was, that being ordered to carry it I might make a claim for the medal of the campaign . . . as for being offered it, why the Commander-in-Chief and Government seem as chary of giving medals to correspondents as though they were made of diamonds and would ruin the public exchequer. They are very ready to ask and expect us to do all kinds of services to assist the army, and in turn charge us full price for the paltry rations we receive . . .

Russell, like Sir Garnet Wolseley, arrived too late to take any part in the Zulu War except for tidying up and capturing Cetewayo. But the journalist made his presence felt by his clash with Sir Garnet Wolseley over the conduct of British troops. Russell wrote in the *Daily Telegraph* about the drunkenness, pillaging and thefts committed by the troops. The affair attracted some space in the press, merited a number of cartoons in the satirical newspapers but, after some harsh words, petered out.

Much of what was now happening in South Africa had been over-shadowed by the recurrence of Afghan activity on the North-West Frontier of India. This time, the newspapers did not have men on hand and if they had, it was unlikely that they would have been able to accompany Roberts's force. Howard Hensman, the special correspondent of the Pioneer (Allahabad) and the *Daily News* (London), wrote that:

It was my good fortune to be the only special correspondent with the gallant little army which moved out of Ali Khedyl in September 1879. The government of India [presumably after the affair of MacPherson of the *Standard*] had notified that 'non-combatant correspondents' would not be allowed to join the force . . .

The newspapers did not only rely on official dispatches as there were '. . . regimental officers, who might in their spare hours supply information carefully *visé*, to such newspapers as chose to accept it'.

Hensman related that the order was issued in such a way that General Roberts was not even aware of it and welcomed him at headquarters. 'I am sure,' wrote Hensman, 'he would have welcomed any other correspondent who had chosen to cross the frontier, and push on without escort and their own baggage animals.' Professional jealousy prompted a number of correspondents to accuse Roberts of this exclusion of the press but Hensman defended him; after all, he could afford to since he obtained scoop after scoop and then wrote his account in book form after the war. The second phase of the second Afghan War was sparked off by the murder of the British envoy and his staff at Kabul. The only force in Afghanistan was the old Kurram Field Force under Roberts, employed on police duties, the other two having been either reduced or returned to India. It was immediately reinforced, renamed the Kabul Field Force and prepared to advance on the Afghan capital to exact retribution. The Field Force moved up the Kurram Valley and fought and won a number of small encounters with the enemy. Amir Yakub Khan was in constant contact with Roberts, denying responsibility for the murder of the British envoy, and entreating the British not to invade. By the beginning of October 1879, Roberts's force was twelve miles from the capital at Charasia where the Afghans had entrenched themselves. By the afternoon at very small cost, Roberts had driven the tribesmen off the entrenched ridge and prepared for his final advance to Kabul. Hensman described the scene of the formal occupation of the city and the triumphant parade of the British and Indian troops: infantry, cavalry, artillery, and sappers and miners:

> Nothing could exceed the splendid form in which these regiments turned out, the bronzed and bearded faces of the soldiers showing but few 'six-year men' [This new short term of enlistment was introduced in 1870 and replaced the previous system of enlistment for twenty-one years.] were in their ranks . . . The sight was a most impressive one, the sun lighting up the double line along which 4,000 bayonets sparkled, and throwing into bold relief the darker forms of men and horses where the cavalry were drawn up. [Hensman was of the opinion that] . . . there was nothing to hinder us marching into the fortress the day after the battle of Charasia . . . But there was no occasion for haste . . .

On 10, 11, and 12 November, the forty-nine 'murderers' of the Kabul envoys, found guilty by a Military Commission, were hanged as an example to others but as Roberts well knew the occupation of Kabul, the imposing of Imperial will on Afghanistan, would not be quite so simple. The Afghans were by nature independent and cunning but they also possessed the characteristic of not knowing when they were beaten. In December, the Afghans rose against the invader and various small armies began marching on Kabul. Roberts was unable to hold the city itself and withdrew his force outside the city to a fortified area, known as the Sherpur cantonment, and the Afghans reoccupied and looted Kabul. Just before Christmas they turned their attention to Roberts's force, but he was so well prepared that the Afghan army was repelled. By March 1880, the British had strengthened their position and Major-General Sir Donald Stewart had moved a force to Kandahar under Major-General Primrose, before marching on Kabul with 14,000 extra troops.

At the end of June, according to Hensman, reports had reached Kandahar that Ayub Khan was on his way bringing a large force to capture the town. A force under General Burrows, comprising 500 cavalry, six horse artillery guns, infantry consisting of the 66th Regiment and 1st Bombay Grenadiers, and various other troops and services, marched to Maiwand on 27 July to intercept Ayub Khan's army and the same day a disastrous battle was fought. The British lost over 1,000 fighting men, all killed, and over a quarter being from the 66th Regiment. Roberts was instructed to march to the relief of Kandahar. On 9 August the force, consisting of nearly 10,000 combatants, marched out of Kabul and twenty days later, Hensman had the satisfaction of wiring his report stating that '. . . more than 300 miles have been covered, giving an average (including one day's halt) of fifteen miles per day. I will leave it to military critics to decide as to the merits of such a march.'

On 1 September 1880, Roberts finally thrashed Ayub Khan's army, captured numerous men and stores, and virtually ended the war. A new amir was placed on the throne and Britain withdrew her armies to India, a rather unsatisfactory end to a campaign whose main attribute was Roberts's march.

During these struggles in Afghanistan, events in South Africa were getting out of control. The Zulus had been effectively dealt with, but the Boers in the Transvaal felt that with the new Liberal government elected in April 1880 and Gladstone as Prime Minister, they would attain self-government once again. Gladstone had vigorously attacked Disraeli's progressive Imperial policies in Afghanistan and South Africa and deplored the excessive spending which resulted when the army was called in. In June 1880, he made it clear to the Afrikaner representatives: 'Our judgment is that the Queen cannot be advised to relinquish her sovereignty over the Transvaal.'

By November the situation had deteriorated into almost open revolt when a riotous crowd assembled at the auction of an Afrikaner's wagon which was being sold for default of taxes. A large open-air meeting in Paardekraal on 8 December demanded that the republic be restored and on 15 December shots were fired between jeering Afrikaners and the British army. Five days later the British suffered the first of three defeats in the first Boer War which lasted nine weeks.

A column under Colonel Anstruther consisting of 235 fighting men plus sundry services was marching to relieve Pretoria which had been encircled by the Transvaal forces. At Bronkhurst Spruit they were confronted by a commando unit which demanded that the column halt until Kruger, Joubert, and Pretorius, the Boer leaders, had received a reply to their letter to Landon, the Governor of Transvaal, informing him of the reconstitution of the Republic. Anstruther refused and ordered his column forward. The commandos, having already taken cover, inflicted heavy casualties on the British, killing and wounding almost half their number, including Anstruther. The Boer fire was so intense that the battle was over in fifteen minutes, and the British survivors disarmed and put to work erecting tents for the wounded. The British position was tenuous as the few troops they had in Transvaal were scattered about in small garrisons. The news of the defeat at Bronkhurst Spruit was greeted in London with deep despair, as the wounds inflicted by the defeats of Isandhlwana and Maiwand were still fresh in the minds of the Victorians. The newspapers stormed against the Boer treachery, *The Times* denouncing the '. . . cold-blooded murder of British troops . . . a deed worthy of savages'. The *Graphic* and the *Illustrated London News* presented their readers with imaginary sketches of the battle, and every London newspaper announced that the rebellion must be put down at all costs, since, as *The Times* stated, the Boer had rejected '. . . the blessing of his adoption into the British Empire . . .'

On 6 January 1881, Queen Victoria at the Opening of Parliament declared: 'A rising in the Transvaal has recently imposed upon me the duty of taking military measures with a view to the prompt vindication of my authority . . .' The newspaper editors needed no more prompting to arrange for their special correspondents to be sent to South Africa, while others with men on the spot issued instructions and the rest made the usual arrangements with local newspapers. Thomas Carter, a local man reporting for the *Natal Times*, was on the spot while the inevitable wave of journalists poured back to South Africa, amongst them the great and established veterans, Melton Prior of the *Illustrated London News*, the small bad-tempered Charles E. Fripp of the *Graphic*, John Cameron of the *Standard*, Hay of the *Daily News* replacing Archibald Forbes. F. R. MacKenzie of the *Standard* was reputed to have beaten out the brains of a fallen Zulu and as a consequence endeared himself to no one, having broken the rules of 'fair play'. The strangest choice was the *Daily Telegraph*'s continued use of the fervent Irish nationalist, Arthur Aylward, a known anti-British journalist and a troublemaker. Most other correspondents kept away from this bitter Fenian, but it proved difficult as Aylward set himself up as the unofficial head of the press contingent.

The correspondents travelled to the front as best they could. The population knew the premium on horses and carts and set a high price, and the difficult country caused many hazards for the newspapermen on their travels. The constant fear of a broken wheel, a horse losing a shoe or poisoned water was made worse by what Melton Prior described as 'jumping', the removal of a vital piece of harness, which was then offered back for sale at an exorbitant price. Fodder cost about fifteen shillings a day, accommodation was bad and expensive, and provisions at a premium. Prior as usual had brought his favourite 'stimulant', whisky, which he disguised in boxes marked 'Drawing materials', as well as his customary thousand cigarettes.

Major-General Sir George Pomeroy Colley, the High Commissioner for South Africa, Governor of Natal and Commander-in-Chief of British forces in Natal and Transvaal, decided to act after this Boer aggression, and marching from Newcastle on 24 January, established a camp at Mount Prospect, planning to move into Transvaal through the Drakensburg mountains at Lang's Nek. His force was opposed by the Boers who had carefully entrenched themselves and, in time-honoured fashion, Colley ordered forward his cavalry consisting of volunteers, police, and some mounted infantry. The initial charge was preceded by an artillery bombardment and as the infantry manoeuvred into skirmishing order, the cavalry charged. This half-hearted attempt was repulsed by the Boers who now trained their accurate fire on the approaching infantry. Complete with colours flying (the last time they were ever carried in battle) the 58th Regiment in typical formation closed on the Boers with fixed bayonets but they were shot to pieces and 150 were killed. Colley had no option but to withdraw to his camp at Mount Prospect. It was another setback for the British army.

First Boer War: Sir George Colley's midnight ascent of Majuba Hill, 26 February 1881 (from a drawing by Melton Prior based on information supplied by the *Standard*'s war correspondent, John Cameron).

Colley decided on a master stroke to restore confidence and to beat the rebels, but on 7 February, he suffered a similar disaster at Schin's Hooghte where only the rain that fell the night after the battle saved his force from greater casualties, total destruction, or capture. Colley's military tactics were influenced by what was happening politically between the home government and the Boers. He decided, drastically, to defeat the rebels that had entrenched themselves at Lang's Nek by securing the flat-topped mountain which overlooked their position named Majuba Hill. Along with the 554 men, who marched out at night to occupy the summit, went a number of war correspondents: Hay of the *Daily News*, who during the march had his girth snap which caused him to fall behind the column, Cameron of the *Standard*, and Carter of

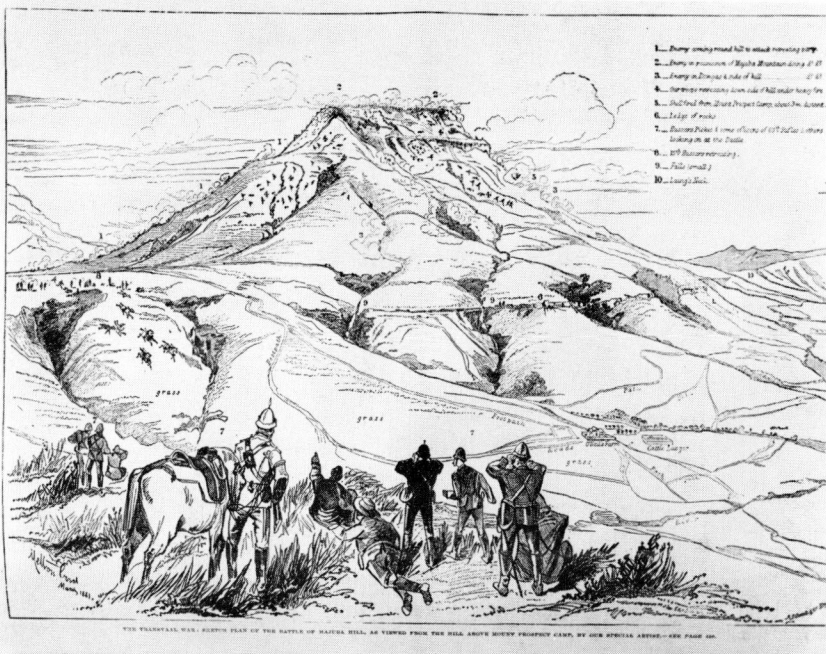

First Boer War: sketch plan of the battle of Majuba Hill, as viewed from the hill above Mount Prospect Camp (from a drawing by Melton Prior).

the *Natal Times*. The night operation was carried out with complete secrecy, '. . . each man,' Cameron recorded, 'carried with him three days' provisions and eighty rounds of ammunition.' If the disaster at Isandhlwana had stunned Britain, the ensuing defeat and rout of British troops at the hands of the Boers at Majuba shook any remaining confidence in British generalship. Cameron's 2,500 word dispatch was a masterpiece of factual reporting which he later found difficult to equal and even rival newspapers agreed, 'The best account of it [Majuba] is that given by the *Standard* correspondent, Mr. Cameron, who was taken prisoner by the Boers and was permitted at once to return to the British Camp . . .' to get medical aid for the wounded. The *Illustrated London News* made use of the *Standard*'s report to accompany Melton Prior's sketch of the incident. 'Dear old Cameron,' wrote Prior, 'was not much of an artist, but he gave me a lot of notes and rough sketches of the fight, which I was able to work up under his guidance . . .' Prior would not forget Cameron's gesture.

According to Cameron, the troops had reached the summit at 5 a.m. about 2,000 yards from the Boers but 2,000 feet above them. The

First Boer War: the scene as the last of our men retreated from Majuba Hill (from the *Illustrated London News,* 23 April 1881).

British were posted at ten-pace intervals around the '... spacious plateau some thousand yards round', with a reserve in the centre. At about 7 a.m. the Boers realized that the British held the heights and after an initial panic started firing at the British at about 9 a.m. Cameron wrote:

We had been exposed to five hours of unceasing fire, and had become accustomed to the constant humming of bullets, which at noon almost ceased, when the General, wearied with the exertions of the previous night, lay down to sleep. Communication by heliograph had been established with the camp, and confidence in our ability to hold our own had increased, rather than abated. A little after twelve he (Lt. Hamilton) came back from his position for a few minutes to tell us that, having seen large numbers of the enemy pass to the hollow underneath him he feared that they were up to some devilment. Reinforcements were promised him and he returned to his post, but these did not reach him until it was almost too late.

Shortly afterwards, Major Hay, of the 92nd, Colonel Stewart, Major Fraser, and myself were discussing the situation, when we were startled by a loud and sustained rattle of musketry, the bullets of which shrieked over our heads in a perfect hail. Lieutenant Wright, of the 92nd, rushed back, shouting out for immediate reinforcements. The General, assisted by his staff, set about getting these forward, and then for the first time it dawned upon us that we might lose the hill, for the soldiers moved forward but slowly and hesitatingly. It was only too evident they did not like the work before them.

It seems that the advance of the enemy had been thoroughly checked, when one of our people—an officer, I believe—noticing the Boers for the first time, ejaculated, Oh, there they are, quite close; and the words were hardly out of his lips ere every man of the newly arrived reinforcements bolted back panic-stricken. This was more than flesh and blood could stand, and the skirmishing line under Hamilton gave way also, the retreating troops being exposed, of course, to the Boer fire with disastrous effect.

I was on the left of the ridge when the men came back on us, and was a witness of the wild confusion which then prevailed. I saw MacDonald, of the 92nd, revolver in hand, threaten to shoot any man who passed him; and, indeed, everybody was hard at work rallying the broken troops. Many, of course, got away and disappeared over the side of the hill next the camp; but some hundred and fifty good men, mostly Highlanders, bluejackets, and old soldiers of the 58th, remained to man the ridge for a final stand.

It was a hot five minutes, but nevertheless, I thought at the time we should hold our own. I expected every minute to hear the order given for a bayonet charge. That order unfortunately never came, although I am sure the men would have responded to it. But our flanks were exposed, and the enemy, checked in front, were stealing round them; across the hollow on the side of the hill facing the camp we had no one . . .

We were most anxious about our right flank. It was evident that the enemy were stealing round it, so men were taken to prolong the position there. They were chiefly bluejackets, led by a brave young officer, and, as I watched them follow him up, for the third time that day, the conviction flashed across me that we should lose the hill. There was a knoll on the threatened point, up which the reinforcements hesitated to climb. Some of them went back over the top of the plateau to the further ridge, others went round.

By and by there was confusion on the knoll itself. Some of the men on it stood up, and were at once shot down; and at last the whole of those who were holding it gave way. Helter skelter they were at once followed by the Boers, who were able then to pour a volley into our flank in the main line, from which instant the hill of Majuba was theirs. It was *sauve qui peut.*

The General had turned round the last of all to walk after his retreating troops, when he also was shot dead, through the head.

To move over about one hundred yards of ground under the fire of some five hundred rifles at close range is not a pleasant experience but it is what all who remained of us on the hill that day had to go through. On every side, men were throwing up their arms, and with sharp cries of agony were pitching forward on the ground. At last we went over the side of the hill.

The Boers were instantly on the ridge above, and for about ten minutes kept up their terrible fire on our soldiers, who plunged down every path. Many, exhausted with the night's marching and the day's fighting, unable to go further, lay down behind rocks and bushes, and were afterwards taken prisoner; but of those who remained on the hill to the very last probably not one in six got clear away.

The reaction to Cameron's dispatch was typical of the Victorian press whose shouts for revenge rivalled the melodramatic prose mourning the death of the General. While some of the public might have been shocked, the readers of the *Referee* were told that 'The novelty of a British army getting thrashed by niggers, and amateurs is wearing off'.

Some newspapers such as the *Natal Mercury*, however, tended to embroider the story with tales of Boers firing on white flags, British soldiers running out of ammunition and being outnumbered thirty to one, and these stories got more preposterous as they were repeated.

On 6 March a cessation of hostilities for eight days was agreed upon and on 21 March a peace conference was assembled. Newspapers who had not previously been represented had dispatched correspondents after the initial defeats and the *Morning Post* bore the ridicule of its rivals when it sent out the first woman war correspondent, Lady Florence Dixie. A devout Imperialist, Lady Florence Dixie had two brothers who were equally eccentric, one being killed scaling the Matterhorn, and the other more famous as the 9th Marquis of Queensberry, who laid out the rules for boxing. She arrived in South Africa just in time for the peace conference, accompanied by her insignificant husband Beau, and soon got bored with reporting peace rather than war. 'With a glass of whisky in her hand,' it was said, 'she could hold her own in any mess tent.'

First Boer War: selling kit belonging to soldiers killed on Majuba Hill, Mount Prospect Camp, May 1881 (pencil sketch by Melton Prior).

She was not only a first-class horsewoman but a crack shot. After the war she returned to England, renounced her sporting activities except for riding and was largely instrumental in obtaining the release of King Cetewayo and arranging his return to Zululand.

Peace terms were negotiated but Cameron and his friends complained of the long inactive wait outside O'Neill's Farm which made tempers short. Many correspondents had their horses saddled ready for the dash to the nearest telegraph at Mount Prospect camp, some two miles away. Prior, who was on intimate terms with General Wood's A.D.C., had asked him to let him know when the Boers had signed. Strolling over to Cameron, he told him quietly to have his horse ready round the corner of a hill out of sight and he would repay his debt for the information used for his Majuba sketch by raising his helmet to show Cameron that peace had been signed. The A.D.C. emerged shortly after to smoke a cigarette and mentioned casually to Prior, 'They have signed'. Prior raised his helmet and Cameron galloped off to the camp.

Twenty minutes later, the General emerged and announced to the pressmen what Prior already knew but added that '. . . the wire to England is closed to all communication until my dispatch has gone'. Cameron's dispatch had already beaten the embargo and the *Standard* was able to publish an *extra* later the same day announcing the peace, even before the somewhat embarrassed officials in Whitehall had received the news. It was, however, as Thomas Carter of the *Natal Times* wrote, echoing the sentiments of the officers and men, 'A miserable ending to a miserable war', one of the very few for which Britain awarded no medal or clasp.

# 5

# A perilous profession

## (1881–7)

*It is an age of hurry, and the war correspondents are in the running.*
Bennet Burleigh, war correspondent of the *Daily Telegraph*.

The last two decades of the nineteenth century provided even more
breathtaking and 'jingoistic' copy than ever before and the demand for
'hot' news increased the competition among the pressmen who
employed any and every means to get the news home first. Newspapers
expended fortunes on their specials and nothing short of a scoop would
satisfy the proprietors. But the era of the highly paid war correspondent with unlimited expenses was soon to come to an end. Reuter's and
other news agencies' telegraphic coverage of wars and campaigns made
editors think twice before sending out their own special whose
egotistical style of writing was becoming outdated. 'We don't want to
read how our correspondent was bitten by mosquitoes, or left his
pyjamas behind him,' commented one editor sourly. War reporting
was entering a new phase where concise factual accounts were all that
was demanded. The temptation to include personal adventures was
still too great even for men like G. W. Steevens, Bennet Burleigh and
Winston S. Churchill, whose direct style became that of the correspondents of the 1890s. Even so the Sudan campaigns of the 1880s and
1890s were followed by a large mixed press corps. Ernest Bennet in
his book *The Downfall of the Dervishes* describes the various types
of correspondents who made up that extravagant fraternity:

> There is the rough man [he wrote], who glories in his roughness, scorns luxury and doesn't wash. An excellent fellow in his way, he yet renders himself more unhappy than he need be by his unstinted devotion to discomfort.

In contrast there were the other correspondents who made themselves as comfortable as possible, men such as Melton Prior of the *Illustrated London News*; but as Bennet conceded, they were always generous towards their colleagues when it came to hospitality and aid with transport. The most detested type was the veteran:

> . . . the self-constituted *doyens* of the pressmen who claim to regulate the camp and lay down the law generally. There was also the new hand . . . clad in all the trappings with which Messrs. Silver (outfitters) adorn the noumenal war correspondent of their imagination . . . the poor man is so festooned with cameras and field glasses and revolvers and haversacks that respiration must be difficult, as he bumps along on his gee gee in an enormous helmet . . .

There were also the non-professionals who paid their own way and hoped to break even with the money received for their letters. Bennet had no comment to make about this category as he was one himself.

Although there were other foreign and imperial campaigns, the newspapers' main attention was focused on Egypt and its disorganized province, the Sudan. Egypt was not an independent sovereign state and the Khedive or ruler was a vassal of the Sultan of Turkey, although in effect, since the opening of the Suez Canal in 1869 and Disraeli's acquisition of a large block of shares for the British government in 1875, British interest was greatly increased. The Egyptian national debt, mainly to France and Britain, had increased from £3¼ million in 1841 to a staggering £94 million, and in 1879 at the insistence of the British and French and with the support of the Sultan of Turkey, Khedive Ismail was deposed in favour of his son, and an international debt commission set up to preside over Egypt's finances. This foreign interference was resented by many Egyptians and in the Egyptian army, already disgruntled by a cut in pay, Colonel Ahmed Arabi gathered support for a *coup d'état*. He wanted to cut the stranglehold of the foreigners who besides controlling Egypt were taking two-thirds of her revenue to repay the national debt. There had been a revolt in the Egyptian army in 1879, but this had been swiftly and ruthlessly put down. The Arabi Revolt, as it is often called, gathered momentum in 1881 as Colonel Ahmed Arabi presented a series of demands to the Egyptian government, each of which were granted. Feeling himself in a strong position he succeeded in getting the Prime Minister sacked and himself appointed as Minister of War, a position which enabled him to challenge the presence of the British and French.

In May 1882, the British and French fleets were anchored off Alexandria in an attempt to intimidate Arabi, who replied by fortifying the area along the waterfront and mounting heavy guns in the forts. Britain's interest in Egypt was not, like that of France, wholly financial. The Suez Canal was the shortest and most direct route to India and the protection of the Canal was bound to involve some form of control over Egypt. The French Prime Minister, Gambetta, was resolved not to abandon Egypt and to side with the British should force become necessary; but at the critical moment he fell from power and the French fleet sailed away leaving Britain to intervene alone. In June rioting broke out in Alexandria and at the news of an impending fight many of the London editors began to warn their correspondents or to make the usual arrangements. Some, however, were content for the moment to rely on Reuter and other agency telegrams. A British ultimatum to dismantle the fortifications was ignored and on 11 July at 7 a.m. the British fleet started the bombardment.

A number of newspaper correspondents had already started to arrive in Egypt: Melton Prior of the *Illustrated London News*, Frank Powers of *The Times*, John Cameron of the *Standard*, Charles E. Fripp and Frederick Villiers of the *Graphic*, Charles F. Moberly Bell of *The Times*, Bennet Burleigh of the Central News Agency, Hilary Skinner of the *Daily News*, Captain Fitzgerald of the *Manchester Guardian*, and John Merry Le Sage of the *Daily Telegraph*. On 10 July, the newspapermen and British subjects were evacuated from Alexandria and put aboard the P. & O. steamer *Tangore* '. . . at ten shillings and sixpence per day per head' but not before the resourceful Fitzgerald had interviewed Arabi for the *Manchester Guardian*, much to its delight, thirty-six hours before the bombardment. Some of the correspondents managed to get invited aboard the warships and so enjoyed a grandstand view of the events. For the entire day, the bombardment raged, mainly against Arabi's stronghold of Fort Mex but towards evening both parties grew silent from lack of ammunition. Some of the warships had been hit, but there was no serious damage, except for the loss of Melton Prior's baggage and the thousand cigarettes he always carried on campaign.

After two days of inactivity, watching the Egyptians firing Alexandria, looting and killing, a party of bluejackets and marines were ordered to land. Cameron, Prior, and a few others obtained permission to accompany the landing party and witnessed scenes of desolation and destruction. Looters were summarily dealt with, usually being shot on sight. Those that were caught, mainly criminals released before Arabi's departure, were tried and hanged. The correspondents seemed more intent on fighting than reporting: 'When we were able to penetrate into the town, revolvers in hand, for we did not know at what moment we might come across a fanatic Egyptian.' It took a time to restore law and order, but Arabi had not been captured and his army, some 60,000 strong, was still at large.

The usual enemy of the war correspondent was officialdom, in this campaign in the guise of Sir Garnet Wolseley. But in some instances, even the ever-fickle public could turn against their favourite newspaper. Archibald Forbes recorded one instance concerning a correspondent in Egypt during the Arabi uprising of 1882:

> He was with the force that was confronting Arabi in the Kafre Dowr position outside Alexandria during the interval between the bombardment of that city and the arrival in Egypt of Lord Wolseley's reinforcements. One afternoon his paper brought out a 'special edition' on the strength of a telegram from him to the effect that one of the pickets of our force had run in on its supports. Whether or not the telegram was 'written up' in Fleet Street, is a question which need not be dwelt on, in the face of the fact that the correspondent did not deny that he had sent intelligence of the misbehaviour of the picket. It was passing strange, the gust of popular indignation against this penman—in this particular matter at least a quite inoffensive although in a professional sense silly person. The angry nation would not have it at any price that a picket of British soldiers could act as described. The correspondent was denounced far and wide as the vilest of calumniators. *Punch* pandered to the undignified and perverse clamour in some doggerel jingle; the correspondent's journal temporised in the face of the storm, and cashiered its representative. Yet his act was in no way blameworthy; it was simply officious and superfluous.

The public liked news of victories and bravery, but this sort of information they preferred to ignore or to disbelieve. It was just not

Egypt 1882: a British square, formed by the Cameron Highlanders in Egypt for the Arabi Revolt.

possible that British soldiers should run away. Although this was considered the standard of behaviour by late Victorians, it was unfortunately far from the truth. Forbes admitted that 'I am not the man, an old soldier myself, to run down the British soldier, but the cheap froth of the cockalorum civilian disgusts me'. He had witnessed a similar occurrence during the Zulu War:

> . . . but it never occurred to me to report it. It was not that
> I shunned doing so, but simply because the thing was not
> worthwhile. My comrade, with his experience, should have
> taken the same view of the petty mischance he happened to
> witness in Egypt; but it was sheer truculence to hound him
> down because he looked at events microscopically.

Sir Garnet Wolseley, 'Our only General', was dispatched to Egypt to lead an expedition to smash the revolt, and to destroy Arabi's army which was situated near Alexandria, Cairo and at Tel-el-Kebir. William Howard Russell arrived in Egypt just after Sir Garnet and he could not resist the temptation to apply for permission to accompany the force. Sir Garnet made it clear that he had forbidden all amateurs to accompany the army and wrote to Russell to tell him that Lord Charles Beresford had been refused permission, even as a Khedive's officer. Beresford was not to be daunted and tried unsuccessfully again to get to the front as the correspondent of the *New York Herald*. Russell's disappointment was great as he witnessed the army march out, 'Alas! why was I not with them? This is my last chance perhaps.'

Melton Prior reported that the troops were going to be in '. . . for some good fighting . . . and the correspondents were cheerful enough in consequence'. In typical Wolseley fashion, news was spread amongst the troops and correspondents that an action was to be mounted against the rebels at Aboukir Bay and the correspondents were encouraged to send the news to London. Although Prior wrote, '...I do not think he seriously believed he had succeeded in baffling the English press', the ruse had the desired effect on the enemy and on some of the press. To help divert Arabi's attention from the Suez Canal which the British were intent on seizing, the intelligence officer, Major Bruce Tulloch, later a *Times* correspondent during the Russo-Japanese war of 1904, 'used' the name of a well-known correspondent. Knowing that all British news telegraphed to and from Cairo passed by Constantinople, where it was copied and relayed back to Arabi, Tulloch concocted a 'false' telegram, which he signed 'John Cameron' and telegraphed to the editor of the *Standard* in London:

> I knew well the correspondent of the *Standard*, Cameron, a splendid fellow ... would be too patriotic to object to my taking his name in vain when it was for the good of our work; so I wired the editor ... as if from Cameron, to the effect that 'rumours of a possible occupation of the canal by the English are now disposed of. M. de Lesseps, who has the French Government behind him, has settled that the neutrality of the canal shall be rigidly observed ... It is now an open secret that whilst the British portion of the force will move from Alexandria and attack Kafr Dewar, the troops coming from India will move from Suez direct on Cairo.'

The telegram had the desired effect. Cameron and Fitzgerald arrived at Aboukir in a specially chartered launch expecting to find exclusive news, but as darkness fell the ships set sail for the Canal where 800 troops were put ashore at Suez. The post and telegraph offices were the first objectives and Wolseley must have felt some satisfaction to find a telegram all ready for transmission from the Frenchman Ferdinand de Lesseps, the builder of the famous canal, which told Arabi 'English not coming here but have assembled at Aboukir'. Naturally Wolseley authorized its transmission before closing the post.

The result of outflanking the enemy made Arabi reinforce his lines at Tel-el-Kebir, and, except for an encounter with the enemy at Tel-el-Magfar in August, there was little activity until the second week in September. Russell who was still in Egypt noted with disgust the changing style of the war correspondents in the field. In his diary for

8 September, eleven days after the famous 'moonlight charge' of the Cavalry Brigade under Sir Drury Lowe at Kassassin, he wrote:

> I received a great pile of papers. It makes me sick to read them. We are quite changing our national character, or showing its worst side, for no Gascon could be more braggart and vain, and the special correspondents vie with each other in gasconnade [boasting].

At 1.30 a.m. on the morning of 13 September, true to Lord Wolseley's publicized promise the troops moved out from Kassassin camp towards the lines of Tel-el-Kebir. Just as dawn was coming up, the British had covered the five and a half miles to Arabi's entrenchments and forming into line stormed and captured the position. Prior, Cameron, and Skinner arrived just in time to see the storming of the earthworks in the early dawn light. Frank Power of *The Times* summed up the attack in his dispatch:

> There was no moon and thus almost within cannon shot, the two armies were resting peacefully, the one side dreaming probably little of the terrible scene of the awakening, when their rest at length rudely disturbed, they awoke to see swiftly advancing upon every side an endless line of dreaded red coats, broken by the even *more fearful* blue of the Marines.

After the battle, Fitzgerald, aided by another correspondent, Le Mesurier also of the *Manchester Guardian*, was the first to telegraph his dispatch of the victory, which should have been a resounding scoop for the paper; but when his telegram reached Alexandria, it was appropriated by the Military Governor and sent to the War Office in London, rather than its true destination, the *Manchester Guardian*. This information emerged when an inquiry was held into the fate of Fitzgerald's missing telegram. Captain G. Field of the Royal Marine Light Infantry sent a number of sketches of this campaign to the *Graphic*, while the *Illustrated Navy and Military Magazine* used *Illustrated London News* material with their permission. The following day, Cairo was captured, the remaining Egyptian troops disarmed and Arabi made prisoner. In Cairo, the British found a number of prisoners, including a French newspaper correspondent, who had been with the Arab army '... and probably wrote something too true', joked an officer of the Scots Guards. Britain now effectively ruled Egypt and set about conscripting a new army there under British officers.

Egypt 1882: interior of one of
the forts of Alexandria showing
the damage done by the British
bombardment.

Egypt 1882: Melton Prior lecturing to the Prince of Wales and members of the Savage Club
about his experiences during the Arabi Revolt.

In gaining a hold over Egypt, Britain had also inherited her problem: the million square miles of scorching sandy, scrubby waste known as the Sudan. G. W. Steevens, the war correspondent for the *Daily Mail* in the Sudan campaign of 1898, wrote that 'Surely enough, "When Allah made the Sudan," say the Arabs, "he laughed". You can almost hear the fiendish echo of it crackling over the dry sand.' The Sudan thrived on its slave trade despite the efforts of the Egyptian government and men such as 'Chinese' Gordon, Governor-General of the Sudan between 1871 and 1880. The Sudanese resented Egypt's presence, their dishonest and corrupt rule, heavy taxation, and above all their attempts to stop slavery.

In 1881, a revolt broke out in the Sudan led by the fanatic son of a carpenter, Mohammed Ahmed, who later dubbed himself Mahdi Allah, the Mahdi of God. He told his followers that he was going to seize the Sudan, conquer Egypt, and establish a kingdom at Mecca. The Sudanese, oppressed for so many years by the Egyptians, saw this as a 'heaven-sent' opportunity to be free. Gordon's successor in the Sudan did not take the matter very seriously until his force sent against the Mahdi and the Dervishes or *Ansars* (helpers) was routed. The Mahdi was delighted with the capture of rifles and his victory encouraged many new recruits. During 1882, the Egyptians were so occupied in trying to defeat the British that the Mahdi did very much as he pleased. He attacked El Obeid, chief city of the Kordofan province, but the attempt failed. He hastily found an excuse for his followers to whom he had previously said that the enemy's bullets could not kill and sat down to starve out the city, which fell on 19 January 1883. Again a quantity of arms was captured and issued to the ever-increasing number of followers.

Although this revolt indirectly concerned the British, Gladstone's foreign policy prevented any intervention by the British army. The Khedive had no choice but to tackle the problem himself, and decided that Egyptian forces led by a competent British officer would be the solution to the Sudan problem. An expedition was mounted at Khartoum under the command of a retired British army colonel, William Hicks, given the rank of Hicks Pasha. At first he defeated the Dervishes in the Sennar district and was then ordered to drive the rebels from Kordofan and retake El Obeid.

Although Hicks would have been only too pleased to have some British regular troops with him British government policy decreed otherwise. The London press were for the most part against any British intervention in the Sudan. 'Whether Hicks falls or conquers,' stated the *Pall Mall Gazette*, 'is not our business; not a single British soldier will be ordered to Khartoum if the Mahdi were to rout the whole force under the orders of the Khedive's officers.' In September 1883 with a force of 10,000 men, and 5,500 camels carrying supplies, Hicks set off from Khartoum towards El Obeid. With the column rode three special correspondents, Edmund O'Donovan of the *Daily News*, the veteran Frank Vizetelly representing both the *Graphic* and the *Illustrated London News*, and Frank Power of *The Times*. All had taken the usual precautions against sunstroke and dysentery and sported large helmets, sun veils, goggles, spine pads as well as carrying the usual comforts, such as whisky, tinned foods by Messrs. Crosse and Blackwell and Leibig soup, the correspondents' standby. Power sported a blue jacket, white helmet, Bedford cord breeches with a scarlet cummerbund but, feeling ill as soon as the march started, he returned to Khartoum. This probably saved his life, as the ramshackle army was drawn further into the Sudan. Warnings were conveyed by leaflets left by the Mahdi (which the Egyptians used as lavatory paper). But eventually, weak with thirst, they were massacred between 3 and 5 November at Kashgil near El Obeid. Both newspapermen died with the column.

The Sudan, with its capital denuded of troops and its smaller outposts menaced by the Dervishes, was virtually in the hands of the Mahdi. It was obvious that unless a full-scale expedition was mounted by the British, which Gladstone had no intention of authorizing, the Sudan was lost. The main problem was how to evacuate the troops and civilians to Egypt.

While the Mahdi was finishing off Hicks's column, his able lieutenant Osman Digna had defeated another Egyptian force and had besieged Sinkat and Tokar. A force under Baker Pasha was sent to relieve these towns and with it went the correspondents and artists of the British press. Melton Prior of the *Illustrated London News*, Francis Scudamore of the *Daily News*, John Cameron of the *Standard*, James Mellor Paulton of the *Manchester Examiner*, Frederick Villiers of the *Graphic*, Bennet Burleigh of the Central News Agency, Godfrey Yeatman Lagden, the famous big-game sportsman and ornithologist, of the *Daily Telegraph* and 'The Solemn' MacDonald of the *Western Morning News*. The troops were landed at Trinkitat, the nearest sea point to Tokar, and marched to its relief. Melton Prior injured his leg and remained on the transports while the other correspondents marched off. Cameron had borrowed Prior's '. . . patent box made of tin, containing cotton wool and methylated spirit, which could be fixed to the bottom of soup tins and preserved meat tins'. Prior had also given Cameron and Scudamore some of his favourite campaigning food, Moyer's tinned Irish stew.

The first battle of El-Teb was fought on 4 February and after what the official dispatch called 'a scene of butchery which has probably never been rivalled', the remnants of Baker's army scurried back to their transports. The action had been witnessed by Cameron of the *Standard* who vividly described the scene in his dispatch:

> I had ridden along by the infantry column, and I saw that it was advancing in the most disorderly manner. There was no sign of discipline or steadiness; it was a mere armed mob tramping along . . . As the cavalry rode wildly in, the order was given for the infantry to form square—a manoeuvre in which they had been daily drilled for weeks. At this crisis, however, the dull, half-disciplined mass failed to accomplish it. Three sides were formed after a fashion, but on the fourth side two companies of the Alexandria Regiment, seeing the enemy coming on leaping and brandishing their spears, stood like a panic-stricken flock of sheep, and nothing could get them to move into their place. Into the gap thus left in the square the enemy poured, and at once all became panic and confusion. The troops fired indeed, but the most part straight into the air. The miserable Egyptian soldiers refused even to defend themselves, but throwing away their rifles, flung themselves on the ground and grovelled there, screaming for mercy. No mercy was given, the Arab spearmen pouncing upon them and driving their spears through their necks or bodies. Nothing could surpass the wild confusion, camels and guns mixed up together, soldiers firing into the air, with wild Arabs, their long hair streaming behind them, darting among them, hacking and thrusting with their spears.

The rest of the night was spent in reloading all the stores and the little fleet sailed hastily back to Suakin.

At last London was stirred into action and a telegram was sent to the occupation force in Cairo ordering them to mount an expedition for the relief of Tokar. The force landed at Trinkitat on 28 February and received the news that Tokar had fallen, but General Graham, much

Sudan 1884-5: disembarking Baker Pasha's forces at Trinkitat for the relief of Tokar.

to the delight of the correspondents, decided to push forward and if possible engage the enemy. The square formation marched towards El-Teb and soon encountered the grisly remains of the massacred army of Baker Pasha. 'Swarms of carrion birds flew off on our approach,' recorded a correspondent. The enemy were found entrenched at El-Teb armed with rifles and supported by two Krupp field guns. General Graham sent forward an officer of his staff with a message on a pole telling the sheiks to disperse. The officer planted the pole and retired. The following morning there was no answer and the pole had been removed.

At 8 a.m. Graham ordered his square to advance towards the left of the enemy position. The same correspondents who had been with Baker accompanied the force in its advance to within 200 yards of the Dervishes and under constant fire, when suddenly the enemy stopped firing and grabbing spears, threw themselves at the British. Cameron of the *Standard* wrote:

So hotly do the Arabs press forward that the troops pause in their steady advance. It becomes a hand-to-hand fight, the soldiers meeting the Arab spear with cold steel, their favourite weapon, and beating them at it. There is not much shouting, and only a short, sharp exclamation, a brief shout or an oath, as the soldiers engage with the foe. At this critical moment for the enemy, the Gardener [machine] guns open fire and the leaden hail soon decides matters.

Although the enemy made several attempts to rush the square, they were driven off. Melton Prior remembers seeing 'Battling Burnaby of the Blues' with shirt sleeves rolled up, '. . . picking off the enemy as they rushed in, in the same way you would kill big game'. During the rounding up operations the British discovered the fanaticism of the Dervishes, who although wounded continued to fight. Severe criticisms were heard in England about the 'murderers' of the wounded, but 'The only choice lay between killing or being killed'. Frederick Villiers of the *Graphic* was sketching a supposedly dying boy-warrior after the battle when the boy rose and chased him with a knife. 'I thought to feel his knife in my back any moment,' he wrote. He called out to some soldiers for help and finally a shot rang out dispatching the Dervish.

It was often useful, as correspondents discovered, to be on good terms with high-ranking officers and Melton Prior and John Cameron were invited by Admiral Sir William Hewitt to send their 'letterpress and sketches' by a naval vessel that was leaving for Port Said to catch the Australian mail steamer. Both correspondents set to work and by offering five pounds to the boat crew, they were rowed over and able to place their work aboard in time, which resulted in Prior's drawing and Cameron's dispatch being published in London a week before any other.

Once the remaining inhabitants of Tokar had been saved, the force returned to Suakin, where Osman Digna and his followers had collected. Another expedition was hastily formed which, with its usual following of correspondents, marched towards Tamai and bivouacked in open square formation within a zareba (a hedged square) some several hundred yards from the enemy who throughout the night kept up a spasmodic fire. At dawn breakfast was taken and the generous and well-equipped Melton Prior offered a number of his colleagues a feast of '. . . bully beef, sardines and cocoa'.

The 1st and 2nd Brigades were formed into separate squares for the attack and the correspondents were allocated their positions in each, so as not to hinder the fighting or the carrying of wounded and ammunition. As the enemy attacked in their usual fashion, an order was given for the 2nd Brigade to advance. 'And now as the pressure increased,' wrote an eye-witness, 'the weak points of a square formation became visible.' The front face composed of the York and Lancaster Regiment and the Black Watch '. . . swept forward against the foe' but the remaining three sides of the formation did not keep up with this movement. Every effort was made to close the gaps as the Dervishes burst through them. Bennet Burleigh of the *Daily Telegraph* described the scene:

> The 65th (York and Lancaster) gave way and fell back on the
> Marines throwing them into disorder, though many men
> disdained to turn their backs, but kept their face to the foe
> firing and thrusting with the bayonet. But both regiments
> were inextricably huddled together, and through the smoke
> of this dire crisis the dark demon-like figures of the foe
> could be seen rushing on, unchecked even for a moment by
> the hailstorm of bullets, and then the fight became hand to
> hand.

Sudan 1884–5: the Battle of Tamai, 13 March 1884.

Sudan 1884-5: Melton Prior of the *Illustrated London News* in campaign kit.

Melton Prior who was also in the square recorded that it was '. . . a
terrible ten minutes . . . Shall I never forget it? I can even now see those
brave Highlanders trying to force back a mass of savages. My God! what
a ghastly fight it was!' Bennet Burleigh, the 'bluff and kindly' Scotsman,
helped to reform the broken square. He was heard crying 'Men of the
65th—close up' and Frederick Villiers remembered hearing Burleigh's
voice above the din shouting, 'Give it to the beggars. Let 'em have it
boys! Hurrah. Three cheers—hurrah.' Villiers himself later confessed,
'. . . how I got out of that fight I hardly know to this day'.

Melton Prior also had a close call while he was sketching:

> . . . an Arab loomed up close to me, and I saw him, spear in
> hand, just in the act of throwing it. Suddenly down it whizzed
> over my shoulder into the back of one of the 42nd, who fell
> to the ground with a groan, dead.

The village of Tamai containing some enemy stores was destroyed and
the force returned to Suakin. Although Osman Digna had lost '. . . a
few of his followers . . . the fights at El-Teb and Tamai did not have the
slightest effect in quelling the Soudan rebellion'.

Sudan 1884-5: 'The desert march. Scene at the wells of Aboo Halfa. Animals no water for three scorching days. Many of the men had only a pint in the morning and a pint at night. Discipline alone prevented a wild confusion setting in' (pencil sketch and notes by Melton Prior).

This sort of adventure inspired not only the correspondents and the public but also the poets and adventure writers who were quick to catch on to this market for patriotic literature. Perhaps the most typical of the popular heroic melodramas, Kipling being far more realistic in his 'Imperial' poetry, was Sir Henry Newbolt's 'Vitaï Lampada', one verse in particular summing up the true Imperial spirit:

> The sand of the desert is sodden red,
> Red with the wreck of a square that broke;
> The Gatling's jammed and the colonel dead,
> And the regiment blind with the dust and smoke.
> The river of death has brimmed its banks
> And England's far, and honour a name,
> But the voice of a schoolboy rallies the ranks:
> Play up! play up! and play the game!

Tamai had been a narrow victory and one correspondent, Cameron of the *Standard*, convinced that the fight was lost, mounted and rode to Suakin to cable his dispatch of the setback. When the troops returned, he found himself in a rather embarrassing situation.

While these actions were being fought in eastern Sudan, the government had decided to send General Charles Gordon to Khartoum to organize the evacuation of civilians and troops. At the same time it was their intention to maintain Suakin as their only hold in the Sudan. On 9 January, the *Pall Mall Gazette* had published an interview between Gordon and its editor, the controversial W. T. Stead, expressing their views about the Sudan. The main criticism Gordon had was the government's announcement of its intention to evacuate the Sudan:

> ... The moment it is known that we have given up the game every man will go over to the Mahdi. All men worship the rising sun. The difficulties of evacuation will be enormously increased, if indeed, the withdrawal of our garrison is not rendered impossible.

Other newspapers hastily reprinted the interview and most were in favour of sending Gordon to the rescue.

Gordon saw his task as the evacuation of all Christians, the government wanted him to be an observer, the Khedive expected total evacuation and the public and press a great re-conquest. It was a confusing situation made more so by Gordon's unpredictable behaviour. By 12 March Khartoum was in a state of siege, but Gordon was still confident that, given the men and the money, he could beat the Mahdi. Gladstone, who had now reconciled himself to a firm policy of non-intervention in Egyptian affairs, believed that Gordon would extricate himself without the need of a costly expedition up the Nile to save him at Khartoum. But Gordon was decided on his course of action. A vigorous press campaign tried to induce the government to act and *The Times* of 1 April published a letter from its special correspondent, Frank Power, besieged in Khartoum, who had assumed the position of acting British Consul. 'We are daily expecting the British troops,' wrote Power, '... We cannot bring ourselves to believe that we are to be abandoned by the Government.' On 16 April, the telegraph lines with Khartoum were cut and news and messages could only be smuggled in and out at risk through the Dervish lines.

It was not until August that, under pressure from public and press, the government at last ordered a relieving force under Sir Garnet

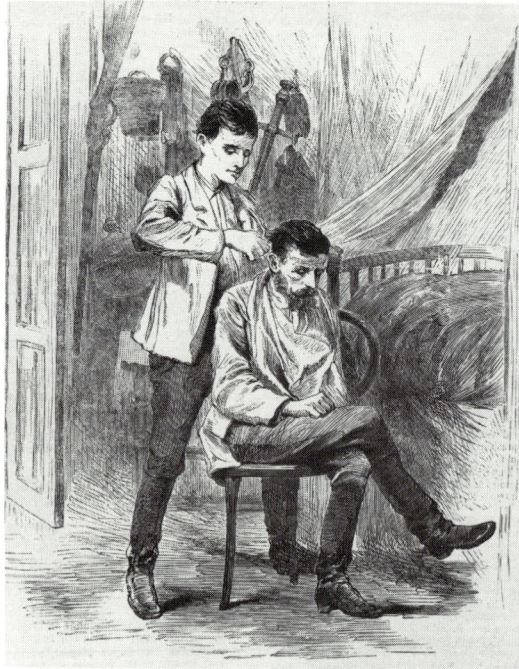

Sudan 1884-5: Walter Paget of
the *Illustrated London News*
gives a haircut to *The Times*'s
correspondent.

Wolseley to prepare. To the British press and public, the thought of
an expeditionary force marching to the rescue of Christians amidst a
sea of heathens gave the expedition an almost crusade-like appearance.
Correspondents and artists prepared their campaigning kit, procured
their permits and supplies and set sail for Egypt. Among the scores of
journalists who descended on Egypt were the familiar and famous
names as well as the newcomers. St. Leger Herbert wrote for the
*Morning Post* while acting as the secretary to General Stewart,
Wentworth Huyshe, 'brother of the Berkshire's Colonel', reported for
*The Times*, H. H. S. Pearse, an accomplished journalist, wrote for the
*Daily News*, Walter Paget, whose brother Sidney Paget would become
the well-known illustrator of Conan Doyle's Sherlock Holmes stories,
and Melton Prior drew for the *Illustrated London News*. Frederick
Villiers and Charles E. Fripp represented the *Graphic*, John Cameron,
the *Standard*, Charles Williams, later senior military correspondent of
the *Daily Chronicle*, *Evening News* and *Morning Leader*, reported his
first campaign for the Central News Agency, while Alex MacDonald
was the *Western Morning News* correspondent, and the now famous
Bennet Burleigh wrote for the *Daily Telegraph*. This gathering of

specials made Rudyard Kipling remark sourly, 'It was absolutely necessary that England at breakfast should be amused and thrilled and interested whether Gordon lived or died, or half the British army went to pieces in the sands.' But nobody wanted stale news and the leading papers had to ensure good representation to equal or better their rivals. It was all a question of economics, the paper with the 'hottest' news sold the most. As Charles Williams of the Central News Agency wrote, 'Military history cannot be properly written over military telegraph wires... Besides promptness is of the essence of correspondents' work in the field, and promptness is seldom compatible with completeness.' However, such was the climate of things that follow up stories were seldom if ever printed. Once the 'telegraphed' news was published it became history. In the case of the expedition to save Gordon things were different and Williams's wordy dispatch filed with the *Fortnightly Review* after the event caused a minor scandal in the British army, resulting in a lawsuit.

By the end of December 1884 Wolseley had assembled most of his troops and supplies at Korti after an arduous journey in whalers up the Nile. The men '... arriving in the boats presented an absolute ludicrous appearance', wrote a correspondent:

> which testifies to the utter unsuitability of the clothes served out to our soldiers for a hard campaign... The tartan trews... have been patched with old sacks, with native cloth... and even portions of biscuit tins... to repair the wear and tear made by rowing.

At Korti, the natives '... finding out we did not wish to rob them...' established a bazaar and soldier and correspondent alike profited by buying fresh vegetables, meat, milk and fruit. At Korti Wolseley formed a Camel Corps to make a dash across the desert as he thought it impossible to reach Khartoum at that time of year along the Nile. From Khartoum, Colonel Stewart and Frank Power of *The Times* had gone out in an attempt to rejoin Wolseley's force but both were murdered on the way. To avenge this a second or river column was formed to proceed up the Nile to exact just retribution from the Berber tribes.

Some correspondents chose to accompany the desert column while others followed the Nile route. Frederick Villiers and Charles Williams at first followed the steamers and were nearly drowned when their boat upturned. This somewhat minor incident was awarded a large space in

Sudan 1884-5: wreck of the press boat which went with the expedition up the Nile in 1885. In the boat were Frederick Villiers of the *Graphic* and Charles Williams of the Central News Agency.

both the *Daily Chronicle* and the *Graphic*. The desert column was equipped with water-skins but still Melton Prior remarked, 'On the march it was quite etiquette to refuse a drink', and he disguised his water-skins as potato sacks to deter would-be thieves.

The column pushed on towards Abu Klea where on 17 January, after a night of desultory fire from the Dervishes, they met the enemy and engaged in battle. General Stewart left the baggage animals in the zareba and advanced in the usual square formation with camels for carrying ammunition and the wounded in the centre. The slowness of these beasts bulged the square at the rear and the guns within also hindered any rapid movement. Alex MacDonald of the *Western Morning News* declined to go with the square, as he thought little of its chances. He rested in the fortified zareba where biscuit boxes and stores had been stacked in defence.

The square was in the act of dressing itself on one of its frequent halts when the Dervishes attacked, throwing their main efforts at the left front corner held by the mounted infantry. This was resisted. The enemy immediately changed their direction to the rear left corner of the square, where a gap had appeared and where mounted infantrymen were hastily trying to drag the camels carrying the wounded inside.

Sudan 1884—5: the Battle of Abu Klea. 'Repulse of the enemy out of our square' (pencil and wash drawing by Melton Prior).

Unfortunately British skirmishers, retiring towards the square, were also in the line of fire and the soldiers were unable to hold the Dervishes at a suitable distance. When the loose men were at last within the square, the enemy was already dangerously close. Lord Charles Beresford with a naval contingent and a Gatling gun was eager to try the machine-gun and rushed it to the gaping left rear corner and pushed it outside the square. At the same time 'Battling Burnaby' wheeled round a company of the 'heavies' and worsened the situation. The right rear corner was rapidly losing contact with the left, violating the most elementary rules of fighting in a square formation. The Dervishes poured through the gap as the Gatling jammed, cartridges stuck, rifles malfunctioned and bayonets bent and twisted.

The camels, who had previously been cursed, now saved the day. Had the square been hollow, total annihilation was almost certain, but with the bunched camels in the centre, the Arabs had to fight their way through in hand-to-hand combat. Burnaby was killed by a Dervish spear while the rear ranks of the front face fired into the crush of friend and foe and the Arabs at last retired. 'The hand-to-hand fighting and confusion for the time was terrific,' wrote Prior, 'but . . . not one of the Arabs that got inside left the square alive.' It was already evident to Bennet Burleigh that there was something sadly wrong with the quality of the weapons used by the British soldier in this campaign and a full condemnation of the cartridges, swords, and bayonets appeared in the *Daily Telegraph* in May 1885 when the campaign was almost over.

The correspondents now feverishly wrote accounts and the artists prepared sketches of the fight in the square, but the main problem was how to get them forwarded. Prior and Cameron paid a camel driver who for fifty pounds was prepared to carry dispatch and drawings. However, neither arrived nor were the driver or cheque ever seen again.

While correspondents were considered a nuisance they were also sometimes praised by the officers. According to Major E. Bambier Parry, correspondents were:

> . . . always in the front when fighting was going on, and always to be found where the bullets fell thickest, and where danger was to be met with. Then after the fighting was over, or perhaps after a long march, they would ride miles in the hot sun, and sit up half the night to write home the doings of the day.

On 18 January the column moved off, leaving the wounded at the wells of Abu Klea, marched all day and most of the night towards Messameh on the Nile. The following morning a large Dervish force was found to be blocking the way to the Nile and after breakfast Stewart ordered his men to construct a zareba. The work was difficult as the enemy started firing at the working parties causing a number of casualties. Eighty yards from the zareba was a prominent mound on which it was decided to construct a redoubt. Boxes, camel saddles, and baggage were carried across under fire and Bennet Burleigh of the *Daily Telegraph* was mentioned in dispatches for his contribution, the first time a war correspondent was so distinguished.

Bennet Burleigh was born in Glasgow in the 1840s and as a young man fought in the American Civil War on the side of the South, during which he was twice sentenced to death. Shortly afterwards he married and later, despite the responsibility of a family of five sons and three daughters, he found life as a special correspondent exhilarating. He first covered the Arabi Revolt for Central News before joining the

Sudan 1884-5: Bennet Burleigh,
war correspondent of the *Daily
Telegraph.*

staff of the *Daily Telegraph* in 1882 where he established firmly his position as their premier special war correspondent. He covered numerous campaigns for his newspaper from 1882 until 1911. He died on 17 June 1914, a few weeks before the outbreak of the First World War. A Scot with typical Victorian moustache, he was described by Melton Prior as '. . . bluff and kindly with a heart far too big for his body, bursting with kindness and good nature for those he liked, endowed with a remarkable energy and pluck and with as much knowledge of soldiering as most generals . . .' As Russell was the star war correspondent during the Crimean War, so was Burleigh during the early Sudan campaign. He showed none of the limelight-seeking of some of the correspondents, was always conscious of his duty and in his own quiet way was as good a reporter as Russell and got the news home as quickly as Forbes had done. He was always kindly towards 'new hands' offering any experience that might be useful and equally generous with his old journalist friends. With Russell, he rose to the higher echelons of his profession by bringing to public notice a military system that was archaic and through his efforts improved the efficiency of the British army.

The haphazard firing at Abu Kru caused a number of casualties amongst the war correspondents as well as the troops. John Cameron

Sudan 1884-5: the death of Cameron of the *Standard* at Abu Kru (pencil sketch by Melton Prior).

Sudan 1884—5: Burleigh, Villiers, MacDonald, Prior and Pearse bearing Cameron's body to the grave.

of the *Standard* was killed as he rose to take a tin of sardines from his servant, while St. Leger Herbert of the *Morning Post*, ever conspicuous in a red jacket, was found dead amongst the camels. John Cameron, a veteran war correspondent, was greatly admired by his colleagues for his professionalism. One of his closest friends, Melton Prior, described him as '. . . a well tried man from north of the Tweed, who was never tired of letting us know it with pride, . . . sharp eyed, imperious, but keen as a razor at his work'. Bennet Burleigh was hit in the throat by a ricocheting bullet and clawing at his neck, thinking he was wounded, shouted to Prior, 'Pick it out, Prior! pick it out!' There was of course no bullet but the blow raised a lump under his ear like half a chicken's egg. Prior himself was hit on the thumb and Villiers on the foot. All but one of the correspondents were hit by ricocheting bullets which were a constant menace to all. Later, Bennet Burleigh, Frederick Villiers, 'the solemn' MacDonald, Melton Prior and H. H. S. Pearse carried Cameron's body on a bier to the grave where Lord Charles Beresford read the burial service, there being no chaplains with the force. The most serious casualty of the day was General Stewart who received a mortal wound and died shortly afterwards, leaving the command of the column to General Wilson, the man so often blamed for the loss of Gordon.

In the three years of campaigning in the Sudan, seven war correspondents had lost their lives and G. A. Henty, at a dinner in 1885 of the Savage Club (founded at the Crown Tavern in 1857 as a haunt for Bohemian artists, authors, and journalists), declared:

> ... why gentlemen, from the days of the Crimean when William Howard Russell, Nat Wood, and in a humble way, myself, began the work of correspondents with the British army all the wars, all the campaigns together, have not caused such a mortality as this.

He greeted those who had returned as having '... come back to us out of the jaws of death!'

A tablet in St. Paul's Cathedral commemorates:

> ... the Gallant Men who in the discharge of their duty as Special Correspondents fell in the Campaigns in the Soudan 1883—1884—1885.
>     EDMOND O'DONOVAN "*Daily News*", Kashgil, November 1883.
>     FRANK VIZETELLY, Artist, Kashgil, November 1883.
>     FRANK POWER "*Times*", El Kamar, October 1884.
>     JOHN ALEXANDER CAMERON, "*Standard*", Abu Kru, January 19, 1885.
>     ST. LEDGER ALGERNON HERBERT, CMG, "*Morning Post*", Abu Kru, January 1885.
>     WILLIAM HENRY GORDON, "*Manchester Guardian*", Korti, January 1885.
>     FRANK J. L. ROBERTS, "*Reuters Agency*", Souakin, May 15, 1885.

Sudan 1884-5: 'The attempt on Metemmeh, throwing up defences in the village of Aboo Krou which we were bound to hold at all costs, 21 January '85' (pencil sketch by Melton Prior).

The whole affair at Abu Kru lasted a few minutes as the Dervish horsemen threw themselves at the square which had formed up and marched towards the enemy. This time it stood firm with the men firing '. . . as they would have done on an Aldershot field day'. The way was open to the Nile and the weary and thirsty soldiers camped there for the night. Before the square was engaged, Burleigh, Pearse, and Prior decided to ride off with the dispatches and sketches but the sight of the Arab horsemen sent them scurrying back to the square, where after the fight they helped to carry the wounded to the encampment which was heavily fortified. Wilson decided to send out his dispatches to Wolseley and Prior noted that as he had the fastest camel it was purchased on behalf of Her Majesty's Government for thirty-five pounds.

Three steamers from Khartoum arrived on 21 January with news of its defence, which now seemed in a very precarious state. Unfortunately Wilson delayed his advance by steamer back to Khartoum and when the boats came in sight of the city on 27 January, they were forty-eight hours too late. Prior had tried to get aboard one but permission to all war correspondents was refused. On 5 February, a telegram which had travelled by various means from Wilson arrived in London: 'Khartoum taken by Mahdi. General Gordon's fate uncertain.' After Gordon's death was known, Bennet Burleigh, braving the dangers of a ride through hostile territory, rode on to Dongola and wired the news of Gordon's death to the *Daily Telegraph*, giving correspondent and newspaper a world scoop. The news appeared in a special edition published on 23 February, a Sunday, some thirty-six hours before it was officially confirmed.

After Gordon's death, the government decided to evacuate the Sudan except for Suakin. While the desert column had fought at Abu Klea and Abu Kru, the column following the Nile under General Earle was laboriously moving towards Khartoum when news arrived of its fall and the column was ordered to remain where it was. On 10 February, the Dervishes were beaten off and in a counter-attack the force completely routed the enemy. Lieutenant-Colonel Brackenbury assumed the command when Earle was killed by a lurking Dervish after the battle was over. When the column marched he had been ordered by Earle:

> ... to inform the English correspondent of a foreign newspaper, ... that owing to the necessity for economising all food for man and beast, and in view of all spare whaler accommodation being required for transport of the sick, he could not allow any civilian correspondent to accompany the column.

The battle over, the column returned to Korti, on orders from Wolseley. Fighting still continued around Suakin, where Osman Digna was convinced of his power to take the town. On 20 March, General Graham broke the enemy concentration at Hasheen and established a fortified position. On 22 March, a force under Sir J. McNeill marched from Suakin to construct some zarebas. At 10.30 the column halted and the work was commenced on the zareba; dinner was served at 2 p.m. but half an hour later, the '... air was rent with the most frightful yells'. The Dervishes attacked in great force on the partially built zareba. The whole attack lasted twenty minutes in which bloody hand-to-hand fighting took place and the very existence of the British was threatened. The Arabs were beaten back with a loss of 1,500 but British casualties were also severe including the loss of some 500 camels.

Wentworth Huyshe witnessed the fight for *The Times*'s readers:

As for the 17th Bengal Native Infantry [he wrote], they could
not face the music, the terrific scream which burst upon the air
the moment of attack, and which those who heard it will never
forget, and they broke and fled . . . and in the next moment the
whole space which had been marked out for the central zareba,
and where the water casks and biscuit boxes were stored,
became a hideous chaos of demoralised men, shouting and
firing in the air, frantic camels and mules struggling, plunging,
kicking, while through the immense cloud of thick dust . . . the
forms of the Hadendowa warriors flitted like armed spectres,
hacking, hewing and thrusting.

The enemy were also inside the Berkshire Regiment zareba:

> . . . swinging sword and hurling spear while Walter Paget of the
> *Illustrated London News*, was calmly making an admirable
> sketch of a single combat between a Hadendowa swordsman
> and a poor little Tommy Atkins of the Commissariat.

In order to clear the enemy, the troops had to fire into their own
baggage animals:

> . . . behind and among which the enemy were in great force . . .
> Not a man of the enemy got out of the zareba alive; they died
> there, a hundred brave men and more, under the shadow of the
> scarred banner which they had planted on the redoubt.

In May 1885, two scandals broke in the press, both provoked by war
correspondents, one being a personal matter while the other put the
Ordnance Department on public trial. Just as Russell's dispatches from
the Crimea had pointed to the inadequate preparations of the expeditionary force, so Bennet Burleigh's dispatches in the *Daily Telegraph*
called into question the quality of the weapons served out to the
British soldier. This triggered off an outcry against the inefficiency of
the Ordnance Department, especially their purchase and inspection
systems. On 6 May, Burleigh had presented '. . . his résumé of his
impressions regarding the British bayonet and the Martini-Henry rifle'.
He had first noticed that something was wrong at the Battle of Tamai
where the enemy, '. . . fairly pitched themselves upon the weapons of
our Black Watch and 65th. The triangular bayonets offtimes bent and
twisted . . .' The swords and sword bayonets '. . . bent like hoop-iron'
and the:

... complex ill shaped Boxer cartridge was the cause of most of the jamming that occurred ... Many a soldier at Abu Klea saw with dismay his bayonet rendered useless at the moment where there was no chance to load his rifle. After that fight you might have noticed brawny foot-guardsmen, herculean Life-guardsmen, and the deft fighters of the mounted infantry ... straightening their bayonets across their knee or under foot ...

The story was reprinted in many newspapers including the *Birmingham Daily Mail*, the *Sussex Daily News*, the *Penny Pictorial*, the *Standard*, *St. James's Gazette* as well as the *Broad Arrow* and the *Globe*. *Punch* on 26 January 1886 published a cartoon and satiric comedy entitled 'Who's to Blame' which in the words of a fictitious special correspondent (meant to be Burleigh) 'seated on an empty biscuit tin with left arm bandaged scribbling with right' denounced the inefficient weapons. Needless to say the whole purchase system of the army was revised.

The second scandal, which also broke in the same month of May 1885, owed its origin to an article filed with the *Fortnightly Review* by Charles Williams, the correspondent of the Central News Agency. Williams directly accused General Wilson of military incompetence for not rushing to Gordon's aid when the steamers arrived after Abu Kru. Williams explained that much of the 'mischief' caused by his profession was the result of officers being unwilling to keep correspondents informed of the situation. This was perhaps an advance excuse for his conduct in questioning the soldiers of the Royal Sussex Regiment about the proximity of the steamers to Khartoum when they eventually sailed. Later some people described this as an attempt to incite mutiny. Williams quoted 'an officer' as saying that Wilson had lost his nerve and then added insult to injury by adding, 'If I differ from this it is only in wondering whether he had any to lose'. He accused the Committee in command as having '... had no more notion of what could or should be done than a bugler'. Williams attributed the loss of Gordon directly to Wilson who knew '... nothing of the science of war' and '... the extraordinary want of nerve which prevented him seeing what a risk he was running ... by hanging about at Abu Klea instead of proceeding forthwith in the steamers ...'

General Wilson, unlike Cardigan after the Crimean Light Brigade affair, made the basic error of commenting on Williams's story which made the controversy all the more public. The *Saturday Review* of

27 June 1885 criticized both parties in an outspoken article entitled 'The War Correspondent'.

> We do not know [they wrote] how it may be with other people, but we, for our part, are very tired of hearing the praises of the War Correspondent. They are much too persistently sung, which is enough to make them a bore . . . If we only had to put up with the hearing of the valour of War Correspondents, the infliction would be endurable. Nobody doubts the readiness of these gentlemen to go under fire.

The *Saturday Review* criticized the correspondent's inclusion of personal adventures in his dispatches and the hero's welcome given him by the Savage Club. At the same time they condemned General Wilson's attitude in allowing himself to be '. . . provoked into a wordy war . . . By merely entering on the dispute Sir Charles has proved how the standard of professional pride in the army has sunk.' They concluded that Charles Williams's job was to 'secure an effect, the more striking the better'. Williams rightly thought the article a stain on his character and that of his profession and issued a writ against the *Saturday Review* for damages amounting to £2,000. After the hearing the court found in his favour, but awarded only £300. The scandal had called into question the right and value of allowing war correspondents on the scene of action and being able to question whoever they wished. The *Saturday Review* concluded its article by recommending that, 'The lesson will be thoroughly learnt if the next of the tribe who is caught at the trick is sent back to base of operations tied by the wrists to the tail of an ammunition wagon'.

The Sudan campaign and the two scandals that followed overshadowed the other fighting in the Empire. In direct violation of the Sand River Convention of 1852, which set up the Transvaal and the Bloemfontein Convention of 1854 which created the Orange Free State, the Boers had in 1884 proposed two further republics in Bechuanaland, Stellaland, and Land Goshen. Cecil Rhodes, the founder of Rhodesia and a great influence in South African affairs, sent a column which forced the Boers to withdraw that December. He seized Bechuanaland, making the north a protectorate and the south a Crown Colony. Julius Mendes Price, who during the First World War was to be a correspondent for the *Daily Telegraph* and official war artist to the Italian government in 1917, enlisted as a trooper in Methuen's Horse to ride with the column for the *Illustrated London News*.

In October 1885 the British government had issued an ultimatum to King Theebaw of Burma. There had been the usual insults to British residents and injuries to British commerce which the Victorians took as a prime motive for a punitive expedition. Again receiving no satisfactory answer, the British troops crossed the Burmese frontier on 15 November to administer suitable correction to the erring monarch. The campaign has been immortalized in Kipling's poem, from the crossing of the frontier until the capture of Mandalay. The annexation of Burma took thirteen days but spasmodic fighting with the Dacoits continued until 1887. Edward Kyran Moylan offered his services to *The Times* and these were readily accepted while Melton Prior, inimitable globetrotter, was present for the *Illustrated London News* with his rival Frederick Villiers of the *Graphic*. A local man, Rose, the correspondent of the *Rangoon Gazette*, was on hand to report for his paper as well as for others in London.

Moylan knew that the English readers wanted dramatic stories and he was prepared to give them the reading matter they liked. He described various episodes after the King had been deported from Mandalay which had taken place in the city. While murder, robbery, looting, and disorder had all occurred, Moylan, intent on a spectacular story, exaggerated the incidents. Worst of all he had disobeyed the regulations which demanded that he submit his copy for censorship, and he sent it direct to London. The Chief of Staff, General Bengough, had no alternative but to have Moylan deported from Mandalay and to return him to Rangoon. What rankled the authorities most was his description of a Mandalay which was supposed to be under British protection:

> Last night [Moylan wrote] the streets were occupied by
> gangs of armed Burmans who looted and murdered almost
> unchecked . . . Unless immediate steps be taken to
> restore order . . . very serious consequences will result
> and Burmah will become completely disorganised. While
> I have been writing two men have been murdered . . . at
> a short distance from this house.

*The Times* of 9 December announced that they were unable to continue their reports from Burma as their correspondent had been sent back to Rangoon; 'We await an explanation of this peremptory act of the General in command.' However, on 20 December, Moylan was allowed to return. Feeling slighted, he was unable to let the matter rest and planned a vindictive campaign against those in command. Enjoying the patronage of *The Times*, he continued to criticize the handling of the campaign and furthermore condemned the way military executions were held. He accused the Provost Marshal of taking pictures of the execution and of holding up the order to fire in order to focus his camera:

> The ghastly scenes which constantly recur in executions carried out by the Provost Marshal constitute grave public scandals. The Provost Marshal, who is an ardent amateur photographer, is desirous of securing views of the persons executed at the precise moment when they are struck by the bullets. To secure this result, after the orders 'Ready' 'Present' have been given to the firing party, the Provost Marshal fixes his camera on the prisoners, who at times are kept waiting for some minutes in that position. The officer commanding the firing party is then directed by the Provost Marshal to give the order to fire at the precise moment when he exposes his plate. So far no satisfactory negative has been obtained and the experiments are likely to be continued. These proceedings take place before a crowd of mixed nationalities, and cannot fail to have a demoralising effect on both soldiers and spectators.

The Provost Marshal was a keen amateur photographer and had taken views of executions but he had not held them up as Moylan had claimed. Moylan continued his vitriolic attacks on the army and the government, but he was found out to be a 'blackguard'. Moylan had had a chequered career. The discovery that while a civil servant in Granada he had been guilty of misconduct and as a barrister and solicitor had caused a number of peasants to lose their land because of improper affidavits, knocked much of the force out of his campaign against the authorities. His involvement in trying to get tenders placed for the Burmese ruby mines did not help his reputation but he continued to wage his personal vendetta until he died in Rangoon in 1893.

# 6
# Pomp and Circumstance
## (1887–98)

*There is sometimes a blatant self-conceit and vulgar swagger*
*about a war correspondent which is very irritating . . .*
Ernest Bennet, war correspondent, *Westminster Gazette*, 1898.

The year of Queen Victoria's Silver Jubilee, 1887, represented for
some of the British public fifty years of Imperial expansion in territory,
trade, and wealth. Britain had not fought a European war since
Waterloo and the only slight cracks in the façade of 'Pax Britannica'
had been the Crimean War and the Indian Mutiny. The various small
wars and punitive expeditions which the Victorians tended to discount
had increased 'the area coloured red' on the globe to nearly eight and
a half million square miles. The Duke of Cambridge at the Aldershot
Review in that jubilee year summed up the army's role in this Imperial
expansion, 'During those fifty years the Army has been called upon to
maintain the interests of the British Empire in every quarter of the
globe . . .', but he might have truthfully added 'every year', for Imperial
arms were constantly engaged.

While the public could learn of the thrilling deeds of Tommy Atkins
through the columns of their newspapers, both illustrated and otherwise, they could also buy the war artist's sketches which gave a more
lifelike image of what actually took place than the printed wood-block
engraver's version. Melton Prior's Sudan sketches were reproduced by
the paprotype process and sold to the public as a collection. It was

essentially a photo-lithographic process which gave an almost perfect copy of a pencil sketch. It was developed by Captain (later Sir) W. de W. Abney at the School of Military Engineering at Chatham. Paper was coated with gelatin and exposed under a negative, then developed to give an image in hardened gelatin; this was spread with greasy ink to form a positive which could be transferred to a stone or metal plate for reproduction.

In 1887, the Burma campaign against the Dacoits was coming slowly to an end, but other expeditions of one sort or another were mounted continually: Hazara in 1888, Sikhim in 1889 and Sierra Leone in the same year. For most editors, it was not worth the expense of reporting these small conflicts first-hand although Claude Champion de Crespigny acted as the correspondent for a number of newspapers from Sikhim on the borders of India. The usual reports were either taken from official dispatches, Reuter's telegrams, or from a 'military' correspondent.

During the latter years of the nineteenth century, the number of 'military' war correspondents increased. These officers in order to follow their profession asked to be sent on every campaign possible, whether their regiment was engaged or not. There were also those who needed to be publicly recognized to gain further promotion or to lay the foundations of a political or other career after they left the service. Winston S. Churchill fell into the last category. He was bored with garrison life in India, and tried to be sent to places of action:

> Poked away in a small garrison town [he wrote in 1897]
> which resembles a 3rd rate watering place, out of season
> and without the seas, with lots of routine work and a hot
> and trying sun—without society or good sport—half my
> friends on leave and the other half ill.

'Military' correspondents were usually more acceptable at headquarters than their civilian counterparts as first and foremost they were soldiers and what they wrote was normally worded to satisfy military etiquette as well as the censor. While the authorities preferred them, newspapers were reluctant to employ them alone and for wars of any importance backed up their coverage with their own civilian journalists.

The easiest way for an officer to get to see any action was as a correspondent. In 1897 General Sir Bindon Blood wrote to Churchill, 'I should advise your coming to me as a press correspondent and when you are here I shall put you on the strength on the first opportunity', which usually meant a vacancy created by a casualty.

It was not until 1893 that an important campaign occurred when the press sent representatives to Matabeleland. South Africa was always a trouble spot and always newsworthy so that at least the *Illustrated London News* and *The Times* thought it worth their while to be represented. The former sent Melton Prior and the latter Edward Frederick Knight, who had previously represented the same paper as a serving officer in the Hunza-Nagar campaign of 1891. He was to lose an arm during the Boer War as his paper's correspondent but this did not deter him from reporting the Russo-Japanese War of 1904.

In 1893, the Ashantis once more threatened the peace and an expedition was sent against them; with them went H. C. Seppings Wright of the *Illustrated London News*, sketching his first campaign. The Ashantis were a permanent source of trouble during the last decade of the nineteenth century and in 1895 a further expedition was mounted accompanied by the representative of the *Daily Chronicle*, R. S. Baden-Powell, later the hero of Mafeking and the founder of the Boy Scout movement.

While these smaller expeditions and the larger wars offered scope for the war correspondent, there was uncertainty amongst 'the luckless tribe' as to their true role. The ever-tightening hand of the censor, both British and foreign, had checked their initiative, and dramatic scoops were a thing of the past. The censor had the power to alter, edit, and delete as he wished and many a correspondent now felt that under these circumstances he could not properly do his job.

The first to see and suffer from this phenomenon was not the general public but the correspondents themselves, who saw that they were unable to fulfil the demands of the public if they were to report their campaigns honestly. Stephen Crane, the American war correspondent of the *New York World* and later the *New York Journal* and the author of the famous *The Red Badge of Courage*, a novel of the American Civil War, wrote:

> Then the censor must go. But he won't. Because of the swiftness of modern means of communication a modern war may not be conducted without the employment of a censor of news. Then the war correspondent must go.
> He must.
> He must go because ocean beds are laid with cables, because range and plain are strung with telegraph, because fast trains and fast steamers are plentiful. His spark of information flies too quickly around the world and into the enemy's camp . . .

Archibald Forbes, himself one of the greatest of war correspondents, confessed that:

> Were I a general, and had I an independent command in war offered me, I should accept it only on the condition that I should have the charter to shoot every war correspondent within fifty miles of my headquarters. The most careful correspondent cannot write a sentence—a sentence which the strictest censor, if he is to pass anything at all, cannot refrain from sanctioning . . . It is a question solely for the public, whose servants the general and the war journalists alike are. If the public deliberately prefers news to victories—for that is the issue in a nutshell as regards a European war — then on the head of the public be it.

War correspondents denouncing matters of inefficiency were seldom taken seriously by the government but were considered as writers of sensational news to boost circulation. Forbes once remarked in this connection, in '. . . the game between him and the correspondent, the official plays with cogged dice'. The censor, working under instructions, could alter or delete as he wished. Winston S. Churchill during the Boer War remarked that the censor had altered one of his dispatches to the *Morning Post* to read 'small parties' of Boers instead of 2,000, a direct untruth if the correspondent was to be believed.

However, the temptation to report exciting incidents within the censor's strict limits was ever prevalent and the correspondents more than ever filled their dispatches with incidental, personal and melo-dramatic stories mixed with the basic facts that were allowed to pass the blue pencil. Donald Macdonald of the *Melbourne Age* and *Melbourne Argus* described a typical interview between correspondent and censor in his book *How we Kept the Flag Flying*:

> *Censor:* Can't let you say this, you know.
> *Correspondent:* Well, it's of interest to the public.
> *Censor:* We're not considering the public, though; we're considering the enemy.
> *Correspondent* (with a weary air): Oh, very well, strike it out.
> *Censor:* And here again you say, 'Great satisfaction expressed here arrival General Buller. Feeling that siege will not long continue.' That's a reflection on our General. You don't mean to say that we're skulking behind rocks, and that General Buller has only to come here and personally drive the Boers away.
> *Correspondent:* No; but he has an army corps with him.

*Censor:* Then why don't you say so? Hum! Ha! What's this?
Question of tactics. Where did you get your knowledge
of military strategy?

*Correspondent* (triumphantly):  It's not so much a matter of
strategy as of common sense.

*Censor:* Your conclusions in that vein, don't you know, are
admirable, if the premises were correct, but
unfortunately they're not. I suppose that doesn't
matter though.

*Correspondent* (seeing an opening):  I shall be very glad, major,
if you will amend them where incorrect.

*Censor:* No doubt; but then, you see, I'm not acting as
correspondent for your paper.

In 1893, a shabby dispute arose between the French and the Siamese
and on 13 July French gunboats settled the question when they entered
the Menam River. With the French forces was Edwin Arthur Norbury
of the *Graphic* and *Daily Graphic*, who sent back a number of sketches
of the advance of the republican troops, but there arrived only those
which the sensitive French censor would allow. The censor's job was
perhaps more difficult than that of the correspondents, as any adverse
comment published automatically became his responsibility and those
officers charged with this work tended for their own reputations to be
more severe than necessary.

Censorship would become even tougher during the Boer War and
during the European conflicts in the Balkans in the early twentieth
century. Max Aghio of the French newspaper *Le Figaro* produced a 600-
word dispatch on the battle of Tchorlou in the province of Thrace
during the Balkan War of 1912, which even the censor considered a
masterpiece of factual reporting. When Aghio returned to collect his
censored dispatch he found to his horror two small pieces of paper
with nine words, the first and last phrase of the original '*La battaille
a recommencé a Tchorlou . . . La battaille continue.*' (The battle has
started at Tchorlou . . . The battle continues.) This form of heavy
censorship, indispensable in a European war, annoyed the correspondents who tried every trick to get their dispatches and photographs out
without passing through official channels. Success, however, was
usually accompanied by a deportation.

The steady westernization of Japan, who had opened up to European
and American trade in the 1850s and 1860s, was almost complete by
1900. Japan possessed a modern if small navy and a well-trained and

equipped army and, like the European powers, she looked around for suitable areas to expand her flourishing trade and her sphere of influence. In short Japan was about to become an imperial power in the great race for colonies and possessions. First choice was Korea which would not only increase her territory but also give Japan a foothold on the Asiatic mainland. Although Korea was a sovereign state, China claimed it to be suzerain to her.

Confident in her materially superior forces, when faced with the outdated and unwieldy power of China, the Japanese government formally declared war on 1 August 1894. A. Hilliard Atteridge, war correspondent for the *Daily Chronicle*, summed up the European opinion of this war, '. . . the first impression . . . was that Japan might win some successes at the outset, but would sooner or later be crushed by the mere numbers of the Chinese'. China did outclass the Japanese at sea, possessing two ironclads while the latter had nothing larger than partially armed cruisers.

> Both navies had the advantage [continued Atteridge] of European teaching in drill, tactics, and seamanship. It was supposed that, everything else being equal, the possession of even a few powerful ironclads would turn the scale in favour of China.

But in war, 'everything else being equal' is a dangerous phrase on which to base supposition.

Fighting had commenced before the formal declaration of war, when a squadron of Japanese cruisers attacked a Chinese cruiser without warning, the latter only escaping capture by a hasty flight. A number of correspondents gathered to report the impending clash, including Charles E. Fripp and Frederick Villiers of the *Graphic*, James Creelman of the *New York World*, and Alfred Cunningham of the Central News Agency. The demand for 'hot news' was very pressing:

> As soon as a war breaks out [wrote one French magazine] in whatever part of the world, the public wants to be informed and to be able to follow all operations, sieges and battles in detail. Do the public really know at what price and through what difficulties these sensational reports are written?

They probably didn't, but then they probably didn't care as long as the reports were there.

Japanese troops had landed in Korea covered by their navy and had pushed up the Korean mainland, defeating the Chinese army at Pin

Yang on 16 September. The battle was witnessed by Frederick Villiers of the *Graphic* among others, who was astounded at the skill and professionalism of the Japanese army. Two days later the battle of the Yalu River took place between the two navies, a decisive action for the Japanese who lost no ships but destroyed half those of their opponents.

On 21 November, watched by copy-hungry war correspondents, the Japanese army took possession of Port Arthur. The overwhelming Japanese success, wrote one correspondent, was due to the Chinese defensive attitude at sea where they were undoubtably superior:

> Had not the Tsung-li-yamen at Pekin dictated a defensive
> attitude to the fleet and forbade its movements outside the
> narrow seas between Port Arthur and Wei-hai-wei, the
> set-backs of the Chinese army might have been equalled
> by an overwhelming victory at sea.

As it was, the Chinese fleet never stood a chance and the Japanese confirmed their victory by taking Wei-hai-wei on 14 February 1895, in effect sealing the gulf of Pe-Chi-Li and denying Peking its access to the China Sea. The war was really decided at sea:

> Had the Chinese had plenty of shells [wrote Hilliard Atteridge],
> they would no doubt have dealt their opponents not one, but
> many such blows as that which nearly wrecked the *Matsushima*
> [the Japanese flagship]. It was the speculation and corruption
> in the Chinese admiralty, so far as supplies were concerned,
> which enabled the Japanese cruisers to make such a good fight
> against the Chinese battleships.

Peace was eventually signed on 16 April 1895 and China ceded Korea and the strategically placed Liaotang peninsula at the tip of which was Port Arthur, an ideal site for Japanese development as a commercial and naval port.

Political commentators were quick to notice that Russia was more than an interested observer. As soon as the Japanese occupation of Port Arthur was confirmed, they lost no time in persuading France and Germany to join in coercing the Japanese to relinquish all territory on the Asiatic mainland, offering the island of Formosa as a war gain. The Russian motives were various. They did not want another Imperial power at their end of Asia nor did they want the Japanese to control Port Arthur, which was secretly proposed as the end of the famous trans-Siberian railway. For the honour of protecting China, the three powers helped themselves to various concessions: in 1897 Germany seized the Bay of Kiaochow, in 1898 France seized Kwangchow in southern China, and Russia leased the strategic Liaotong peninsula and occupied Port Arthur. In the same year, however, ever watchful of the rise of powers that challenged her superiority Britain occupied the Chinese harbour Wei-hai-wei on the opposite side of the gulf of Pe-Chi-Li. Britain's friendly attitude towards Japan did not go unnoticed in the press and a treaty concluded in 1902 between both countries set the scene for the confrontation of Russia and Japan in 1904.

The year 1895 was a busy one for the war correspondent in various parts of the globe. In February the Cubans rose against their Spanish occupiers; while in April a British force marched to the relief of British representatives in Chitral. The Italians were engaged in a disastrous venture in Abyssinia; the French invaded Madagascar and the British again marched against the Ashanti. A number of war correspondents went to Cuba, mainly Americans including Richard Harding Davies and Frederick Remington, the famous artist of western scenes, both representing *Hearst's Journal*. Another who sent dispatches to the *Daily Graphic*, the first daily illustrated newspaper, was a newly gazetted officer to the 4th Hussars, Winston S. Churchill. Taking his annual leave with a friend, Churchill decided to travel to the West Indies but, on the outbreak of the revolt, went to Cuba in November 1894. He had arranged that he would send letters to the *Daily Graphic* for which he would be paid five guineas. They eventually appeared in five parts entitled 'The Insurrection in Cuba'. On his twenty-first birthday Churchill recalled, '. . . for the first time I heard shots fired in anger and heard bullets strike flesh or whistle through the air'. His opinion of American journalism and the dispatches of American war correspondents was not high:

> The essence of American journalism [he wrote to his brother] is vulgarity divested of truth. Their best papers write for a class of snotty housemaids and footmen and even the nicest people here have so vitiated their taste as to appreciate the style . . .

Another correspondent writing for *The Times* was Hubert Howard, whom Churchill admired. He later wrote about him on his death in 1898 at Omdurman:

Mr. Hubert Howard was a man of some reputation, and of much greater promise. The love of adventure had already led him several times to scenes of war and tumult. In 1895 he passed the Spanish lines in Cuba, and for six weeks fought and was hunted with the Cuban insurgents, whose privations and dangers he shared, and whose cause he afterwards pleaded warmly. At this time I was, as you know, with the Spanish forces witnessing their operations, and the fact that we had been on opposite sides proved a bond of union. Thereafter I saw him frequently. His profession—that of the Law—gave him more opportunities for travelling than fall to the lot of a subaltern of horse. On the outbreak of the Matabele War he hurried to South Africa, and in the attack on Sekombo's Kraal in the autumn of 1896 he acted as adjutant of Robertson's Cape Boys, and displayed military qualities which left no doubt in the minds of those who saw that he should have been a soldier, not only for his own sake, but for that of the army. Having, on his own initiative, captured a steep and nearly precipitous hill, which proved of considerable tactical value, he was severely wounded in the ankle. He refused to leave the field and continued till the end of the day to drag himself about, directing and inspiriting his men. His services on this occasion, not less than his known abilities, obtained for him the position of Secretary to Lord Grey. The recrudescence of trouble in Mashonaland and Matabeleland in 1897 led him again to the field, and in many minor engagements—those unheeded skirmishes by which unknown men build up our Empire—he added to his reputation as a soldier and as a man.

Churchill returned to his regiment in India but not before some newspapers had made scathing remarks about his acting as a war correspondent. The *Newcastle Leader* concluded that:

> Sensible people will wonder what motive could possibly impel a British officer to mix himself up in a dispute with the merits of which he had absolutely nothing to do . . . Spending a holiday in fighting other people's battles is rather an extraordinary proceeding even for a Churchill.

However, Churchill's opinion of the revolutionaries was low and in March 1896 he wrote a long article in the *Saturday Review* describing them as 'undisciplined rabble'.

While the rebels in Cuba were fighting the Spanish, the North-West Frontier of India called for an expedition which was much more to the liking of the general public. Chitral, which lay on that ever troublesome border of northern India, had first interested Britain in 1876 when the Chitralis asked for the protection of the Maharajah of Kashmir, himself under the protection of British India. The series of murders, plots, and counterplots for the throne between the various relatives of the late ruler became the excuse for a general tribal revolt. Surgeon-Major George Robertson was the British Agent in Chitral and he quickly reorganized matters. The son of the late Mehtar, or ruler, was got rid of and his twelve-year-old younger brother installed on the throne ripe for British manipulation. However, an uncle of this large family, Umra Khan, saw this as an opportunity to make himself the ruler of Chitral and after invading, beat a Kashmiri army on 3 March 1895. The following day Chitral was in a state of siege.

A few journalists rushed to the camp where a relief expedition was being prepared. Lionel James went for Reuter's Agency, W. T. Maude for the *Graphic*, and the brothers Younghusband, both serving officers, arranged to report for *The Times*. People were so optimistic of the outcome of the expedition that some newspapers did not bother to send correspondents and relied on Reuter's man on the spot and on accounts and sketches sent back by serving officers, including the '. . . well known Roddy Owen'.

After an arduous march and a number of bitter fights with the enemy, the expedition relieved the fort of Chitral. The besiegers had retreated and left the way open. Captain G. J. Younghusband wrote after the campaign:

> . . . Now in Chitral the people once and for all recognising
> that we are a power who can and will exercise the proper
> duties of a suzerain and yet we have no wish to tamper with
> their customs or set aside their ruler, will join us instead of
> opposing us . . . and help us in the defence of our great
> Indian Empire.

This was unfortunately a soldier's point of view not shared by many politicians whose misunderstanding of many situations viewed at a distance had caused numerous punitive and relief expeditions. South Africa was always in the news, but more so in 1895 when a band of 'capitalists', as Melton Prior termed them, formed the National Union

Bulawayo: a false alarm in Bulawayo (drawing by Melton Prior).

Tirah Expedition: 'the disaster to the Dorset Regiment. Hand to hand fighting with the enemy in a nullah' (pencil sketch by Melton Prior).

of Reformers intent on opposing the Boers' unyielding rule in the Transvaal even though they were not the majority of the population.

In 1889, Cecil Rhodes had acquired a Royal Charter for his British South Africa Company as well as an 800-mile area of territory, much of it under the government of the Matabele. By various means, including armed force, Rhodes established his superiority over the Matabele in his hunt for gold and his eventual domination of South Africa. The Boer treatment of the majority of *Uitlanders* and gold-miners led Rhodes to believe that with a little organization and an armed attack, the Transvaal would rise against the Boers. Then he would be able to include the largest gold-producing area in the world in his British South Africa Company. The raid over the border to inspire the revolt was a dismal failure. Led by Rhodes's right-hand man, Dr. Jameson, the force of 800 men deliberately attacked the Transvaal without waiting for the *Uitlanders'* revolt, which never came, and they were ambushed and captured. *The Times* admitted that the raid was '. . . technically incorrect' but added that 'technicalities could not have been allowed to stand in the way where the lives and property of thousands' was threatened. Melton Prior, on hand in the Transvaal, beat the other newspapermen with his direct sketches of the survivors being marched into Pretoria. Although two were sentenced to death and the rest to long prison terms, most were soon released. But the main outcome of this singular and apparently insignificant event was, as the press were obliged to point out, the final and damning end of British influence in the Transvaal and some uncomfortable moments for both Cecil Rhodes and the Colonial Secretary who had condoned the raid, Joseph Chamberlain.

The Matabele were not all content to sit and do nothing against Rhodes's encroachment of their lands and in March 1896 a revolt threatened the town of Bulawayo. The *Illustrated London News* and other newspapers who had representatives in South Africa ordered them immediately to Bulawayo. Prior, still sketching, immediately made arrangements to travel to Bulawayo via Mafeking, an arduous journey made by train and coach and as can be expected tinged with personal adventure. He arrived at his destination, complete with his overweight 'clothes basket' filled with two dozen bottles of whisky. Prior witnessed the 'siege' and the arrival of the 'relief' column under Cecil Rhodes which had come up from Salisbury. Every time the force could it attempted to get '. . . at the Matabele, and we gave them an awful doing', wrote Prior. He also recorded the hardships of a correspondent's life: 'I only had my boots off three times in fifteen days, for we all had to sleep in our clothes, with our arms beside us, in case of a surprise visit from the enemy.' At least life was made endurable with Moyer's tinned Irish stew and Prior's 'clothes basket'.

Events were also happening in the northern part of Africa and many an old and some new campaigners assembled in Egypt to await the outcome of a proposed advance into the Sudan. One of these was G. W. Steevens, later the star war correspondent of Harmsworth's *Daily Mail*, which the proprietors claimed to be 'The Busy Man's Paper' which stood for power, supremacy, and greatness of the British Empire, but which Lord Salisbury described as 'Written by office boys for office boys'. 'The old campaigner,' Steevens asserted '. . . starts out with the clothes he stands up in and a tin opener. The young campaigner provides the change of linen and tins for the old campaigner to open.'

The Dongola expedition of 1896, led by the young and ambitious Sirdar, Horatio Kitchener, was a purely Egyptian affair whose lack of money, good troops, and armaments prevented a complete reoccupation of the Sudan. As a compromise, it was decided to advance to Dongola which did not seem to impress any of the newspapers or correspondents. Bennet Burleigh, an 'old campaigner', thought that:

> To proceed no further than Dongola meant, I contend,
> quitting a safe frontier for a dangerous one: and merely
> to go no further than El Ordeh, otherwise New Dongola,
> involved that the province in question would be harassed
> by raiders, and would not repay its keeping.

While the 1896 expedition was according to Burleigh '. . . regarded in army circles as a fixture' it did prove that the Dervishes were not as invincible as had been believed. On 7 June, Kitchener's army defeated the Dervishes at Firket and by September Dongola was occupied. While the Imperial hold was pushed 'further up the Nile' the consensus of opinion was that the expedition had been mounted solely to help the Italians who had been soundly thrashed at Adowa in February 1896. Burleigh wrote that the Dongola expedition, whatever its driving motivation, proved that '. . . first the Khedival troops could be depended upon in action; second that Mahdism was on the wane, and that the local population everywhere unmistakably friendly'. The undoubted success led the British government to finance and aid Egypt in winning back its lost province. Reuter's chief correspondent was H. A. Gwynne, who later organized Reuter's effort during the Boer War.

In 1897, a force under Sir Archibald Hunter retook Abu Hamed and pushed on to secure Berber. The stage was now set for the final and absolute re-conquest of the Sudan. But in 1896 and 1897, other areas under the control of the crumbling Ottoman Empire attracted the war correspondents. In two years the Sultan's agents had disposed of over 100,000 Armenians in a massacre of inhuman proportions, while in Crete a revolution was attempted, with Greek aid, to get rid of Turkish rule.

> A very plucky resistance shown by the Greek Army [wrote
> the Marquis of Lorne] only showed the hopelessness of
> their anticipations, for, great as was the horror excited by the
> Armenian massacres, Europe was not yet ready to face the
> far greater slaughter which a general war in the East would
> have inevitably brought about.

The Cretan insurrection was only the start of the ever-present crisis in the Near East which eventually led Europe to the 'war to end all wars' in 1914.

But while some war correspondents and artists followed the troubles in Crete and the Greco-Turkish War, others were back over the mountains of the North-West Frontier of India as the British army moved north to re-secure the Khyber Pass and to punish the Afridis, the most dissident of dissident tribesmen. The expedition was accompanied by Melton Prior of the *Illustrated London News* who rode with Rene Bull of *Black and White,* who claimed to hold the record for reporting on three different campaigns in three different continents in a space of ten months. Newspapers owed much not only to the tenacity of their correspondents but to the travel arrangements of Messrs. Thomas Cook, whose agents, like those of Reuter, seemed to be in every corner of the globe.

The North-West Frontier campaign was also reported by a serving officer, Winston S. Churchill, writing for the *Daily Telegraph*. He had offered his services previously to the *Daily Chronicle* to go to Crete, but had been refused unless he was prepared to finance his own way. Alexander Edward, Viscount Findcastle, A.D.C. to General Sir Bindon Blood, wrote for *The Times* as did Colonel Hutchinson. Eventually

Afridi War: uncomfortable experiences of war correspondents (drawing by Rene Bull, who added: 'The drawing represents Mr. Melton Prior and myself having dinner. A bullet struck our water bottle and showered it to atoms.').

British arms triumphed but Winston Churchill in one of his dispatches remarked philosophically that:

> We have killed men as targets. Tribesmen fighting for their homes and hills have been regarded only as the objective of an attack; killed and wounded human beings merely as the waste of war. The philosopher may observe with pity, and the philanthropist deplore with pain that the attention of so many minds should be directed to the scientific destruction of the human species; but practical people in a business-like age will remember that they live in a world of men—not angels — and rule their conduct accordingly.

Churchill's dispatches were vivid, as was expected by the public, but they overstepped the accepted scope of the war correspondent many times to offer political and other controversial comment. While he no doubt used this public platform to further his proposed political career, his writings, observations, and comments provided war correspondence at its finest, devoid of 'jingoism' but none the less popularly acceptable.

216

*Pomp and
Circumstance*

Afridi War: Melton Prior and another war correspondent surprised in a village in the Maidan valley. 'Mr. Rene Bull and myself,' wrote Prior, 'with two officers, were nearly cut off . . . But for the arrival of a party of Sikhs, acting as escort to a convoy, I should not be alive to send you this sketch. We had fired away all our cartridges and could not have kept our assailants at bay much longer.'

Melton Prior had arrived in Crete, via China where he had observed the Germans taking possession of Kiaochow, while Rene Bull arrived directly from India to swell the press corps of American, French, British, and other war correspondents who had arrived to sketch and report the struggle between Greek and Turk, who in Crete were, '. . . cutting each other's throats and burning each other's houses in the good old style,' commented one war correspondent. Ernest Bennet also arrived at the same time for the *Westminster Gazette*.

On 17 April Turkey declared war on Greece after the Greek government had sent a force to annex Crete. The island was soon blocked by the major European powers including Britain. The war was short in duration but its build up, as the political commentators wrote, had been long. The press corps was a mixed bunch, some reporting on the Turkish side, others with the Greeks. Stephen Crane, the author, arrived with his fiancée, Cora Taylor, who wrote various reports for the *New York Journal* under the name of Imogene Carter, 'Woman Correspondent at the Front'. She was not the only woman correspondent, for the same newspaper used the services of Harriet Boyd and made the mistake of describing her as, 'Only Woman War Correspondent at Front' in one of their editions (5 May). Frederick Palmer, another American, was there, also Richard Harding Davis representing the London *Times* and John Bass, heading the field force of the *New York Journal* and a notorious adversary of Stephen Crane who had not only accepted a commission from the *New York Journal* but also the *Westminster Gazette*. James Creelman represented the *New York World* and the *Journal*, Edward Frederick Knight, *The Times*, Frederick Villiers, the *Graphic*, Melton Prior and H. C. Seppings Wright the *Illustrated London News*, and Percival Phillips reported his first campaign from the Greek side for the *Daily Telegraph*; W. T. Maude of the *Graphic*, Julius Mendes Price of the *Illustrated London News*, and Rene Bull of *Black and White*, who was later captured by the Turks but escaped, wrote and drew from the Greek side with G. W. Steevens of the *Pall Mall Gazette*. Among the correspondents with the Turkish army was Charles Clive Bigham, 2nd Viscount Mersey, who wrote for *The Times* and was later to be Admiral Seymour's intelligence officer in the relief of Peking in 1900. Bennet Burleigh was also on hand leading the *Daily Telegraph*'s reports which like others were afterwards skilfully written up in book form.

Correspondents and artists not only wrote and sketched, but carried cameras. The Kodak camera with roll film, invented in 1888, revolutionized photography and meant that any correspondent could be a war photographer. Many took pictures of fighting not for publication but as *aides-mémoire* used when describing scenes later and for their own published accounts of the campaign which flooded on to the market after any controversial or sizeable war.

In the Greco-Turkish War the animosity between certain members of the American press corps, namely Stephen Crane and Richard Harding Davis, undoubtedly the star reporter of his day, who resented any competition, drew a number of smirks from the gentlemanly representatives of the British press who tended to describe the Americans as 'good fellows' and leave it at that. John Bass, however, merited Melton Prior's admiration more than the others. Prior admired the American's courage and they were both soon friends. Crane had somehow annoyed Harding Davis because of an article on the battle of Velestino which Crane had filed.

> Crane came up for fifteen minutes and wrote a 1300 word story on that [he complained bitterly]. He was never near the front but don't say I said so . . . . If he had not had that woman with him [Cora Taylor] he would have been with us . . . and could have seen the show, toothache or no toothache.

While Harding Davis enjoyed his confirmed superiority, Crane cared little or nothing about the jibes. 'Of the first two days' combat some other correspondents saw more than I did—namely Davis and Bass, I was rather laid up . . .' Crane's dispatch about Velestino in the *New York Journal* had headlined the 'Blue Badge of Cowardice', but Crane was as always oblivious of adverse comment. A professional and highly talented writer, he had no conception of the needs of a popular newspaper and wrote only what interested him. His name attracted the reading public in spite of his indifference to their reading habits and refusal to offer prose in the Harding Davis tradition. 'If they had appeared in a more literary medium, they would have carried more weight,' commented the *Literary Digest*. Stephen Crane was perhaps to American journalism what G. W. Steevens would be to English newspaper war reporting. 'I only say what I saw,' wrote Steevens, while Crane in much the same spirit stated, 'You've got to feel the things you write if you want to make an impact on the world.' Undoubtedly both men did.

In January 1898, newspapers could not decide where to send their best men. In the Sudan, Kitchener was preparing for the final blow against Mahdism, but then Kitchener was a notorious press-hater and liable to hamper the special correspondent. In the Caribbean tensions were mounting between the United States and Spain over their sole New World possession, Cuba. After the destruction by a mysterious explosion of the American battleship *Maine* while lying in Havana Harbour on 20 February, the United States demanded the withdrawal of Spain from Cuba and proceeded to blockade the island. While the Americans invaded Cuba and the journalists revelled in the escapades of Roosevelt's Rough Riders, the war was mainly fought at sea, in the Caribbean and the Philippines. Both Cuba and Manila were blockaded and besieged and held out for considerable time against overwhelming American superiority. The Spanish-American War was followed avidly in both Cuba and the Philippines by numerous correspondents. Newspapers as always considered anybody's war their own. Opinions were offered, sides taken and battles refought; readers demanded it and proprietors provided it.

Besides the journalists of the American press who took more than a casual interest, there were also representatives of the British, French, Spanish, and German newspapers. Frederick Palmer was with the American force in Cuba, while Alfred Cunningham of the *New York Journal* was with the Spanish. Edward Marshall, a much revered and respected newspaper correspondent, was also reporting for the *New York Journal* as was James Creelman. Of the British press, Percival Phillips and Lieutenant-Colonel Robert Joseph MacHugh represented the *Daily Telegraph*, George Lynch the *Daily Chronicle*, Richard Harding Davis *The Times*, who also had Edward Frederick Knight. The *Illustrated London News* sent H. C. Seppings Wright while the *Graphic* was represented in the Philippines by Charles E. Fripp. Charles Hands was in Cuba for the *Daily Mail* while the *Navy and Army Illustrated*, using photographs almost exclusively, had their 'own correspondent in besieged capital of Cuba', their special correspondent at the front, one of the besieged in Manila and M. T. Cowan in the same island. The Spanish had numerous correspondents, but strict censorship made working difficult. Miguel Ageyro wrote for a number of Madrid newspapers and was the first correspondent to be killed in action in Cuba. The heroic little Spaniard was watching an American attack through his binoculars, while making notes of the action. An American sharpshooter, seeing his silhouette, mistook it for a Spanish officer and shot at Ageyro. A French correspondent nearby wrote of the incident:

> . . . the unfortunate correspondent received a bullet in the base of the neck and his blood covered the notepad on which he had set down his observations. With superhuman courage, he finished his dispatch with a play on words. 'The enemy retires . . . so do I.'

In their issue of 28 January 1899, the *Navy and Army Illustrated* extolled the courage of their correspondent:

> Mr. Cowan has run many risks on their account. As he has intimated in the letters which have appeared in these pages from time to time, he was several times arrested by the Spaniards during the recent fighting at Manila, and threatened with the extreme penalty of martial law for the offence, persistently committed, it must be confessed, of photographing the forts, troops, and defences of Manila. But, as the *Westminster Gazette* says, 'Mr. Cowan was venturesome even to recklessness, now joining the Spanish defenders of the city, now penetrating into the camp of the Filipinos and interviewing Aguinaldo (whom, it may be added, he contrived to photograph), and now visiting the United States Fleet and headquarters at Cavite.' He did, however, so far cultivate prudence as to retire more into the background, as will be gathered from the relative position of the troops in one of the accompanying snap-shots. His memorandum, pencilled upon the back of this picture, is as follows, 'Native troops marching to Iloilo. *Slouching* would be the correct word. I took them from the rear because I do not want to be potted, and to stand up in front and photograph is the surest way to get shot.'
> On the corner of one of the envelopes containing photographs Cowan had written, 'Have to be dreadfully cautious. It is death to be seen photographing the war or anything about it.' [The paper continued] Mr. Cowan in his letters modestly made light of the danger he was running, spoke contemptuously of the marksmanship of the Spaniards and rebels alike, and seemed to relish the sensation which he once experienced of getting between the two cross-fires of Spaniards and Filipinos during an engagement. Although he concealed, rather than displayed, the risks he took upon himself on behalf of the 'people at home' he was not insensible of the perils of his position,

and several times let slip an admission, in a few significant words, of his narrow escapes . . . We anticipate that should the Filipino insurgents be misguided enough to enter upon open hostilities against the Americans, our correspondent will be found, as usual, in the front . . . If hostilities should unfortunately ensue, we believe, as we have indicated that no hospital will hold our correspondent.

T. Cowan had also covered the Sino-Japanese War of 1894 as a *Times* correspondent. The son of the editor of the *Yorkshire Evening Press*, Cowan was at that time editor of the *Hong Kong Telegraph*.

> While sitting at his desk [wrote the editor of the *Navy and Army Illustrated*] he received the following telegram from *The Times*. 'Proceed Japanese front. Remain there till close of war.' He at once put on his hat and coat and then walked down to the docks, chartered a special steamer, bought a few note books and a pair of heavy boots and within half-an-hour had left Hong Kong behind, and was on his way to the scene of hostilities.

He was, as the same paper pointed out concerning the *Standard* correspondent John Blondelle-Burton:

> . . . one of that little band of intrepid journalists who, with portmanteau always packed, are ready to start at a moment's notice to the far ends of the earth and brave every sort of danger to paint vivid word pictures for newspaper readers at home.

After the surrender of Cuba and the Philippines, America turned her attention to Puerto Rico which was invaded on 21 July 1898. Peace was signed on 12 August 1898 and over three hundred years of Spanish rule and influence in the New World were at an end.

On the very same day, 12 August, Kitchener was assembling his army at Atbara for the final thrust at Omdurman and the re-occupation of the Sudan. Events had been building up since December 1897 when the Sirdar, Kitchener, demanded reinforcements of British troops for his final suppression of the Khalifa, the Mahdi's successor. Kitchener, being an engineer, had thoroughly planned his advance on Omdurman and the revenge of General Gordon. Railways had been laid, for this was the best means of transportation in a country that possessed little water and where the laborious camel was the only means of transport. Wadi Halfa was the hub of the expedition. G. W. Steevens now writing for the *Daily Mail* commented:

Halfa has left off being a fortress and a garrison; today it is all workshop and railway terminus. Today it makes war not with bayonets but with rivets and spindle-glands . . . Halfa looks for all the world like Chicago in a turban.

The Sudan had acquired a compelling mystique. Whether it was the heat, the terrain, or the bleakness of shimmering wilderness is uncertain, but in some way this parched, scrubby country held a fatal fascination for journalist, editor and public alike.

> Yes, it is a murderous devil, the Sudan [wrote G. W. Steevens], and we have watered it with more of our blood than it will ever yield to pay for. The man-eater is very grim, and he is not sated yet. Only this time he was to be conquered at last.

By the beginning of January, Winston Churchill, who was still in India, had published his account of the Malakand Field Force using much of the material sent to the *Daily Telegraph* and *Pioneer* (Allahabad) with whom he also had a contract. He hankered to get to Egypt where he was sure a fight was imminent, but he had stirred up so much controversy that Kitchener replied to a letter from General Sir Evelyn Wood, instigated by the Prince of Wales and asking for Churchill to be seconded, '. . . I do not want Churchill as no room'. Churchill was determined and explained to his mother that he would take his leave and go as a correspondent if necessary. As it happened not only was he seconded to the 21st Lancers but he acted as a war correspondent for the *Morning Post*. On 20 July he received official confirmation of his attachment to the 21st Lancers but he had to proceed at his own expense, which he hoped to cover by his pay from the *Morning Post*'s editor, Oliver Borthwick, and possibly by publication of an account of the campaign.

Other newspapers were frantically applying for permission to send their special correspondents to the Sudan, and they were a mixed bunch, all equally detested by Kitchener. Ernest Bennet, an amateur who had managed to get accredited through the *Westminster Gazette* for the final attack on Omdurman, attended a press conference given by Kitchener:

> I did not enjoy the interview. The only parallel to it which I can think of is that of a row of curates before a brusque and autocratic bishop . . . The general impression conveyed to me was the immeasurable condescension of our chief in even deigning to address the representatives of a Press which has

Sudan 1898: Frederick Villiers
of the *Graphic.*

Sudan 1898: Earl Kitchener of
Khartoum, the Sirdar (oil painting
by Sir Hubert von Herkomer and
F. Goodall, 1890).

never failed to extol even to the verge of exaggeration the achievements of the Anglo-Egyptian Army and its leaders! . . . In short I would advise anybody who cannot put his pride in his pocket to avoid the role of amateur war correspondent in Egypt. The professionals are, I suppose, to some extent innoculated by this time, and cling to the delusion that correspondents during a campaign are treated like officers . . . There is sometimes a blatant self-conceit and vulgar swagger about a war correspondent which is very irritating . . . Of course there are pleasant exceptions . . . men like Steevens, Scudamore, Villiers and others whom I could name.

Amateur correspondents, those who paid their own expenses and hoped by receipt of a fixed fee per letter at least to break even, were considered by the professionals, Burleigh, and others as 'interlopers'.

Whether professional or amateur, they all flocked to Egypt and Cairo where their permits to follow the army would be issued. *The Times* and *New York Herald* were represented by a lawyer, Hubert Howard, an intrepid follower of imperial campaigns who was later killed at Omdurman. The *Daily News* sent their veteran correspondent, Francis Scudamore, whose cool professionalism was the envy of his colleagues, the *Graphic* was represented by W. T. Maude, whose method of getting back his sketches even astounded the past master himself, Melton Prior, and Frederick Villiers who spurned the use of camels and arrived in Cairo complete with his dark-green 'roadster' bicycle. Charles Williams, who had stirred up so much argument in 1885 with his article on 'How we lost Gordon', was now commissioned by the *Daily Chronicle*, Rene Bull and Mr. Ross wrote and photographed for the *Black and White*, *The Times* sent Edward Frederick Knight. Bennet Burleigh headed the *Daily Telegraph*'s team and Hilliard Atteridge added to the coverage of the *Daily Chronicle*. Reuter as usual was represented, this time by Colonel Lionel James, later to switch to *The Times* and to command King Edward's Horse after the First World War. The *Manchester Guardian* employed Henry Cross, a great friend of Ernest Bennet, who had rowed in the Varsity boat race of 1888 and who, inspired by Bennet's accounts, 'Such delights as these I had experienced during the Cretan troubles in the spring of 1897', secured a permit through the *Manchester Guardian* for the last stage of the campaign. Ernest Bennet himself wrote for the *Westminster Gazette* and terminated his amateur status by becoming the press censor on the Turkish staff during the Balkan wars of 1912. H. H. S. Pearse, an old friend of

Melton Prior, was the artist and correspondent of the *Graphic* but during times of peace wrote on hunting for the *Field*. Winston Churchill, as we know, wrote for the *Morning Post*. G. W. Steevens of the *Daily Mail* claimed to feel a bit lost when he arrived in Sudan:

> I sat on a box of tinned beef, whisky, and other delicacies, dumped down on a slope of loose sand. Round me lay another similar case, a tent, bed, and bath, all collapsible and duly collapsed into a brown canvas jacket, two brown canvas bags containing saddlery, towels, and table linen, a chair and a table lashed together, a wash-hand basin with shaving tackle concealed beneath inside its green canvas cover, a brown bag with some clothes in it, a shining tin canteen, a cracking lunch-basket, a driving coat, and a hunting crop . . .

Other correspondents were similarly equipped although the old campaigners had eliminated some of the superfluous items. Francis Scudamore had his baggage on two camels together with tenting and, as Ernest Bennet called it, 'his drink camel, i.e. the animal which carried his stores of alcohol and soda water . . .' To the dismay of some of the other correspondents Frederick Villiers of the *Graphic* turned up with a large leather case containing a moving picture camera. Villiers had tried to use this type of camera before during the Greco-Turkish War but with little result. The other correspondents, however, knowing the important inroads made by photography and its invaluable use on the field of battle, immediately telegraphed to Cairo for cameras and equipment to be sent to them at the front. Villiers later described his delight when the packages arrived and were found to be lantern slide projectors together with a set of slides '. . . of the racy type likely to please an Egyptian audience'.

Although some correspondents had made **prior** arrangements through Thomas Cook and Sons, others arrived to find no transport for their load of equipment. 'One consequence of the inrush of officers and correspondents,' wrote Bennet, 'was a dearth of horses. The neighbourhood had been ransacked for animals . . .' Bennet eventually paid £17.10s. for a horse which somewhat pleased him as the government was paying £20. Servants were indispensable and a problem, and a large number of illiterate, incoherent, thieving Arabs were employed by unwary correspondents. The old campaigners, especially those who had been on the 1884-5 campaign, knew better. Supplies were obtained in Cairo from Messrs. Walker whom Bennet described as a '... veritable Egyptian Whiteleys from whom one can buy anything from condensed milk to a trotting camel'. Each correspondent had, or at least claimed for journalistic purposes to have, a faithful, comic cook and Ernest Bennet was no exception, his sporting a large sword as Bennet had refused to buy him a rifle. 'To have a cook bending over the fire,' he wrote, 'with a belt full of cartridges, or walking round one's tent with a loaded rifle—these were indeed added terrors to the perils of a Sudan campaign.' G. W. Steevens fared no better with his horse:

> Experts opined [he declared] that he might in the remote past have been a Dervish horse . . . His teeth, what remained of them, gave no clear evidence of his age, but on a general view of him I should say he was rising ninety. Early in the century he was probably a chestnut, but now he was a silver chestnut . . . He wore a pessimistic expression . . . and no flesh of any kind in any corner.

Steevens, who like others had assembled a presentable and well-organized campaign kit, procured in London on the advice of salesmen of the larger outfitters who had been no further south than Brighton, found once it was loaded an embarrassing tangle:

> . . . As piled by Sudanese Arabs on to donkeys it was a disreputable, dishevelled, and humiliation beyond blushes. The canteen, the chair and table that had looked so neat and workmanlike, on the donkey became the pots and sticks of a gipsy encampment. My tent was a slipshod monstrosity, my dressing-case blatantly secondhand, my washing basin was positively indecent. To make things worse, they had trimmed my baggage up with garbage of their own—dirty bags of dates and cast-off clothing . . . And to finish my shame, here was I trudging behind cracking and flicking at donkeys and half-naked black men, like a combination of gipsy, horse-coper and slave-driver.

Even Bennet Burleigh had trouble with baggage and transport. 'Drenched to the skin, I reached the shelter of a friendly bar,' wrote the bluff Scotsman who once dismally remarked to Melton Prior in Somaliland that the nearest public house was a thousand miles away. 'My baggage was soaked, and so was my negro boy and my polyglot interpreter . . . Meanwhile I had been trafficking for six mules and two guides, and with some pressing secured them.'

But even before the Dervishes had been sighted, trouble loomed in the British force. It was not bayonets and swords this time but the boots and the cartridges of the Lee-Metford rifle.

The boot scandal came to light during the forced march of Major General Gatacre's brigade from Abu Dis to Berber, 134 miles covered in five and a half days. Steevens recorded that:

> The brigade had only been up-river about a month, after all, and no military boot ought to wear out in a month. We have been campaigning in the Sudan, off and on, for over fourteen years; we might have discovered the little peculiarities of its climate by now. The Egyptian army uses a riveted boot; the boots our British boys were expected to march in had not even a toe-cap. So that when the three battalions and a battery arrived in Berber hundreds of men were all but barefoot: the soles peeled off, and instead of a solid double sole, revealed a layer of shoddy packing sandwiched between two thin slices of leather . . . It is always the same story—knavery and slackness clogging and strangling the best efforts of the British soldier. To save some contractor a few pence on a boot, or to save some War Office clerk a few hours of work he is paid for not doing, you stand to lose a good rifle and bayonet in a decisive battle, and to break a good man's heart into the bargain. Is it worth it? But it is always happening; the history of the Army is a string of such disgraces. And each time we arise and bawl, 'Somebody ought to be hanged.' So says everybody. But nobody ever is hanged.

The controversy following the publication of Steevens's dispatch even affected Parliament and the War Office. Steevens continued the argument in his classic book, *With Kitchener to Khartum*:

> The official reply to them was in effect that the boots were very good boots, only that the work done by the brigade over bad ground had tried them too severely. It is a strange sort of answer to say that a military boot is a very good boot, only you mustn't march in it. Having walked myself over most of the same ground as General Gatacre's brigade, I am able to say that, while there is a good deal of rock and loose sand, the greater part of the going is hard sand or gravel. The boots I wore myself I have on at the moment of writing, as sound as ever.

Bennet Burleigh further embarrassed the War Office when he denounced the bullet of the Lee-Metford Rifle:

The War Office authorities have reams of correspondence on
the valueless character of the Lee-Metford rifle bullet. Indeed,
the rifle itself has come in for severe strictures, as being
inferior in its magazine arrangement to the German and Italian
weapons; whilst the cordite is described as 'an indifferent
explosive compared to the powder of other countries'.
However, all that may be, certainly the soldiers have no faith
in the stopping qualities of the Lee-Metford bullet. Under
superior orders, issued at Dekesh camp, large details from each
regiment were engaged daily in filing off the tips of the
Lee-Metford bullet. One million rounds had to be so dealt with.
They were doing the same thing in Cairo arsenal. It is little
short of a scandal that an army in the field has to sit down
whilst the men re-make its ammunition.

# 7

# The end of Pax Britannica

## (1898–1902)

*As the correspondent approaches the theatre of war he will
naturally endeavour to observe every sign along the line of
communications which indicates an unusual state of affairs.*
Winston Spencer Churchill, war correspondent, *Daily
Telegraph*, 1897

During January 1898, reports from the front showed that the Dervishes
were planning a move of some importance but Bennet Burleigh noted
sourly:

> . . . an order was sprung . . . upon the English press that
> correspondents would not be allowed south of Assouan.
> There was, however, a reservation in the case of a press agency,
> that one of its representatives, aptly dubbed 'a tame
> correspondent' by a critic, would be allowed at Wady Halfa
> or rail head, and that he should be the sole medium of non-
> official (?) communication between the army and the press.

It was a bold move by Kitchener and Lord Cromer which not even
Sir Garnet Wolseley would have dreamed of trying. In reply to the
stormy protests from the London press, Kitchener and Lord Cromer
gave as a reason the shortage of transport. Within twenty-four hours,
however, Burleigh wrote '. . . the regulation had to be relaxed, and
war correspondents from all representative British newspapers received
permission to proceed to Wady Halfa and railhead'. Later Lord Cromer
told Burleigh that the order had been in the interests of the newspapers
and to cut their costs of keeping a representative on hand during the

dull season while adding, according to Burleigh, '. . . editors did not exercise enough care in making their selection of representatives, and unfit men were often sent out, who did much harm in many ways'.

Kitchener's restrictions on correspondents also included permitting them only two hundred words per dispatch over the wires. The *New York Herald* and London *Times* among others had agreed to exchange reports and, much to the annoyance of some of the other correspondents, Hubert Howard and Colonel Frank Rhodes composed their reports, each of two hundred words, to form a complete dispatch of four hundred words.

By March, Steevens noted:

> The only restrictions . . . laid upon correspondents . . . were that they were not to go out on reconnaissances, and especially not to go near the Sirdar. They were advised not to stand in front of the firing line during general actions, but even this was not insisted upon.

With their newly granted permission the correspondents rushed to the railhead for as Ernest Bennet realized '. . . no Sudan campaign has ever possessed a quarter of the interest which, for some reason or other, the present one has aroused in the British public'. Great precautions were taken with the press telegrams and once they had passed the scrutiny of Colonel Wingate, they were put on the wires.

> All the clerks employed on this service [recalled Bennet] were bound over in sureties of £240 not to divulge the contents of any telegram . . . as during the last campaign several important telegrams . . . were revealed to others than the lawful recipients.

This probably referred to the *Manchester Guardian*'s telegram about Tel-el-Kebir.

Kitchener was preparing slowly and methodically to crush the Dervishes and to retake Khartoum to avenge Gordon's death, a crusade-like and romantic notion that accounted for much of the public interest in the campaign. But G. W. Steevens pointed out, 'The real enemy he [Kitchener] has seen, is not the Dervishes, whom we have always beaten, but the Sudan itself.' Kitchener's cautious, well-prepared forward movement would eventually pay off even if it left the correspondents rather bored. Besides minor contacts with the enemy, nothing happened until the beginning of April, when the Egyptian cavalry brushed with the Dervish force under Mahmoud on 4 April. As the

Sudan 1898: war correspondents en route for Khartoum on press barge number 9. The group includes W. Maxwell of the *Standard,* H. Weldon of the *Morning Post* and Bennet Burleigh of the *Daily Telegraph* (drawing by Rene Bull of *Black and White*).

force moved forward correspondents struggled to mount their horses. 'Mounting into the saddle,' wrote Steevens, 'had been like sitting down suddenly in a too hot bath . . .' The action, if small, was successful. 'It was Maiwand over again, only properly done', Steevens heard one soldier remark. Two hundred Dervishes were killed mainly by the Maxim guns and the lances of the Egyptian cavalry. The action certainly cheered up army and correspondents alike who were getting heartily sick of the Atbar camp, '. . . which had been such a paradise of green when we first camped on it'. Officers in the Sudan whiled away the time colouring pictures from the *Illustrated London News* and *Graphic*.

On 8 April, the enemy were seriously engaged in a decisive action at Atbara, where the Dervishes fought under Mahmoud who had assembled his followers in a fortified zareba. In his dispatch, Bennet Burleigh wrote:

. . . Mahmoud did not anticipate the presence of British troops with the Sirdar's forces when he quitted Shendy to seek battle with the Egyptian army. When he learned that 'Inglesi' were with the Sirdar, he altered his tactics, and, though sorely pressed for food, awaited attack in an encampment of his own choosing, which he strengthened by various devices . . .

The attacking force had moved out of camp at Emdabiya where the fires were kept burning to deceive any 'prowling Dervish scouts'.

At 1.15 a.m. on 8 April, Good Friday, the troops were roused and assembled; soldiers and correspondents made final adjustments to equipment and weapons before moving forward closer to the enemy zareba. As dawn came up the men awoke from the final night-halt.

> The squares shifted into the fighting formations [wrote
> G. W. Steevens]. At one impulse, in one superb sweep,
> near 12,000 men moved forward towards the enemy. All
> England and all Egypt, and the flower of the black lands
> beyond, Birmingham and the West Highlands, the half-
> regenerated children of the earth's earliest civilisation,
> and grinning savages from the uttermost swamps of
> Equatoria, muscle and machinery, lord and larrikin,
> Balliol and the Board school, the Sirdar's brain and the
> camel's back—all welded into one, the awful war machine
> went forward into action . . . The line went on over the
> crunching gravel in awful silence . . . till it was not half
> a mile from the flags. Then it halted.

The artillery opened a tremendous barrage on the zareba just after 6 a.m. as the assaulting force lay on the ground waiting. It lasted over an hour and a half. At 8 a.m. the Sirdar, from a vantage point on a knoll overlooking the zareba and at a distance of about 900 yards from it, ordered the general advance.

> An advance [noted Burleigh, following Gatacre's brigade],
> was begun as if in review order but was lifted out of that
> staccato performance by a tremendous shout, which resounded
> from right to left of our lines—a brotherly challenge 'twixt
> white and black to intrepidity. We were in for it now.

Steevens takes up the account of the action as the line moved forward:

> . . . the bullets were swishing and lashing now like rain on a
> pond. But the line of khaki and purple tartan never bent nor

swayed . . . It was not so difficult to go on—the pipes picked
you up and carried you on—but it was difficult not to hurry . . .

The advancing troops, with war correspondents following close behind,
reached the zareba amidst a 'furious gust of bullets' and the low hedge
of dry camel-thorn was quickly pulled at.

'Just half a dozen tugs,' wrote Steevens, 'and the impossible zareba
was a gap and a scattered heap of brushwood.' Bennet Burleigh and
some other correspondents, Scudamore, Steevens, and Maude ducked
the bullets and scribbled their notes. 'Dervish bullets,' wrote Burleigh,
'were flying thick and fast, viciously noisy and near . . .' Inside the
troops found a labyrinth of holes, shelter-pits, trenches, and palisades
intermingled with huts, and baggage animals. Burleigh compared the
action to, '. . . clearing out by hand a hive of hornets . . .' The fight
inside the zareba was furious and deadly. The attacking troops were
fired at from all directions, from the open and from concealed shelter-
pits. Line formation was useless and the attack was one of broken
rushes against trenches and other objectives. The fight was made all
the more desperate because the Dervishes '. . . gave no quarter and
rarely asked for it themselves, fighting like beasts till death relaxed
their thews'. Inside the zareba, Steevens described the fight:

> For now began the killing. Bullet and bayonet and butt, the
> whirlwind of Highlanders swept over. And by this time the
> Lincolns were in on the right, and the Maxims, galloping right
> up to the stockade, had withered the left, and the Warwicks,
> the enemy's cavalry definitely gone, were volleying off the
> blacks as your beard comes off under a keen razor. Farther
> and farther they cleared the ground—cleared it of everything
> like a living man, for it was left carpeted thick enough with
> dead. Here was a trench; bayonet that man. Here a little straw
> tukl; warily round to the door, and then a volley. Now in
> columns through this opening in the bushes; then into line,
> and drop those few desperately firing shadows among the
> dry stems beyond. For the running blacks—poor heroes—
> still fired, though every second they fired less and ran more.
> And on, on the British stumbled and slew, till suddenly there
> was unbroken blue overhead, and a clear drop underfoot. The
> river! And across the trickle of water the quarter mile of dry
> sand-bed was a fly-paper with scrambling spots of black. The
> pursuers thronged the bank in double line, and in two minutes
> the paper was still black-spotted, only the spots scrambled no

more . . . It has lasted forty minutes; and nobody was quite certain whether it had seemed more like two minutes or two years. All at once there came a roar of fire from the left; and half-sated British saw the river covered with a new swarm of flies only just in time to see them stop still as the others. This was Lewis's half-brigade of Egyptians at work. They had stood the heavy fire that sought them as if there were no such things as wounds or death; now they had swept down leftward of the zareba, shovelled the enemy into the river-bed, and shot them down. Bloodthirsty? Count up the Egyptians murdered by Mahdism and then say so if you will.

The battle was over and won, but at what cost. Bennet Burleigh and his colleagues started writing their telegrams and dispatches. Equally worn out as the soldiers, their work had just begun. During the action, the correspondents followed the troops but they were also involved in the fight. Francis Scudamore was noticed by George Steevens, inside the zareba under a distracting volley of shots, very coolly tying up Colonel Murray of the Seaforths who had been wounded.

> After the fatigues of the march [wrote Burleigh], and the excitement of the action, and when I had finished dispatching my long but hastily written telegrams, which were scrawled out whilst sitting upon pebbles under a blazing desert sun, half blinded and wholly wearied, and terribly thirsty and hungry, I managed to procure some refreshment.

Steevens fell asleep with a half eaten biscuit having, 'scraped a short hieroglyphic scrawl on a telegraph form'. Later on Burleigh wrote a long description of the battle of the Atbara; this was the usual procedure for the war correspondents. Accurate, short telegrams were hastily dispatched immediately after the action or event, although the censor rarely allowed casualty figures to be given.

> The rules of military censorship [complained Burleigh] did not permit the transmission of my figures . . . It is perhaps after all a merciful regulation that breaks news of loss and suffering by degrees . . . I confess that I never like to be the first to wire or write, giving the information of the death of any person . . . except in special circumstances, such as where the public interest overweighs those of the few.

After the battle, there was some concern felt by correspondents about the safety of Frederick Villiers of the *Graphic*. However, Villiers, to the delight of the press corps, eventually reappeared, armed with a bulging sketch-book and with a pencil between his teeth.

The long dispatches always posted after the telegrams were usually written with more style and contained anecdotes and smaller details of the fight as well as the main narrative of the action. Sometimes, however, a newspaper was embarrassed when its rivals followed up their telegraphic stories with long accounts and it was not able to produce a single word from its correspondent due to a loss of mail. The *Daily Graphic* correspondent remarked that after the siege of Hafir in 1897, '...I paid tribute to the services rendered by the N.C. Officers of the Royal Marine Artillery ... that letter went to the bottom of the Nile when the nuggar carrying the mail was wrecked near Haneck Cataract ...' War artists followed the precedent set by Melton Prior and usually kept tracings of their sketches, a prudent precaution when they had to rely solely on the mail. W. T. Maude of the *Graphic* however, not content to wait for either boats or dispatch riders to cross the desert, hired natives to carry his sketches in waterproof packets in their turbans on their heads while they swam

Sudan 1898: how W. Maude of the *Graphic* got his sketches of the battle of Omdurman away. A native swimmer with sketches in his turban swims downstream to catch a steamer.

down the Nile, ever wary of crocodiles, to the nearest steamer, for quick transmission. 'The morrow of the fight,' recorded Steevens, 'brought a quiet morning for all but the correspondents, who had now to pay for many days of idle luxury.'

The army now moved into summer quarters and there was little action for the correspondents to report, most of them returning to Cairo or even to England for a rest. At the end of July, Cairo was again bustling as troops, officers, and correspondents prepared to move towards Fort Atbara. New correspondents swelled the press corps to fifteen including Ernest Bennet of the *Westminster Gazette*, Henry Cross of the *Manchester Guardian*, Colonel Frank Rhodes of *The Times* and Hubert Howard of the *Times* and *New York Herald*, who had not witnessed the campaign of the earlier part of the year. The trains were crowded and described by Steevens, '. . . rather like the special trains that take boys back to school'. Winston Churchill, on his way to join the 21st Lancers, wrote in his dispatch to the *Morning Post* that the soldiers were '. . . arrayed in what they call "Christmas Tree Order", and dangling with water bottles, haversacks and canteen straps, cloaks, swords, and carbines from every part of their body . . .'. The native troop trains and steamers on the Nile were even worse. 'You may have seen sardines in tins,' wrote Steevens, 'but you will never really know how roomy and comfortable a tinned sardine must feel until you have seen blacks packed on one of the Sirdar's steamers.'

The final goal was Omdurman, the symbol of Mahdism whose capture would avenge Gordon and subdue the Sudan. There was a quickening excitement in the atmosphere during August, but the Sirdar was not to be rushed. While correspondents idly kicked their heels, Kitchener engineered with thorough planning his final move for the capture of Omdurman and the smashing of the Khalifa's forces.

The correspondents and artists meanwhile set about describing the advance in every detail from troop movements to the steamers and trains carrying stores and fodder. Their narratives excited the reading public at home, who, like theatre audiences, were on the edge of their seats waiting for the final act. However, most correspondents complained, for such was their nature, about inadequate arrangements, especially the functioning of the so-called Post Office. At Fort Atbara, Steevens recorded with disgust that, 'You can ask when the next post goes out or comes in: the dirty Copt boy they call the postmaster will answer "Tomorrow".' The correspondents had always been considered as hard drinkers, and tough characters had nothing else to think about except what Steevens called the 'Sudan thirst'. This was usually slaked with whisky and soda, gin and soda, gin and lime juice and soda, gin and bitters, or 'that triumphant blend of all whetting flavours an Abu Hamed', said to have been concocted by Francis Scudamore, consisting of gin, vermouth, Angostura, lime juice, and soda. Ernest Bennet had other tastes, 'When the whisky mule halts, it is kindness to lighten his burden.'

Besides 'Sudan thirst' there were other discomforts such as scorpions which frequently and without distinction stung soldier and correspondent alike. Frederick Villiers was the first to succumb to a bite but after having some ammonia rubbed on and drinking a bottle of neat whisky he arose the following day, somewhat bleary-eyed but cured. The torrential rain did not improve tempers during the desert march, although Francis Scudamore seemed oblivious of anything out of the ordinary. Bennet recorded that 'Mr. Scudamore was sitting and calmly shaving himself before a looking glass, with a piece of waterproof over his shoulders'. Neither Arabs nor camels liked the rain, and Bennet loaned his splendid red-lined mackintosh to his two native servants. During the night they rolled in opposite directions with disastrous results for the mackintosh.

There was great friendliness amongst the correspondents. W. T. Maude and G. W. Steevens had lent a couple of horses to Cross and Bennet who had intended to walk in front of their camels, overladen with bathtubs, tents and Messrs. Silver's campaign bed, 'The Salisbury'. Camels were seldom ridden but used as transport and, as horses were in short supply, the ever-eccentric Frederick Villiers of the *Graphic* again brought along with him his bicycle. This machine, '. . . of a dull green tint, was usually to be found in the charge of his servant, who had acquired considerable skill in controlling the movements of his master's donkey with one hand and his master's machine with the other'. The sight of Villiers pedalling off at speed in search of material for a sketch must have been comical. Bennet noted that a Greek correspondent went through the entire Greco-Turkish war on a bicycle and later published his memoirs which greatly accelerated the sale of bicycles in Athens. With regard to Villiers's machine he wrote:

> . . . this lugubrious-looking bicycle bore the battle and the breeze wonderfully well, and the maker ought to secure a splendid advertisement out of it; for the tyres which can

237

*The end of Pax Britannica*

pass unpunctured through the terrors of the mimosa scrub, and refrain from bursting under the rays of a Sudan sun in August, may fairly be recommended for 'strong roadster' work in the country lanes of England.

The Sudan had perhaps provided more column inches, more comment, more interest than many more important campaigns of the late Victorian era. After Atbara, correspondents rushed into print with their memoirs of the campaign. Bennet Burleigh's book *Sirdar and Khalifa* was finished and ready for the press in July 1898, three months after the battle. Steevens's account and that of Ernest Bennet included in addition accounts of the battle of Omdurman; they were finished in September and November respectively, and published a few months later. These books were an added bonus, which brought their names home to the British reading public who were usually ignorant of the identity of their favourite correspondent, as telegrams and follow-up stories were usually headed 'From our Special Correspondent'. Emile Zola spoke at one of the annual conferences of the Institute of Journalists:

> I wish to speak of anonymity in journalism . . . and if you consider an English newspaper, in which not a single article is signed, and a French newspaper, in which everything is signed, you will find yourself, I believe, confronted by the two races, with all that national temperament, the manners and the history of the last hundred years have made them.

Published accounts of campaigns were very popular until the advent of photographs in newspapers, as the correspondents were able in their printed works to elaborate more than they could in their dispatches for reasons of space or censorship. At the turn of the century, magazines such as *Black and White*, Harmsworth's part work, *With the Flag to Pretoria* and *After Pretoria, the Guerilla War* established photography and half-tone prints as an essential part of mass circulation journalism.

Coverage of the Battle of Omdurman, while bringing to a head a controversy between war correspondents and the army, also showed the public for the first time in printed photographs what war was all about. The mass slaughter inflicted by the Maxim guns may have appeared tame when compared with the photographs of the First and Second World Wars and other modern conflicts but to the Victorians, who knew only second-hand graphic and 'acceptable' illustrations of war, the sensational illustrations of the Omdurman campaign had the same effect as the violent pictures in the supplements of today.

Ernest Bennet of the *Westminster Gazette* tried to explain the horror felt by the Victorians at tales of Dervish mutilation of British wounded in his dispatches:

> Indignation against the Dervishes for such mutilations may easily be exaggerated. Sickening as it is to gaze upon a comrade's features hacked out of all human semblance, one cannot forget that the men who did the deed had seen thousands of their brethren slain by our awful fire without a possibility of retaliation. It is worth remembering, too, that the mutilation of the human body is not the exclusive monopoly of barbaric people; anyone who has seen the effects of shell fire—bodies ripped open, jaws torn off, and kindred horrors—may find it difficult to differentiate very markedly between the accursed usages inseparable from every system of warfare—civilised and barbarous alike.

'It was the last day of Mahdism and the greatest,' wrote G. W. Steevens. The battle started, according to Winston Churchill, at 5.50 in the morning and by 11.30, '. . . Sir H. Kitchener shut up his glasses and remarked that he thought the enemy had been given a "good dusting" '. The specials devoted large portions of their dispatches to the heroism of the ill-armed enemy in the face of the sophisticated and destructive weapons of the British. 'No white troops would have faced the torrent of death for five minutes,' wrote G. W. Steevens, '. . the torrent swept into them and hurled them down in whole companies . . . It was not a battle but an execution.' Bennet Burleigh, a seasoned war correspondent, wrote his dispatches in much the same style, '. . . In sheer blundering brutishness, the ferocious Dervishes tried to stem the storm . . . Death was reaping a gigantic harvest . . .'

It was G. W. Steevens's description of the Battle of Omdurman that has remained a classic piece of journalism and raised him to the ranks of the great war correspondents. He did not see it as a triumphal victory of British Imperialism or of Kitchener's generalship. Since 11,000 Dervishes had died for a small British loss, he wrote in his book, *With Kitchener to Khartum*:

> The battle was almost a miracle of success. For that thanks are due to the Khalifa, whose generalship throughout was a masterpiece of imbecility . . . The Sirdar would have won in

any case: that he won so crushingly and so cheaply was the gift of luck and the Khalifa.

It was the Dervishes who lost rather than Kitchener who won.

Some glory still remained thanks to the charge of the 21st Lancers against the Dervishes. While written up by some as a charge in the heroic style, to others such as Steevens it was pure luck that there were any survivors. Correspondents were perhaps a little brutal towards Kitchener but as he had classed them as a race of 'drunken swabs' they felt no love for him. Only perhaps G. W. Steevens and Hubert Howard enjoyed anything like cordiality with the Sirdar. Churchill, soldier and correspondent, described the charge:

> In a deep fold of the ground—completely concealed by its peculiar formation—a long, dense, white mass of men became visible. In length they were nearly equal to our front. They were about twelve deep. It was undoubtedly a complete surprise for us. What followed probably astonished them as much. The Lancers acknowledged the unexpected sight only by an increase of pace. A desire to have the necessary momentum to drive through so solid a line animated each man. But the whole affair was a matter of seconds.
>
> At full gallop and in the closest order the squadron struck the Dervish mass. The riflemen, who fired bravely to the last, were brushed head over heel in the khor. And with them the Lancers jumped actually on to the spears of the enemy, whose heads were scarcely level with the horses' knees.
>
> In this case the two living walls crashed together with a mighty collision. The Dervishes stood their ground manfully. They tried to hamstring the horses. They fired their rifles, pressing the muzzles into the very bodies of their opponents. They cut bridle reins and stirrup-leathers. They would not budge until they were knocked over. They stabbed and hacked with savage pertinacity. In fact, they tried every device of cool determined men practised in war and familiar in cavalry. Many horses pecked on landing and stumbled in the press, and the man that fell was pounced on by a dozen merciless foes.
>
> The regiment broke completely through the line everywhere, leaving sixty Dervishes dead and many wounded in their track. A hundred and fifty yards away they halted, rallied, and in less than five minutes were reformed and ready for a second charge. The men were anxious to cut their way back through their enemies. But some realisation of the cost of that wild ride began to come to all of us. Riderless horses galloped

Sudan 1898: the charge of the 21st Lancers at Omdurman (from the painting by Stanley Berkeley).

across the plain. Men, clinging on to their saddles, lurched
hopelessly about, covered with blood from perhaps a dozen
wounds. Horses streaming from tremendous gashes limped
and staggered with their riders. In one hundred and twenty
seconds five officers, sixty-six men, and one hundred and
nineteen horses out of less than three hundred had been
killed or wounded.

The Dervish line, broken and shattered by the charge, began
to reform at once. They closed up, shook themselves together,
and prepared with constancy and courage for another shock.
The 21st, now again drawn up in line of squadron columns,
wheeled and, galloping round the Dervish flank, dismounted
and opened a heavy fire with their magazine carbines. When
the Dervish change of front was completed they began to
advance against the dismounted men. But the fire was accurate,
and there can be little doubt that the moral effect of the
charge had been very great, and that these brave enemy were
no longer unshaken. Be this as it may, the fact remains that
they retreated swiftly, though in good order, towards the
ridge of Heliograph Hill, where the Khalifa's black flag still
waved, and the 21st Lancers remained in possession of the
ground—and of their dead.

For some the charge of the 21st Lancers was the redeeming feature
of the battle, meaty actions to describe, heroic and romantic tales to
be told, but to many of the war correspondents, and among them
G. W. Steevens, it was '... indisputable folly'. But the clamouring
British public saw it otherwise.

> It is perhaps an unfortunate consequence of the modern
> development of war correspondence [wrote Steevens] and
> the general influence of popular feeling on every branch of
> our Government, that what the street applauds, the War
> Office is compelled at least to condone. The populace has
> glorified the charge of the 21st for its indisputable heroism;
> the War Office will hardly condemn it for its equally
> indisputable folly ... For cavalry to charge unbroken
> infantry, of unknown strength, over unknown ground ...
> was as grave a tactical crime as cavalry could possibly commit.

While the battle had caused casualties on the side of the British and
most of all on that of the Dervishes, the war correspondents had their
share of dead and wounded. Out of the fifteen who entered the battle,
two died and two were wounded, one seriously. Hubert Howard of
*The Times*, who had ridden with Churchill in the charge of the Lancers,
was inspecting with others the Khalifa's Palace when 'Suddenly four

shells burst in rapid succession'. Everyone rushed for cover but Howard was already in the Palace and:

> Another shell screamed over the houses [reported Bennet], and as it burst a fragment struck Howard on the back of the head, and killed him instantly—a tragic and untimely death, when the perils of the day seemed over . . .

Colonel Frank Rhodes of *The Times* was an early victim of the battle, shot through the flesh of the right shoulder and carried protestingly to the rear. 'From the very beginning,' wrote Steevens, 'no Sudan campaign has been complete without Colonel Rhodes, and it must have been a keen disappointment to miss Omdurman.' Churchill saw him afterwards and reported in his dispatch that he was '. . . propped up against the railing of a barge with a bullet through his shoulder, but brave and cheery as ever, the life and soul of the hospital as formerly of the camp'. Charles Williams of the *Daily Chronicle* had his cheek cut by a bullet or chip of stone, '. . . it was nothing and he made of it even less than it was'. Henry Cross of the *Manchester Guardian* had fallen victim to enteric fever from which he later died. Bennet, his great friend, wrote sadly:

> At last I came by accident upon Cross. The poor fellow was again in a state of prostration, and was lying under the blanket-tent of Captain Luther, R.A.M.C. in the camp of the Lancashire Fusiliers. He told me that on the previous night he had, like the rest of the correspondents, failed to get any food and had slept on the sand without a blanket though Steevens, with his usual kindness, had lent him an overcoat when the night became chilly.

Ernest Bennet, amongst others including Henry Cross of the *Manchester Guardian* and Charles Williams of the *Daily Chronicle*, were horrified with the excesses indulged in after the battle:

> Our native battalions were soon busily engaged in killing the wounded. The Sudanese undertook this task with evident relish, and never spared a single Dervish along their path . . . a large number of servants and camp followers were also busy . . . Some carried clubs or spears, others had managed to secure old rifles. They advanced with great caution, and I saw them fire repeatedly into bodies which were already quite dead before they dared to rush in and strip the corpse of its arms and clothing. These cowardly wretches ought most certainly to have been prevented from carrying on this irresponsible

Sudan 1898: looters after the battle. '. . . It was a most appalling slaughter. The Dervish army was killed out as hardly an army had been killed out in the history of war,' said G. W. Steevens.

shooting . . . The barbarous usage of killing the wounded has become traditional in Sudanese warfare, and in some cases it must be looked upon as a painful necessity. The wounded Dervishes—as I saw with my own eyes, and on one occasion nearly felt with my own body—sometimes raised themselves and fired one last round at our advancing line . . . Still when all has been said in defence of this practice, it is certain that in many cases wounded Dervishes, unarmed and helpless, were butchered from sheer wantonness and lust of bloodshed. The whole formed a hideous picture, not easy to forget.

However, not only were the African troops accused of the excesses but the British troops were said to have killed wounded men who asked for quarter and to have done nothing about the welfare of the enemy wounded. The various rumours and accusations were brought to a head by an article in the *Contemporary Review* written by Ernest Bennet. Various newspapers took up the fight against the War Office including the *Manchester Guardian*, whose correspondent Cross had died, and even some of the small provincial newspapers joined in. The *Guardian* reproduced the controversy raging in the *Daily Telegraph* between Burleigh and Bennet over the charges as well as reproducing a number of Charles Williams's dispatches from the *Daily Chronicle*. The campaign might have fizzled out as the *Guardian* relied too much on quotations from other papers, even including reports of Churchill about the wounded left for three days on the burning sands, and had not attempted to get any accounts from soldiers or officers present. But the matter was kept alive by the debate in the House of Commons which voted a grant of £30,000 to Kitchener. Churchill in his book *The River War* expressed himself more definitely on the question than he had done in his dispatches to the *Morning Post*:

> I must personally record that there was a very general
> impression that the fewer the prisoners, the greater would be
> the satisfaction of the commander. The sentiment that the
> British soldier is incapable of brutality, is one which never
> fails to win the meed of popular applause; but there is in fact
> a considerable proportion of cruel men in every army . . .
> The unmeasured terms in which the Dervishes had been
> described in the newspapers, and the idea which had been
> laboriously circulated, of 'avenging Gordon' had inflamed
> their passions, and had led them to believe that it was quite
> correct to regard their enemy as vermin—unfit to live. The
> result was that there were many wounded Dervishes killed.

Concerning these killings, Charles Neufeld, a German merchant who had been a prisoner of the Khalifa for twelve years, wrote in his book *A Prisoner of the Khaleefa* (1899) against newspaper correspondents who had condemned the killing of wounded Dervishes:

> . . . let each correspondent accompanying an expedition into
> the heart of Africa declare whether he votes for first aid to the
> wounded Dervishes or not. If he does not, then let him hold
> his peace . . . If he declares for first aid, then give him a packet
> of bandages and a water-bottle, and let him put his principles
> into practice, while his more enlightened brother knights of
> the pen tag on to their dispatches his obituary notice.

Meanwhile other correspondents preferred to highlight the scandal of how the Dervishes managed to be so plentifully supplied with ammunition. Many of the correspondents noticed the large number of Martini-Henry rifles of British manufacture the enemy possessed at the time of the occupation of Berber, as well as an abundant supply of ammunition and guns. 'Part, it had been suspected,' wrote Burleigh, 'found its way from the West, a little from the North, and more from the East Coast...' The papers found on a prisoner captured by General Hunter revealed those who were engaged in shipping the shells and ammunition. Ernest Bennet recorded that he found some invoices:

> ...which showed clearly that a certain Manchester firm had supplied the Khalifa with lead for the manufacture of bullets! It is difficult to believe that an Englishman could sink so low as to supply his country's enemy with munitions of war for the sack of filthy lucre!'

But the international armaments salesmen, such as the legendary Basil Zharov, were now an integral part of modern warfare.

The Khalifa remained at liberty for a further two months and Osman Digna was free until 1900 but the campaign was no longer news. The Fashoda crisis between the French and British over spheres of influence now took the limelight, to be resolved by Kitchener. The nineteenth century and the Victorian age was, however, to close on one of the last and most brutal of Imperial wars; that of the Boers against the British in South Africa.

The prolonged negotiations between the Boers and the British Government failed to produce a solution to the problem of the rights of the *Uitlanders*, or settlers, in the Transvaal who had petitioned the Queen. As the negotiations at Bloemfontein had broken down, despite a final offer by the British government to accept the enfranchisement of the settlers on the Boers' original conditions, the two parties seemed destined to collide. To unbiased observers it seemed ridiculous that a small number of Boer farmers should think themselves capable of taking on the greatest Empire the world had ever seen but many were convinced that war was inevitable, including the proprietors of the leading London newspapers. Alfred Harmsworth telegraphed Winston Churchill offering him the post of *Daily Mail* war correspondent, but Churchill was loyal to the *Morning Post* and told Oliver Borthwick about this offer. Borthwick offered Churchill amazing conditions, which included the complete copyright of his work. The terms were 'higher, I think', wrote Churchill, 'than any previously paid in British journalism to war correspondents.' He was to receive £250 per month, all expenses paid, with freedom of movement and four months guaranteed employment. The *Morning Post* also arranged for other correspondents to cover the war, including Lord Cecil Manners, Mr. Blundell and Mr. Duncombe-Jewell. Lord Cecil Manners was later wounded outside Johannesburg in the fight for Knight's Station. Other newspapers were making similar arrangements as the war fever mounted.

Ultimatums flew back and forth between the two countries until the Boers' demand for the withdrawal of British troops remained unanswered by the expiry time, 11 October. On that day, a Wednesday, '... at tea time' as *The Times* humorously put it, war broke out between Great Britain and the Transvaal. In South Africa, martial law was proclaimed and newspaper dispatches subjected to censorship. The following day a large number of correspondents left for South Africa. On board the *Dunottar Castle*, Churchill was accompanied by a host of press colleagues who posed for their photograph on their arrival at Cape Town. They came from different countries and with differing backgrounds, some of whom had never before served their newspapers as special correspondents. There were American as well as British correspondents: William Dinwiddie (*Harper's Weekly*), Alister Campbell (Laffan's Agency), J. B. Atkins (*Manchester Guardian*), Douglas Story (*Daily Mail*), G. H. Seull (*New York Commercial Advertiser*), R. C. Booth (*Pearson's War News*), R. M. B. Paxton (*Sphere*), Major A. W. A. Pollock (*The Times*), Basil Gotto (*Daily*

Boer War: a group of war correspondents on their way to the front, photographed on their arrival in Cape Town aboard the *Dunottar Castle*.

Boer War: Winston S. Churchill, as the war correspondent of the *Morning Post,* 1899.

*Express*), Winston S. Churchill (*Morning Post*), F. W. Walker (*Daily
Express*), M. H. Donohue (*Daily Chronicle*), H. J. Wigham (*Daily Mail*),
W. B. Wollen (*Sphere*), J. O. Knight (*Chicago Times and Herald*), and
Ernest Prater (*Sphere*).

Most of the correspondents looked after the inner man and Churchill
was no exception. Shipped aboard the *Dunottar Castle* for him was the
following from his wine merchant, Rudolph Payne and Sons:

| 6 October 1899 | | 61 St. James's Street S.W. | | |
|---|---|---|---|---|
| | (per dozen) | | | |
| 6 Bottles 1889 Vin d'Ay Sec | 110/- | 2 | 15 | 0 |
| 18 bottles St. Emilion | 24/- | 1 | 16 | 0 |
| 6 bottles light Port | 42/- | 1 | 1 | 0 |
| 6 bottles French Vermouth | 36/- | | 18 | 0 |
| 18 bottles Scotch Whisky (10 years old) | 48/- | 3 | 12 | 0 |
| 6 bottles Very Old Eau de Vie landed 1866 | 160/- | 4 | 0 | 0 |
| 12 Rose's Cordial Lime Juice | 15/- | | 15 | 0 |
| 6 x 1 dozen cases for same packing, marking etc. | | | 10 | 0 |
| Cartage Dock charges & Insurance | | | 13 | 0 |
| | | 16 | 0 | 0 |

Sent by S.S. *Dunottar Castle* to South Africa

Other correspondents had made similar provisions for refreshment, bringing with them quantities of tinned foods and bottled fruit, indispensable on campaign. Camp beds, portable wash-stands, valises, all selected from the catalogues of the prominent suppliers were in evidence. Melton Prior ordered his customary thousand cigarettes and his numerous bottles of specially blended whisky, Steevens procured himself a new campaigning suit, while Charles E. Fripp took the trouble to order a sword from Messrs. Wilkinson of Pall Mall, especially made for his diminutive stature. This strange weapon, with a cavalry hand guard and cutlass blade, was eventually 'lost' or perhaps stolen during the campaign. John Latham of Wilkinson's (great-grandfather of the author) noted in his diary that '. . . we eventually satisfied the man of the *Graphic* with his idea of what a sword should be'.

Most of the correspondents aboard the *Dunottar Castle* on passing the S.S. *Australasian* displaying various signs of good news thought that it would be over by the time they arrived. The enthusiasm of the British war correspondents was always evident at this stage. They had a swagger that tended to annoy the authorities and intimidate the newcomers, and armed with pencil and note-pad sped around the camp making copious notes to work up into a dispatch that tended to terrify the novices.

The South African War was the most closely followed and had the largest British and foreign press corps to date. Various European countries had already made clear their intentions to side with the Boers against Britain, Germany being the most powerful and significant while America, France, and others stood by as interested spectators. If the British Lion had his tail severely twisted, it might prove the end of British world domination. The twentieth century was dawning and a resounding setback might change Britannia's global influence. While the war concerned only Britain and her Empire, the world press watched and waited.

The careers of a number of the correspondents aboard the *Dunottar Castle* are of interest. A. W. A. Pollock of *The Times* and *United Services Magazine* was a former regular army colonel who, at the age of sixty-two, commanded the 10th Service Battalion of the King's Own Yorkshire Light Infantry at Loos in France in 1915 where he was gassed and invalided home. Basil Gotto, a sculptor by profession, who first publicly exhibited in 1892, later reported the Boer War and joined the army during the First World War to become a staff officer for musketry. He sculpted the Army and Navy Club war memorial and also the Newfoundland battle memorial. Douglas Story reporting from the Boers' side for the *Daily Mail* went on to report the Russo-Japanese War for the *Daily Express* before finishing his career as Director of the Bureau of Information of the Government of Bengal. Martin Henry Donohue was captured by the Boers and released after the fall of Pretoria and continued to report wars and revolutions for the *Daily Chronicle* until the First World War when he served as an officer in the Intelligence Corps. John Black Atkins, the first staff war correspondent of the *Manchester Guardian*, had served his newspaper in other capacities before arriving in South Africa. He became London editor of the *Manchester Guardian* in 1901, assistant editor of the *Spectator* in 1907, and finally editor of the *Manchester Guardian* in 1931. Besides his own account of the Boer War, *Relief of Ladysmith*, he wrote the monumental two-volume work on the life of William Howard Russell.

The British troops had gone off to the war on the same wave of public exuberance as their predecessors had gone to the Crimea. The Guards' farewell at Waterloo Station, is described by the *Daily Mail*:

> The gathering crowds swept in on the ranks, and so impeded the march that the band had to stop short again and again before Waterloo Station was reached in order that they might not lose the troops altogether. The isolated cheers of the first part of the route swelled into one grand chorus of welcome. Handkerchiefs, hats, sticks and umbrellas waved wildly above the pressing crowd, and by the time the Houses of Parliament—grimly grey, and indistinct masses in the murky gloom—were reached the Guards were literally fighting their way through. Women hung sobbing to the arms of husbands, and sweethearts, relatives and even total strangers, carried away by the enthusiasm, broke into the ranks and insisted on carrying rifles, kitbags . . . the chorus of cheers seemed never-ending, and at Waterloo all semblance of military order had disappeared. The police were swept aside and the men were borne, in many cases, shoulder high to the entraining platform, while others struggled through in single file.

'Good-Bye Dolly Grey', a flop when it was first written for the Spanish American War, now became the song of the moment. Bands played, flags were waved, the crowds shouted and cheered, and once more Britain went to war, confident that it would be over before Christmas 1900. The American press contingent included Richard Harding Davis of the *New York World* with 'three ox carts of luggage and equipment including a portable bath tub . . .', and also his new bride, whom he was later to divorce when he fell under the charms of the 'Yama Yama Girl', Miss Bessie McCoy, the famous musical-comedy star. He died in 1916 passing the last two years of his life reporting for the *Daily Chronicle* in France and Flanders.

As the troops and correspondents rushed to South Africa the world of commerce moved to cater for their needs. Pontings Brothers of Kensington High Street, offered all the extra necessaries: cholera belts, 'The best preventative against dysentery', priced at 2*s.* 6½*d.* each, cardigans, white flannel undershirts, army 'greyback' shirts, the 'Roberts' Valise at 39*s.* 6*d.*, and presumably the superior 'Wolseley' Valise at 41*s.* 6*d.* Blankets, groundsheets, pillows, and canvas buckets, in fact everything and anything; and 'orders of any magnitude executed within a few hours' was the boast of most outfitters.

But the opening stages of the war could hardly have been said to have gone well for Britain. The Boers moved swiftly to avoid invasion, and fast-moving 'commandos' pushed east and west from the Orange Free State and the Transvaal to paralyse the vital railway system on which the British placed paramount importance for the speedy movement of troops. On the western side Mafeking and Kimberley were vital targets while to the east Ladysmith, lying at the junction of two railway systems running from Natal into the Boer Republics, was doubly important. So the three famous sieges of the Boer War started. The first prisoners were taken on 15 October 1899 at Vryburg, a small town between Mafeking and Kimberley which had been evacuated by the Bechuanaland police and seized by the Boers. Among the prisoners were Mr. Hellewell of the London *Daily Mail* and *Cape Times* and Mr. Townshend of the *Bechuanaland News*. Seemingly not too dismayed they posed for a photograph with a compositor of the local newspaper and a native guide, and accompanied by three Boer guards.

Early in November, all three towns were in a state of siege, while the largest expeditionary force ever sent overseas, 50,000 men, was converging on South Africa, accompanied by an equally impressive number of correspondents. Some correspondents had found themselves locked up with the troops and civilians in the besieged towns while the luckier ones, such as Rene Bull and Bennet Burleigh, were still free to report the events of the war. *Black and White* proudly boasted to its readers that '. . . while many of the correspondents of other illustrated papers have been shut up in beleaguered towns, Mr. Bull has been

251

*The end of Pax Britannica*

sagacious enough to keep in open country "hopping about at his own sweet will", as a humorous contemporary remarks'.

Rene Bull was a veteran correspondent of considerable talent and ingenuity who served the *Black and White* for many years. Born in Ireland, he first covered the Armenian massacres as a war artist in 1896 and during the Greco-Turkish War he fell into the hands of the Turks but managed to escape. He went on to report the North-West Frontier campaigns and the Sudan expedition. He had originally studied in Paris to be an engineer but gave it up in 1892 to become an artist. During the Boer War he managed to maintain his usual superiority. In the Greco-Turkish War, the *Black and White* informed its readers, '. . . his camera played a large part and he was successful on many occasions in portraying scenes of actual fighting, such as had never before been recorded by an artist . . .' and succeeded in beating all the pictorial records previously established. During the second year of the Boer War he was severely wounded and invalided home. He never resumed the arduous career of a war artist but during the First World War joined the Royal Naval Volunteer Reserve as a lieutenant and was attached to the Royal Naval Air Service, ending the war as a major in the newly formed Royal Air Force. In 1940, he once again offered his services and entered the Air Ministry on technical duties. He died on 14 March 1942. His photographic and artistic talent is immediately evident in his pictures and photographs which reveal his keen sense of priorities.

The number of war correspondents in South Africa meant that competition for news was extremely tough. *The Times* had twenty-four correspondents in the field by the end of the war and the *Black and White* in January 1900 boasted fifteen correspondents. There was, however, a new and different aspect of war reporting present in ever-increasing numbers, photography both still and moving. W. K. Dickson who claimed to be the first man to take moving pictures in the field vied with John Bennet Stanford, an amateur newsreel cameraman. The biograph was a moving picture camera taking its name from the American patent company which exhibited the camera in London in 1897. John Bennet Stanford had travelled to South Africa at his own expense to take pictures of the war and his films were shown with great success at the Alhambra Theatre. They caused such a stir that the leading British film company, the Warwick Trading Company, sent out three staff cameramen. This new means of communication was avidly grasped at and numerous propaganda films were produced showing Boers firing on first-aid men as they 'heroically under fire tended the wounded'. These anti-Boer films were quietly shot on Hampstead Heath, using professional actors, stage 'blood', and blank ammunition. Even for the photographer of still pictures, the war proved an advance; Reinhold Thiele, a talented German artist who had previously worked and reported for the *Graphic*, had the honour to be the first staff photographer to be sent to South Africa, the rest being freelance, financed by themselves or companies hoping to sell their results.

The illustrated newspapers made it a more vivid war: 'The Best pictures by the Best men' announced the *Black and White*. Photographs were increasingly used and being increasingly demanded by the reading public but there was still an even greater demand for the dramatic and well-written reports of the 'specials' whether they were with the relieving forces or besieged in Mafeking, Kimberley, or Ladysmith. Such was the speedy means of communication that censorship was strict and necessary. Newspapers were always well received in camp, however. 'They make warm blankets,' wrote D. Barnett, a talented photographer of the *Black and White* team, 'though the *Daily Chronicle* is considered too thin even for this purpose.'

Newspapers were still an excellent medium for propaganda, either anti- or pro-Boer, and certain journalists or newspapers were soon known for their sympathies. W. T. Stead, as always a controversial figure, was described as 'a friend of every country but his own' and Henry Labouchere who had reported the Franco-Prussian War for the *Daily News* and had been proprietor and editor of *Truth* for a number of years drew the following remark, 'There is enough perversity in "Labby's" composition to make one doubt whether his pro-Boer utterances are altogether serious'. While the British government realized the usefulness of the press so did the Boers. Mr. Statham, an Englishman who had lived for many years in the Transvaal, was sent to London by the Boers to drum up pro-Boer sympathies, but once editors realized who he was they stopped printing his articles. Dr. Leyds, the Boer Secretary of State, '... bought silence or even mild approval' from certain newspapers although after the war he confessed that his campaign had not been as useful as was thought. 'The papers I should have liked to buy,' he remarked, 'I couldn't, and those I could, were not worth it.'

# 8

# Difficult times

## (1902–14)

There is lacking but one thing — war. The troops want it to prove
their efficiency, the journalists demand it to justify their
existence . . .
J. Angus Hamilton, war correspondent, *The Times* and
*Black and White Magazine*

The declaration of war with South Africa had a mixed reception in the
press, some considering it as no more than another colonial war while
others, such as the *Manchester Guardian*, were more inclined to think
of it as a 'shady attempt of Cecil Rhodes and his financial friends to
engineer an official war to carry out what Dr. Jameson had failed to do
by a private war', namely the inclusion of the rich goldfields of the
Transvaal under the banner of the British South Africa Company,
controlling the diamond fields of Kimberley, and the unification of
African States under British rule.

No one, not even correspondents or public, had envisaged the
dramatic turn of events that marked the beginning of the war. It was
certainly not to be a leisurely campaign and as Winston Churchill
remarked, ' "as far as you can as quickly as you can" must be the
motto of the war correspondent'. On 20 October, British and Boers
clashed at Talana where the British repulsed the enemy but with high
losses. The town of Dundee was abandoned the next day, the troops
falling back on Ladysmith. When General Sir Redvers Buller arrived at
the end of October to take up his position as Commander-in-Chief,
South Africa, the Boers were already in a strong position. They had

isolated a large number of troops in Mafeking, Kimberley, and Ladysmith, and controlled the north of Natal to the Tugela River and were only 120 miles from the vital sea port of Durban.

The essence of Buller's plan was the lifting of the three sieges before his troops could invade the Boer Republics and defeat the enemy. He accordingly ordered Lord Methuen with his column to advance up the Western Railway and relieve Kimberley and Mafeking, while he would move in to Natal to the rescue of Ladysmith. While the various columns of the London press gave headlines to the concentration of troops from 'Our War Correspondent', they also extolled the heroism of the *Morning Post* war correspondent, Winston S. Churchill, during an engagement between the Boers and an armoured train. Churchill had travelled quickly to the front. Arriving at Estcourt, he once again encountered an old Harrovian friend, Leo Amery, now the chief war correspondent of *The Times*. After the war Leo Amery edited with B. Williams the mammoth seven volumes of *The Times History of the War in South Africa*. Winston Churchill was ironically to write in one of his dispatches, 'A week ago I pointed out the many defects in the construction and the great dangers of employment of that forlorn military machine ... nicknamed "Wilson's death trap".' It was precisely one of these 'forlorn military machines' that caused him to be captured and to raise a controversy in the press about the rights of war correspondents in the field.

The *Daily Mail* among others gave numerous versions of the story, some from their own men in the field, others from agency or Boer sources:

### ARMOURED TRAIN FIGHT
#### Boer account of the engagement near Colenso
##### *Mr. Churchill wounded and a prisoner*

Lorenco Marques, Nov. 18

A despatch, dated Pretoria, November 16, says: General Joubert advises the Government that a Transvaal force had a sharp engagement with the British on Tuesday between Colenso and Estcourt.

An armoured train came out suddenly round a kopje and fired on the burghers with a Nordenfelt and Maxims. The burghers on the other side of the kopje made a detour and placed stones on the line. Three armoured trucks and two

Boer War: the action between the Boers and the British armoured train at Estcourt when Winston Churchill was captured (watercolour by Rene Bull).

ordinary carriages were derailed. Firing ensued, during which the locomotive managed to uncouple, and retired with the rest of the train. The British lost two killed, ten wounded, and fifty six taken prisoners. Among the latter was Mr. Winston Churchill, correspondent of the 'Morning Post'. The prisoners are being brought to Pretoria. Our loss was five slightly wounded.

Although Churchill protested from his prison in Pretoria that he was a correspondent, not entitled to be held, the Boers refused to release him. Churchill's claim for non-combatant status was also under discussion as there was some doubt of the role he played that day. Some newspapers were openly hostile towards Churchill and the *London Phoenix* (23 November 1899) went as far as recommending to the Boers that he be shot:

> It is to be sincerely hoped that Mr. Churchill will not be shot. At the same time the Boer General cannot be blamed should he order his execution. A non-combatant has no right to carry arms. In the Franco-Prussian War all non-combatants who carried arms were promptly executed, when they were caught; and we can hardly expect the Boers to be more humane than were the highly civilized French and Germans . . .

The *Westminster Gazette* of 26 December 1899 was also hostile towards him:

> . . . we confess that we hardly understand the application which
> Mr. Churchill is reported to have made to General Joubert
> asking to be released on the ground that he was a newspaper
> correspondent and had taken no part in the fighting. We
> rubbed our eyes when we read this—have we not read glowing
> (and apparently authentic) accounts of Mr. Churchill's
> heroic exploits in the armoured train affair? General Joubert,
> apparently, rubbed his eyes too. He replied that
> Mr. Churchill—unknown to him personally—was detained
> because all the Natal papers attributed the escape of the
> armoured train to his bravery and exertion . . . Mr. Churchill's
> non-combatancy is indeed a mystery, but one thing is clear—
> that he cannot have the best of both worlds. His letter to
> General Joubert absolutely disposes of that probable V.C.
> with which numerous correspondents have decorated him.

Before the Boers had had time to make up their minds, Churchill escaped and his story cabled to the *Morning Post* was widely used by other newspapers. An insignificant event in itself, the escape of Winston Churchill was grasped by the public as an adventurous interlude in the war. To Churchill, his capture and escape was an unexpected bonus in bringing his name before the public.

> Lorenco Marques. Dec. 21 (10 p.m.)
>
> On the afternoon of the 12th the Transvaal Government's
> Secretary for War informed me that there was little chance
> of my release. I therefore resolved to escape. The same night
> I left the State Schools Prison at Pretoria by climbing the
> wall when the sentries' backs were turned momentarily.
> I walked through the streets of the town without any
> disguise, meeting many burghers, but I was not challenged.
> In the crowd I got through the piquets of the Town Guard
> and struck the Delagoa Bay Railroad. I walked along it,
> evading the watchers at the bridge and culverts. The out
> 11.10 goods train from Pretoria arrived, and before it had
> reached full speed I boarded with great difficulty, and hid
> myself under the coal sacks. I jumped from the train before
> dawn and sheltered during the day in a small wood in
> company with a huge vulture, which displayed a lively
> interest in me.

I walked on at dusk. There were no more trains that night. The danger of meeting the guards of the railway line continued, but I was obliged to follow it, as I had no compass or map. I had to make wide detours to avoid the bridges, stations, and huts, and in the dark I frequently fell into small watercourses. My progress was very slow, and chocolate is not a satisfying food. The outlook was gloomy, but I persevered with God's help for five days. The food I had to have was very precarious. I was lying up at daylight and walking on at night time, and meanwhile my escape had been discovered and my description telegraphed everywhere. All the trains were searched. Everyone was on the watch for me. Four wrong people were arrested. But on the seventh day I managed to board a train beyond Middelburg, whence there is a direct service to Delagoa. I was concealed in a railway truck under great sacks. I had a small store of good water with me. I remained hidden, chancing discovery.

The Boers searched the train at Nomati Poort, but did not search deep enough, so after sixty hours of misery I came safely here. I am very weak, but I am free. I have lost many pounds in weight, but I am lighter in heart, and I avail myself of this moment, in the condition in which I find myself—which is a witness to my earnestness—to urge an unflinching and uncompromising prosecution of the war.

Chievely Camp, Dec. 26 (10.30 a.m.) Mr. Winston Churchill is once more in the British camp. *Central News.*

Churchill found himself the idol of the public, the star war correspondent and the subject of a popular music hall song, sung by T. E. Dunville, the Lancashire music-hall comedian:

> You've heard of Winston Churchill
> This is all I have to say
> He's the latest and the greatest
> Correspondent of the day.

Because of what Churchill wrote and the way he wrote it, Lord Roberts was not anxious to have him as a correspondent but eventually condescended '. . . for your father's sake'. Largely because of Churchill's dispatches, soldier correspondents were highly discouraged, so it is doubly puzzling to see Churchill still as a war correspondent but also commissioned in the South African Light Horse. Sir Francis Patrick Fletcher Vane as a Captain in the 3rd Battalion, Royal Lancashire Regiment, also acted as a soldier correspondent and wrote for the

*Daily News*, *Manchester Guardian*, and *Westminster Gazette*. Another soldier correspondent was Lt. T. J. Dunn of the Scottish Horse, while Lt. C. H. Temple represented the *Navy and Army Illustrated*. But Churchill was not contented to rest on his laurels and he continued to report the war for his newspaper, until 28 June 1900 when he finished his last dispatch for Oliver Borthwick:

> Such as it is, the work at least represents the changing moods
> and forecasts of the camp, and if in this fashion it has helped
> to bring those who have borne the long anxiety at home into
> sympathy with their soldiers at the wars, I shall be content,
> and even be bold to ask the reader to dismiss me with a smile.

Not all the correspondents enjoyed unlimited telegram expenses and both John B. Atkins and Filson Young of the *Manchester Guardian* were told that only short news telegrams were to be sent and that fuller reports were to be sent by mail. This did not seem to appeal to Filson Young, whose brother was forced to act as a peacemaker between the editor and correspondent in the field. Filson Young became the literary editor of the *Daily Mail* after the Boer War, and in 1914 as a lieutenant, R.N.V.R., went to France with the B.E.F. as *The Times* correspondent. The *Manchester Guardian*, being short of material for fuller accounts, returned to their old practice of reprinting accounts from other newspapers, usually the *Daily Telegraph*, whose team led by the veteran Bennet Burleigh were providing excellent coverage for their readers.

Amongst the correspondents of the *Daily Telegraph* were Charles Falconer, Percy Sutherland Bullen, awarded the first gold medal ever given to a foreign correspondent by the University of Missouri, and Lieutenant-Colonel Robert MacHugh, a veteran of the Spanish-American War who would go on to report the Russo-Japanese War and the Balkan War for his newspaper. Bennet Burleigh, like Rene Bull, was careful to keep in the open and as the Boers closed on Ladysmith remarked to the artist of the *Illustrated London News*, 'Prior my boy, it is all over; we are beaten, and it means investment. We shall be all locked up in Ladysmith.' Organizing his horse and cart, Burleigh left the other correspondents including MacHugh of the *Daily Telegraph* who, like Melton Prior, elected to remain. But life in the open was equally as disagreeable and dangerous as being besieged. While Richard

Boer War: Melton Prior of the *Illustrated London News* sketching, 1899.

Harding Davis was accompanied by his portable bath-tub, Rene Bull and Bennet Burleigh used to '... before breakfast ... ride out in our pyjamas to the river to bath.'

As *The Times* had done during the Crimea, various newspapers started funds, the most famous of which was the *Daily Mail* 'Absent-Minded Beggar' fund, named after Rudyard Kipling's famous poem. Everywhere in Britain were to be seen statues, medals, and reproductions of the famous R. Caton Woodville painting, 'The Gentlemen in Khaki'. Messrs. Kinnear Ltd., the cigarette-makers, announced that '... by special arrangement with the London *Daily Mail*' they were including an exquisite miniature reproduction of the picture in each packet of their various brands of cigarettes; while famous actors, actresses and music-hall stars held public recitals of the poem to raise money. The *Daily Mail* had reached circulation of a million by 1900 and it chartered special trains to distribute copies beyond the traditional Home Counties boundary. The fund organized by the *Daily Telegraph* and *Scotsman* was less publicized but had an equal response and by January 1900 raised £100,000. Various commercial concerns sent salt and other commodities to the troops. Private individuals organized collections, the knitting of socks, the getting together of pipes and other items for troops. Even Queen Victoria ordered that each of her soldiers should be given for Christmas a box of chocolates in a specially designed tin. Some of these gifts never arrived and one soldier told a correspondent that the only safe way to send out cigarettes was to label them boot-laces, and whisky as 'Books for our Boys from Y.M.C.A.' The war correspondents also contributed to the various funds and on the capture of Bloemfontein by Lord Roberts's force they organized a concert on behalf of the Widow's and Orphan's Fund of London and Bloemfontein, where they raised £300.

Of the three sieges which the soldiers now set out to relieve, Mafeking was considered by the public far the most important. There was something about Mafeking that inspired the public, something intangible that neither Kimberley nor Ladysmith had, although of the three it was the least important from a military point of view. The correspondents who were still at liberty or had newly arrived had a life of action with plenty to write about, if the censor let it pass; those besieged spent a life of boredom. 'Beyond is the world—war and love', wrote G. W. Steevens of the *Daily Mail* bottled up with others in Ladysmith:

261

*Difficult times*

Boer War: Boers and British fighting (pencil sketch by war artist François).

You are of it, but not in it—clean out of the world. To your world and to yourself you are every bit as good as dead—except that dead men have no time to fill in. I know how a monk without a vocation feels. I know how a fly in a beer bottle feels. I know how it tastes too.

In Mafeking the feeling was the same. J. Angus Hamilton, correspondent and photographer of *The Times* and *Black and White*, wrote, 'distress is wholly absent and danger is largely a question of accident'. Vere Stent of Reuters had dispatch runners leaving every day but confessed, '. . . I have to make bricks without straw in the shape of despatches without news'. F. D. Baillie of the *Morning Post*, nicknamed 'The Major' by his press colleagues, complained that, 'In this war of "Sit down" I, for one, have worn out much patience and several pairs of trousers'.

While the Boer encirclement of the three towns was considered by some to be a mild set-back, the relieving forces suffered what could only be called in Redvers Buller's own words 'a serious reverse'. During what the public aptly dubbed 'Black Week', the largest British expeditionary force ever to leave England suffered severe defeats at Stormberg, Magersfontein, and Colenso. 'The week which extended from 10th December to 17th December, 1899,' wrote Conan Doyle, 'was the blackest one known during our generation, and the most disastrous for British arms during the century.' While some claimed that the sensationalism of the British press magnified the defeats out of all proportion, the casualty list showed otherwise. Patriotic fervour remained at its highest, and the public still took some comfort from the fact that Mafeking was still holding on. But for how long? The recruiting offices in London were besieged by volunteers eager to reverse the situation, '. . . noblemen and grooms rode knee to knee in the ranks; the Imperial Yeomanry was formed. Newspapers were also besieged with offers to act as special correspondents in South Africa, and abroad the colonies and the Empire answered the call. Patriotic pictures were painted and columns of print extolled the closeness of the Empire. 'Sons of the Blood' was a popular phrase and there was considerable pride felt in being considered British.

Especially during this campaign, the war correspondents had to have as Kipling wrote '. . . the constitution of a bullock, the digestion of an ostrich and an infinite adaptability to all circumstances', whether they were besieged or with the relieving forces. The disastrous 'Black Week' caused the War Office to appoint Lord Roberts to command in South Africa and with him, Sir Horatio Kitchener. Redvers Buller, whom a popular joke renamed 'Pigger' because he was always getting stuck, was relegated to the command of the Natal Field Force. The main task of Roberts, who arrived in Cape Town on 10 January 1900, was to follow the initial plan and relieve the three besieged towns.

The new burst of enthusiasm initiated by Roberts's appointment and that of the hero of Omdurman, Kitchener, prompted a new rush of correspondents to South Africa in various guises. Although military officers acting as correspondents were now frowned on, a number contrived to act for newspapers while also serving mainly in the newly formed Imperial Yeomanry or one of the mounted troops that abounded. But the interest was not solely British and the regular army had to contend with temperamental Frenchmen and stern and 'heavy' Germans, who more often than not were a cause of annoyance. Most of the foreign correspondents of French and German papers were with the Boers, including at Colenso the war correspondent of the French *Petit Bleu*. At Eland's River in 1900, Jean Carrere of the French paper *Matin* slid out of the trench and knelt behind it to observe the effect of the British fire through his field glasses. He only added to the troops' anxiety by drawing the Boer fire until hastily dragged by the lapels back into the trench by a cursing sergeant of some considerable service. His newspaper, however, only praised the heroism of their special correspondent under fire. The Austrian correspondent of the *Reichpost* suffered the same fate when he was unceremoniously bundled into a trench by two long-suffering privates of the Highland Light Infantry who had attracted no attention from the Boers until the correspondent appeared. Correspondents naturally drew curses from the soldiers as they attempted to observe, sometimes at great personal danger, what was happening. In Mafeking, Emerson Neilly, 'a world traveller for the *Pall Mall Gazette*', returned to his hotel to have breakfast one morning and, as his horse had hit a thorn fence, returned to the scene of action on a bicycle only to be greeted by an old soldier who shouted, 'For 'eaven's sake, Sir, dismount, yer 'andle bars' drawing fire'.

The Boer War was considered the 'last of the gentleman's wars' and this attitude was observed by the British soldiers and correspondents. If censorship was strict, the correspondents accepted it; if postal facilities were bad, they accepted it; although they often complained:

'the postal arrangements throughout the campaign have been most infamous', wrote F. D. Baillie of the *Morning Post*. Rarely did a correspondent for the sake of sensationalism or to obtain a scoop step outside the rigid rules laid down by the military censor. If there was any censure to be made, it was usually made by the press corps itself against an offending member and three French and two German correspondents were made so unwelcome that they left the action.

In Kimberley, the siege had begun on 14 October when '... the telegraph instruments in the office, which had been clicking away like a lot of noisy crickets, one by one in rapid succession, ceased their chattering and within a few seconds a dead silence reigned in the room'. The overpowering Cecil Rhodes flagrantly disobeyed nearly all the regulations with regard to dispatches put into force by the long-suffering military commander, Lieutenant-Colonel R. G. Kekewich, and insisted that Kimberley be relieved forthwith. He succeeded in getting messages through to influential people in London and the daily press. His main concern was for the safety of his diamond empire. The correspondents besieged in Kimberley found their task of sending out dispatches difficult since Kekewich's imposed censorship and also that of Cecil Rhodes cut down any relevant dispatch to the minimum. As the relieving column under Methuen pushed to the relief of Kimberley, it seemed in the town that the siege would be over before it had started. Moving up the railway line, the troops were engaged at Belmont on 23 November where they won a victory over the Boers. Edward Frederick Knight of *The Times* witnessed the action but was severely wounded and had to have his right arm amputated. Modder River, a battle fought on 28 November, was even less of a victory and many did not know whether they had won or been beaten. At Magersfontein, Lord Methuen launched a night attack on 11 December, but at daybreak the troops were held back by a line of wire and through lack of maps and intelligence the attack fell into a Boer trap and collapsed. Kimberley would have to wait and endure bombardment.

*The Times* correspondent, a wife of one of the De Beers directors, managed to get dispatches to London, mainly through the influence of Cecil Rhodes, while other correspondents were subject to the strictness of Kekewich's orders. The *Daily Telegraph* correspondent managed to send some dispatches before the siege became absolute:

> No doubt there was secret terror and alarm in many a
> household, but out of doors the people behaved exactly as

I have read of their doing during the bombardment of Paris. When they had got over their first shock of surprise and trepidation, they looked upon the Boer shelling much as they would have done upon an exhibition of fireworks. They gathered on the debris heaps and on the house tops of double-storeyed buildings, and, oblivious of any personal risk, watched with curious interest for every flash and explosion; then, when a bomb burst anywhere near them, they rushed to the spot to pick up fragments. In vain was the danger thus incurred pointed out by the military authorities; the recklessness of the Kimberley gamins, and even of many adults, in their desire to obtain gratuitous supplies of an easily-marketable commodity, knew no bounds. The price of a complete shell, of which there were several in the market, was £5, the base of a shell sold for about a sovereign, and smaller pieces fetched anything from two shillings and sixpence to fifteen shillings.

Many of the newspapermen saved up their stories for the end of the siege which they hoped would be not far away. Even then, they were not at liberty to write what they wanted. Filson Young of the *Manchester Guardian* was obliged to insert in his copy that 'The condition of the town would have been deplorable but for the administration of the De Beers Company' while Cecil Rhodes revelled in personal interviews, in his usual way. He told Charles Hands of the *Daily Mail*, a veteran of Cuba, who was later wounded on 12 May in a Boer attack on the Mafeking relief force:

> The marvellous thing about England is her luck. We have made the silliest mistakes, we have had some most incompetent generals, but we are coming out all right, as we always do. Glad to have Kimberley relieved? Of course, we are all glad, but, in Heaven's name, why was it not done sooner? Why did they not do at first what was so readily done at last? The earlier plans were different, you say? I should think they were. Do you know what General Buller's orders to Lord Methuen were with regard to Kimberley? They were these: Methuen was to come here, relieve the town, carry all the people away out of it, and then fall back to Orange River. It is scandalous. It would have been a disgrace upon England had it been carried out. It is simply monstrous.

During the siege of Kimberley, Major O'Meara in his capacity as Intelligence Officer and military censor claimed that two editorials of the local newspaper, *The Diamond Fields Advertiser*, were 'extremely injurious to the interests of the Army and the defence of the town'. The editor was so furious that he stopped publication of the newspaper completely.

There were many correspondents in the other two besieged towns, especially Ladysmith, which suffered perhaps the worst, and most of them managed by some means to get news through to their papers. One was Nevinson of the *Daily Chronicle* and another George Lynch of the same newspaper, who remained only for the early part of the siege and was captured when he ventured out of the town to try to join General Buller's column. He was imprisoned at Pretoria, released on the fall of the town and invalided home. He then set out for China and the relief of the Legations. During the First World War he represented the *Illustrated London News* and *Westminster Gazette* and invented a special pair of gloves for handling barbed wire. Lieutenant-Colonel Robert MacHugh remained behind for the *Daily Telegraph* when Bennet Burleigh left, W. T. Maude represented the *Graphic* while his friend Melton Prior as always sketched for the *Illustrated London News.* H. H. S. Pearse not only represented the *Daily News* but with other journalists produced the *Ladysmith Bombshell*, a free cartoon-type newspaper. While the *Ladysmith Lyre*, edited by G. W. Steevens, prided itself on the inaccuracy of its news, the *Bombshell* tried to distract the population by such pertinent remarks as: 'If the Relief Column takes a day and a half to march a yard and a half, how much longer will the price of eggs be at 10*s*. 7*d*. per dozen'. Both papers were produced by the stylographic process.

The veteran brother of Cecil Rhodes, Colonel F. Rhodes, was in Ladysmith reporting as always for *The Times* while a fellow colonel, Lionel James, also represented the same newspaper as well as Reuter's. Corporal Ferrand, a trooper in the Imperial Light Horse, wrote for the *Morning Post* and, like G. W. Steevens of the *Daily Mail*, died at Ladysmith. Ernest Smith, a photographer as well as a spirited journalist, wrote for the *Morning Leader* and Reid seconded Steevens for the *Daily Mail.* During Steevens's illness which eventually led to his death, the *Daily Mail* reported that 'Mr. Reid, . . . is acting during his chief's short, we trust, indisposition'. Melton Prior noted that there were about eight other correspondents in the town from various newspapers. Lieutenant Stabb, R.N.V.R., represented the *Times of India* and died from enteric a few days before the same illness killed G. W. Steevens.

*Difficult times*

Boer War: correspondents in
Ladysmith — Ernest W. Smith,
Melton Prior and H.H.S. Pearse.

Boer War: Melton Prior's shelter on the banks of the Klip river.

W. Maxwell, later to head a section of the British Secret Service, reported for the *Standard*.

The bombardment of the town was intense sometimes but boredom was the worst enemy and G. W. Steevens undoubtedly expressed the thoughts of many others when he wrote:

> Weary, stale, flat, unprofitable, the whole thing. At first, to be besieged and bombarded was a thrill; then it was a joke; now it is nothing but a weary, weary, weary bore. We do nothing but eat and drink and sleep—just exist dismally. We have forgotten when the siege began; and now we are beginning not to care when it ends.
>
> For my part, I feel it will never end. It will go on just as now, languid fighting, languid cessation for ever and ever. We shall drop off one by one, and listlessly die of old age.

When the news of Steevens's death reached Lord Roberts he cabled to the *Daily Mail* in London, 'Deeply regret death of your talented correspondent, Steevens'. Kitchener expressed his sorrow at his death:

> I wish all correspondents were like him. I suppose they will try and follow in his footsteps. I am sure I hope they will. He was the model correspondent, the best I have ever known and I should like you to say how greatly grieved I am at his death.

Mafeking was also in the same plight, although for some reason the spirited messages of Baden-Powell stating 'All's well' seemed to inspire a confidence out of all proportion to the importance of this small railway town. Besieged correspondents also made the best of it. They knew, unlike those in Kimberley and Ladysmith, that all eyes were on them and their copy carried out by native runners at great expense was tinted with what the public wanted, personal adventure. As Angus Hamilton, representing both *The Times* and the *Black and White*, wrote, indifferent to the siege and its importance, 'There is lacking but one thing—war. The troops want it to prove their efficiency, the journalists demand it to justify their existence.' With his 'bomb-proof' horse however, even Hamilton, indifferent as he was, could not help but capitalize a personal experience. A shell landed in his room and he had a fellow correspondent photograph him holding what remained of his kit, a slipper. He was undoubtedly the most perceptive and experienced reporter in Mafeking. Reuter's had their man on the spot, Vere Stent, a great favourite amongst the other journalists as he was

*Difficult times*

Boer War: the grave of G. W. Steevens of the *Daily Mail* in Ladysmith. On the right is W. K. Dickson, one of the first moving-picture cameramen in South Africa.

Boer War: the meeting of Sir George White and Lord Dundonald on the relief of Ladysmith.

Boer War: Lady Sarah Wilson, special war correspondent for the *Daily Mail* (watercolour by Rene Bull).

well supplied with money. Many of the correspondents were nearly broke as they had not expected to be away from Cape Town so long, but Stent was well supplied with money by his agency. 'Major' F. D. Baillie representing the *Morning Post* was not only short of money but had incurred heavy gambling debts when the relief finally arrived. He managed to hand over to a relief and head for Kimberley. Emerson Neilly wrote for the *Pall Mall Gazette* and seemed thoroughly to enjoy the inconvenience and discomfort of the siege while Whales of the *Daily Mail* managed to get some dispatches out of the town. Lady Sarah Wilson offered her services to the *Daily Mail* which were readily accepted but she was taken by the Boers on 4 December as she attempted to enter the town. She was later exchanged for a Boer prisoner and established a bomb-proof shelter in the town displaying a large Union Jack. She was rather put out when J. Angus Hamilton held a dinner on 2 January 1900 for Baden-Powell's staff and other correspondents but excluded her because she was an amateur. The tragedy of Mafeking was the death of E. G. Parslow of the *Daily Chronicle*, which many newspapers preferred to headline as 'Accidental'. The correspondents had a reputation for hard drinking and the circumstances of Parslow's death could easily have been misconstrued by the public. A verdict of accidental death saved any embarrassment. As it was, Parslow had become assistant editor of the *Mafeking Mail*, a siege paper which incidentally is still in business today, printed by the local printer Mr. Townsend who was also responsible for the siege money. On the second day of publication, at 10 a.m. on 2 November 1899, Parslow got into an argument with Lieutenant Murchison of the artillery in the bar of Dixon's Hotel. Eventually pushed too far, Parslow exclaimed to Murchison 'You're no gentleman', to which the officer replied by pulling out his revolver and killing the correspondent. The offender was ordered to be tried and when Mafeking was relieved served his sentence on the Isle of Wight. Parslow was buried that evening at a ceremony attended by the other pressmen. His coffin, draped with a Union Jack, was carried to the grave by F. D. Baillie, J. Angus Hamilton, Hellewell, Emerson Neilly and the correspondent of the Press Association.

But Mafeking was not so cut off as one might have thought. At the beginning of the siege, an American journalist of Reuter's, Pearson by name, visited the town and inspected the defences before riding south to Cape Town to cable his report.

The correspondents in the besieged towns had the advantage of a captive audience and any trivia they wrote was well received. Those in the open found their task more exacting. When Kimberley was relieved on 15 February 1900, various journalists collected for the march to relieve Mafeking. The newspapers sent their best men as the relief of the heroic little town would be the climax of the war. Charles Falconer represented the *Daily Telegraph*, Charles Hands the *Daily Mail*, A. W. A. Pollock *The Times*, John Stuart the *Morning Post*, and Filson Young the *Manchester Guardian*. Meanwhile Roberts's plan had paid off well. The newly reinforced British army relieved Kimberley on 15 February 1900 and Ladysmith on 26 February.

But a much more important event in the course of the war occurred during February when on 27 February, the nineteenth anniversary of the disaster of Majuba Hill, Roberts captured the Boer General Cronje at Paardeberg. The plan of the attack at Paardeberg was kept entirely secret and various misleading orders for troop movements were given

Boer War: Bennet Burleigh brings the news to Lord Roberts that Bloemfontein has surrendered.

over the wires and then cancelled in code. To aid in the deception, Roberts used Wolseley's old trick and 'confidential tips' about the troop concentration were given to a correspondent of the English press with strict orders to keep it to himself. However, when the dispatches of the unfortunate correspondent were published in his newspaper, the government telegraphed Lord Roberts that there had been a 'serious indiscretion on the part of someone of his staff'. Later, when the true line of advance became evident, the correspondent in question complained to Lord Roberts about 'unfair and dishonest treatment'. On 13 March the British entered Bloemfontein, capital of the Orange Free State. Fred. W. Unger, a correspondent of the *Daily Express*, had the honour of carrying not only his but Lord Roberts's dispatch from Bloemfontein to Kimberley. Unger had already become somewhat of a legend as the man who had interviewed Kruger, and by plainly explaining his situation managed to be enrolled as an official dispatch rider and so claimed the South African war medal.

The correspondents actually made news on the entry into Bloemfontein as the *Black and White* recorded:

> The war correspondents have been muzzled so much, that it is
> a pleasure to find some of them distinguishing themselves.
> When the Boers left Bloemfontein, three of the newspapermen
> with Lord Roberts dashed forward on horseback, and after a
> hard race for the honour, a correspondent of an Australian
> paper was the first to enter the town ... The three corres-
> pondents involved were Bennet Burleigh of the *Daily
> Telegraph*, the correspondent of the *Daily News* and the
> winner, the war correspondent of the *Sydney Herald*.

When he entered the town, Roberts suppressed the Boer newspaper, *The Friend of the Free State*, paid an indemnity for use of the plant and published a paper for the soldiers called the *Friend*, with Rudyard Kipling as editor and P. Landon, H. A. Gwynne, F. W. Buxton, and Julian Ralph, a *Daily Mail* war correspondent, as contributors.

The demand for news was such that no expense was spared by the leading papers.

> Since the moment of the outbreak of hostilities [wrote the
> editor of the *Black and White*], we have been enabled each
> week to present an unrivalled selection of pictures, sketches
> and photographs dealing with the progress of events ... This
> has been possible only through the untiring efforts of the
> little army of correspondents which the proprietors raised
> to chronicle on the spot the stirring events of the campaign ...

These included a gentleman whose '... name we may not give' and at Pretoria, '... two gentlemen whose names we must withhold for very obvious reasons'. The *Black and White* was not the only paper and others employed more correspondents than they had ever done before.

Newspapers reinforced their teams of correspondents even though censorship was strong and newspapers were often forced to announce that '... though many actions have probably taken place ... so strict is the censorship at present that very little news has come through'. In these circumstances sensational papers were tempted to fabricate news.

> News comes via Aden [wrote the editor of *Black and White*],
> where most severe censorship takes place. It is said that the
> authorities there have ordered copies of all English papers ...
> with a view to picking out how far the telegrams published
> differ from those ... allowed to go through ... It should

Boer War: City Imperial Volunteers manhandling a Maxim gun (pen and ink sketch by Charles E. Fripp of the *Graphic*).

> throw an interesting light on the news manufacturers of
> our most sensational papers!

The list of correspondents in the field is imposing, so important did the press and public view the war, but their task was difficult. News was difficult to find, and what could be found was subject to rough censorship. Correspondents even lacked 'news of the camp gossip' as, it was reported, soldiers had strict orders not to speak to war correspondents. Sending the news was also difficult as the Boers, like the Afghans, enjoyed cutting the telegraph wires. However, by the end of 1899, 'The Marconi system has just been established at De Aar. Considering all the difficulties of the cutting of wires it seems a pity that the use of the wireless system was not thought of earlier.'

The number of men in the *Black and White* team was formidable but not quite as many as that of *The Times* which boasted twenty-four correspondents; C. E. Finlason, Lester Ralph, son of Julian Ralph the *Daily Mail* war correspondent, George Clark Musgrave, 'Late Special from Cuba', Mortimer Menpes, the famous artist and sculptor who later

Boer War: a war correspondent amidst the wreck of his tent after a violent rainstorm.

held a one-man exhibition of his work entitled 'The War in South Africa', the American, S. M. Lawrence, plus G. W. Wilson, A. A. Sykes, Harrington Mann, F. A. Stewart, H. McCormick, and D. Giles among others made up the *Black and White* team which the other illustrated newspapers found hard to equal. In 1900 the famous Bennet Burleigh also joined their ranks. The *Graphic* headed their effort with the work of their best man, Frederick Villiers, who still used his green roadster bicycle while the rival *Sphere*, a newcomer to illustrated newspapers, used the talented Lance Thackery and the services of the Earl of Rosslyn who, while serving in Thornycroft's House, managed to write for the *Sphere* and the *Daily Mail*. He was captured by the Boers, managed to escape but was recaptured and sent to Waterval prison. He succeeded '. . . in getting a telegram through to the *Mail*, days ahead of official news, announcing the release of the prisoners and conveying the welcome information that Pretoria would offer no resistance to Lord Roberts'. The *Navy and Army Illustrated*, always renowned for its photographic content and fine printing, had on the spot as one of their men the talented Hartford Hartland while the *Morning Post* employed among others Henry Provost Battersby. He was wounded and invalided home but took the field again during the Somaliland campaign and also during the First World War when he represented Reuter's until gassed and invalided home in 1918. The *Morning Post* also had a female correspondent, Mrs. Mary Kingsley, who had performed sterling work nursing Boer prisoners and who eventually died on Whit Monday, 1900. In accordance with her wishes she was buried at sea. The large number of Empire troops also brought the correspondents of their newspapers, such as Cameron, an Australian war correspondent who represented a number of newspapers, and also a representative of the *Melbourne Herald*. From Canada, the press corps was headed by Frederick Hamilton of the *Toronto Globe*. John Rathom reported for the Australian press and Andrew Paterson covered the war for the Sydney *Morning Herald* and Melbourne *Argus* as well as acting for Reuter's.

Reuter's were as usual strongly represented by such men as Roderick Jones, later to succeed the Baron Reuter, son of the founder, in 1915 and to be Director of Propaganda in the Ministry of Information from 1916 to 1918, and Thomas William MacKenzie. The Hon. John George Maydon reported the war from Magersfontein to the capture of Bloemfontein as did Alfred Kinnear, the veteran star correspondent of the Central News Agency, and Theodore John Valentine Fielden who during the First World War was thanked by Lord Kitchener for his services to recruiting. Charles Sydney Goldman could not get enough news of the war and after riding with Buller's relief force to Ladysmith joined the cavalry on the western side in their advance north. He later became Member of Parliament for Penryn and Falmouth. Ernest Bennet still reported for the *Westminster Gazette* but his main work was done as a volunteer medical orderly. Edgar Wallace, later to become famous as a novelist, represented the Reuter Agency up to 1900 when he transferred to the *Daily News* and then to the *Daily Mail* with A. G. Hales. One of his dispatches reported Boer atrocities at Vlakfontein, which caused the Secretary of State for War to threaten punishment unless he toned down his reports.

Not all correspondents were journalists or ex-military or serving men. The *Western Morning Post* employed Dr. James Alexander Kay, accredited to the staff of Lord Roberts as their correspondent. James Alexander Kay had been a doctor in the Transvaal but was not fully qualified before the war and had returned to Dublin to take his finals examination, leaving a 'locum'. On his return he found his house ran-

Boer War: Edgar Wallace,
war correspondent for
the *Daily Mail*.

sacked and his practice stolen. Suspected of being a British spy, he offered his services as a surgeon in Ladysmith where he served during the siege and returned in 1900 to Pretoria as a special correspondent.

Many of the correspondents were wounded and captured and a number killed. Two correspondents with the Australian forces, A. G. Hales of the *Daily News* and Mr. Lambie of the *Melbourne Age*, met the Boers attempting to escape from an ambush, which killed Lambie and wounded Hales.

> We drifted a few hundred yards behind the advance party [wrote Hales], when a number of horsemen made a dash from the Kopjes which we were skirting . . . There was not time for poetry, it was a case of sit tight and ride hard or surrender and be made prisoners. Lambie shouted to me: 'Let's make a dash, Hales,' and we made it. The Boers were very close to us before we knew anything concerning their presence. Some of them were behind us, and some extended along the edge of the kopjes by which we had to pass to get to the British line in front; all of them were galloping in on

Boer War: Lambie is killed and A. G. Hales wounded attempting to escape from the Boers.

us, shooting as they rode, and shouting to us to surrender, and had we been wise men, we should have thrown up our hands, for it was almost hopeless to try and ride through the rain of lead that whistled around us. It was no wonder that we were hit, the wonder to me is that we were not filled with lead, for some of the bullets came so close to me that I think I should know them again if I met them in a shop window. We were racing by this time . . . . A voice called in good English: 'Throw up your hands, you d . . . fools.' But the galloping fever was on us both, and we only crouched lower on our horses' backs, and rode all the harder, for even a barnyard fowl loves liberty.

All at once I saw my comrade throw up his hands with a spasmodic gesture. He rose in his stirrups, and fairly bounded high out of his saddle, and as he spun round in the air I saw the red blood on the white face, and I knew that death had come to him sudden and sharp . . .

Hales was wounded in the temple and losing consciousness fell from his horse and was captured. The fate of the two correspondents was discovered by Mr. Cameron, the representative of the *Melbourne Herald,* who crossed the Boer lines under a flag of truce. Lambie's body was brought back for burial.

The public at home were soon in much the same frame of mind about Baden-Powell and Mafeking as they had been about Gordon and Khartoum and daily they scanned their papers for news of fresh developments. The news of the relief of the town after 216 days was greeted with unprecedented outbursts of enthusiasm and rejoicing throughout Britain, in many towns the police having to be called out to keep order. The news that the Boers had abandoned the siege of Mafeking was obtained by the enterprising Reuter's correspondent in Pretoria and smuggled out of the town and over the border in a sandwich before being put on the wires to London. At exactly 9.17 pm on 18 May the message arrived in Reuter's London office. In twenty minutes the news had spread down Fleet Street to the west end of London. The *Daily Telegraph* was the first newspaper to place a placard outside their office while in the composing rooms the pages of the various newspapers were being made ready to be first on the street. So infectious was the atmosphere that many a young newsboy gave away copies of his paper in the excitement, while others with a better head for business charged double the price and were quickly sold out. The relief of Mafeking spawned a new word in the English language, 'to maffick', and a popular song started, 'Mother may I go and maffick, run around and hinder traffic.'

There were mixed feelings among the correspondents in the various besieged towns as they were relieved. Emerson Neilly remarked that 'Frankly our defender's pluck did not save Mafeking, great and heroic though that pluck was. The cowardice of the enemy saved us.' He admitted that, as the town was relieved, 'I did not think it was possible for human joy to reach such a white-hot pitch.' June 1900, with the action at Diamond Hill, seemed to most to be the turning point in the war and the general opinion was that the end was in sight. In fact the Boers continued to fight until 1902.

During this war in South Africa, fifteen correspondents were killed or lost their lives through disease. Those who succumbed to disease were Albert F. Adams and Albert Julian Adams of the Exchange Telegraph Company, James Innes Calder of the Reuter Agency; William

Boer War: war correspondents by their shelter in Mafeking — Emerson Neilly, Vere Stent, F. D. Baillie and J. Angus Hamilton.

Sidney Inder, an ex-sergeant of the 2nd Volunteer Battalion of the Border Regiment, who was appointed in 1900 to the Imperial Military Railways at Bloemfontein while also acting for the *Westmorland Gazette,* died of pneumonia; while Robert Mitchell of the *Standard* died of fever at Ladysmith, as did the famous G. W. Steevens. Another to die of fever was H. H. Spooner of the Sydney *Evening News* and Mrs. Mary Kingsley of the *Morning Post.* Those who were killed were: George Alfred Farrand, acting for the *Morning Post* and serving in the Imperial Light Horse; W. J. Lambie of the *Melbourne Age;* E. G. Parslow of the *Daily Chronicle,* who was murdered in Mafeking; E. D. Scott of the *Manchester Courier,* a veteran traveller and expert on South Africa who immediately put his knowledge at the disposal of the *Courier* on the outbreak of war; and two 'soldier correspondents', Major G. L. Sidney Ray of the Northumberland Fusiliers and Lieutenant

T. J. Dunn of the Scottish Horse. A memorial to these men was erected in the crypt of St. Paul's Cathedral by the Institute of Journalists.

In mid-1900, another incident ousted the South African War from the headlines. With little opposition from the Dowager Empress of China or the Imperial Army, a rebellious faction known as Boxers had created havoc in the countryside around Peking, murdering and looting Christian mission stations in an effort to drive out all foreigners. On 28 May 1900 the *Corps Diplomatique* had requested guards from the respective fleets anchored off the coast. By 16 June matters had so deteriorated that Sir Claude MacDonald, the British Ambassador, had telegraphed for additional help. Admiral Seymour quickly assembled a force to march on the capital but was baulked by the Boxers and was unable to get through to Peking. In the Legations a decision was being reached as to what action should be taken, 'If to stay meant probably massacre, to go meant certain destruction'. On the afternoon of 20 June, the Legation quarter was in a state of siege. The following day, rumours in London announced that Seymour's column had reached Peking and without any concrete details, the newspapers continued to speculate.

On 29 June the last telegram was received from the Legations, 'Foreign community besieged in Legations. Situation desperate. *Make Haste!*' On 7 July doubt about the fate of the Europeans in Peking was felt when a Reuter dispatch announced: 'Prepare to hear the worst!' Nine days later the fate of the Legations seems to have been sealed when the *Daily Mail* published the dispatch of their Shanghai correspondent, F. W. Sutterlee, headed 'The Peking Massacre'.

The dispatch described the monumental attacks and the heroic defence of the inhabitants. Those who did not fall under the hail of bullets were '. . . put to the sword in the most atrocious manner'. 'It would be foolish and unmanly,' concluded *The Times*, 'to affect to doubt the awful truth.' The *Black and White* in their issue of 28 July carried a photograph of the British Legation staff who had been 'murdered' and commenced their leader article, 'The heroic manner in which Europeans, especially the English men and women, died at their posts in Peking, was perpetuated by a national requiem in St. Paul's Cathedral last Monday . . .'. The same magazine continued that the:

. . . British Legation, a structure surrounded by grounds,

bordered by high walls which isolated it from the putrid
filth of the town was perfectly adapted . . . to social
gatherings, but it was, alas, less capable of enduring the
horrors of a long siege.

The public had renewed its hope when the American State Department announced the receipt of a message from their Legation. Loud
and violent accusations were soon being flung at the *Daily Mail. The
Times* examined the relevant documents and facts and reported that
they '. . . are conclusive as to the good faith of the *Daily Mail* in
publishing it'. Sutterlee it appeared had been a swindler and a gun-
runner amongst other things and 'You will see,' wrote Morrison of
*The Times*, their correspondent in Peking, 'that the *Daily Mail* did not
exercise a very wise choice in the appointment of their correspondent.'
The defenders still managed to hold out as an international relief force
struggled to save them.

Dr. Ernest Morrison, *The Times* Peking correspondent who kept a
diary throughout the siege and later wrote it up in two gripping
dispatches for his paper, noted during the first onslaught that 'I killed
at least six!' With the relief force were other journalists eager for a
repeat of Mafeking. George Lynch, who had immediately left South
Africa and the *Daily Chronicle* when he heard the news, had been
commissioned by the *Daily Express* and *Sphere*, Alfred Cunningham
represented the *Daily Mail* and *New York Sun*, Emile Joseph Dillon
the *Daily Telegraph* and J. C. Williamson reported for a large number
of New Zealand newspapers while Pierre Loti among others represented
the French and foreign press. Andrew Paterson represented the
Sydney *Morning Herald*, as previously and as he was later to do
during the First World War. On the morning of 14 August, the
defenders heard the guns of the advancing relief force. By 2.30, the
first British troops had entered the city and advanced up Canal Street
to the British Legation. Peking was relieved and the newspaper reports
caused nearly as great a reaction as the relief of Mafeking. 'It was a
tremendous score our people being first,' wrote the British Ambassador
with pride, while Dr. Morrison was still putting the finishing touches to
the account which he had been writing under the most difficult circumstances for the last fifty-five days. His was the first eye-witness dispatch
to appear and it shocked the public with its grim details:

> As darkness came on [ran a typical passage], the most terrible
> cries were heard in the city, most demoniacal and unforgettable,

the cries of the Boxers, *Sha Kweitze*, Kill the Devils—mingled
with the shrieks of the victims and the groans of the dying.
For the Boxers were sweeping through the city massacring
the native Christians and burning them alive in their homes.

Later other eye witnesses, not always journalists, published their
accounts of the ordeal in Peking; that of Corporal William Gregory of
the Royal Marines, one of the original Legation guard, appeared in the
*Daily Malta Chronicle,* for which the corporal received ten pounds. The
newspapermen and their editors once again returned to the prime
important question of South Africa.

Besides news of the fighting, the specials reported facts concerning
the treatment of prisoners by the Boers and acts of treachery committed
by them. The *Standard* correspondent in Pretoria wrote, 'However
humane the Boers may have shown themselves in the treatment of the
wounded . . . their conduct towards prisoners has violated almost every
principle of justice and has been directly at variance with the usage of
civilised nations.' The public were beginning to tire of the war which
seemed to drag on without positive results. Kitchener soon became
Commander-in-Chief, South Africa, and embarked on a firm offensive
policy to break the Boers. He constructed concentration camps,
perhaps one of the most controversial aspects of the war, and divided
up the area of war into various pockets with wire and block houses.
These areas were then invaded and the Boers rounded up; but success
was slow and the Boer still showed himself capable of inflicting
humiliating defeats on the British. At last in 1902 the government
decided that the only logical outcome was a negotiated peace, which
was signed and concluded with the treaty of Vereeniging which gave
generous terms to the Boers.

Newspaper correspondents had been excluded from the peace
discussions at Vereeniging but, as usual, were not to be thwarted.
Edgar Wallace of the *Daily Mail* kept passing the spot by train, having
arranged with one of the soldiers guarding the camp to signal him when
peace was signed. The action of the soldier blowing his nose with a
white handkerchief, one of Wallace's pre-arranged signals, gave the
correspondent the information he wanted. Arriving at the telegraph
office, he wired to the *Daily Mail,* the following: 'Have bought you
1,000 Rand Collieries'. This inoffensive message passed the censor and
arrived in London on a Sunday before the news had even reached the
government. Unfortunately, the *Daily Mail* did not publish a Sunday

edition and the correspondent was robbed of a world scoop. The following morning's edition, however, carried the full story forty-eight hours ahead of the government and many rival newspapers. To prevent any leaks of information, the entire production and editorial staff of the *Daily Mail* had been locked in Carmelite House for the night until the news was public property. Edgar Wallace's resourcefulness in getting the news home first annoyed Lord Kitchener to such an extent that he caused the following letter to be sent to the special correspondent in an attempt to end his journalistic career:

Censor's Office, Johannesburg,
July 1, 1902.

Dear Sir,
I have been instructed to write and inform you that in consequence of your having evaded the rules of censorship subsequent to the warning you received, you will not in future be allowed to act as a war correspondent: and further, that you will not be recommended for the medal.

Edgar Wallace, far from being outraged or annoyed, treated the letter with amusement and gave the story to the newspapers, commenting that, 'one scarcely knows whether to be amused or saddened by the puerility of the War Office'.

The extent of the newsgathering effort by the larger daily and weekly newspapers during the war in South Africa was neatly summed up by the editor of *The Times* when he gave evidence before the Elgin Commission, set up to report on the conduct of the war. Concerning the conduct of the Intelligence Department, the editor stated:

We did not spend nearly enough money, or send enough officers. The eight or ten who went out did very good work, but they were fewer than the men I employed myself as *Times* correspondents, and I should have been ashamed to have sent correspondents anywhere, or even a commercial traveller with the sums of money they were given.

'We are living in difficult times', wrote Edward VII as the new century dawned. Imperial expansion had virtually ceased with the death of Queen Victoria and the various great powers now jostled for position in Europe forming alliances and consolidating their gains.

A minor punitive expedition was undertaken in Somaliland in 1903 and various correspondents arrived on the scene, some like Melton

Prior of the *Illustrated London News* direct from the Delhi Durbar of 1902, proclaiming Edward VII, Emperor of India. Prior landed and 'approaching some tents saw a flag denoting "Post Office" and knowing that my dear old companion would not be far from there, I yelled "Burleigh" '. Bennet Burleigh of the *Daily Telegraph* was his usual self. When he saw that Prior had not brought any servants or equipment he informed him '. . . there is not a camel to be had in the place . . . there is only sand . . . the shortest road to the public house is a thousand miles long'. H. P. Battersby represented the *Morning Post* during the brief campaign which was not without its usual share of disasters for British arms, including the massacre of a column under Colonel Plunkett which left only a handful of native survivors. In Melton Prior's own words, 'This was not a satisfactory campaign'.

The following year, British troops invaded Tibet as the people had not fulfilled their obligations under a treaty. Edmund Chandler of the *Daily Mail* accompanied the force and during the battle of Hot Springs four Tibetans made for him. He was wounded in twelve places. The Tibetans were no match for the superior arms of the British, whose artillery tore the Tibetans with shrapnel and mowed them down with

Somaliland: Colonel Plunkett's fight to the death near Gumburu, 17 April 1903 (a sketch by Melton Prior made' . . . from notes and information furnished direct to Bennet Burleigh').

Tibet 1904: dead Tibetan soldiers after the battle.

Tibet 1904: shelling the Niam Monastery, 26 July, with 'screw guns' of the Mountain Batteries in action.

a deadly fire. 'The whole affair did not last ten minutes,' wrote a correspondent, 'but in that short space of time the flower of the Tibetan army perished.'

In the same year, the Far East became a focal point, as Japan challenged the Imperial might of Russia. As usual there were correspondents with both armies but those with the Japanese found a tough censorship imposed and almost complete refusal to accompany troops or go to the front. Correspondents still flocked to the war; Alfred Cunningham of the *Daily Mail* and *New York Sun* was with the Russian forces and so was Julius Mendes Price of the *Illustrated London News*, who was later to cover the First World War; Douglas Story now represented the *Daily Express* and Charles Hands the *Daily Mail*. With the Japanese troops and suffering from almost total censorship and hindrance of movement were Martin Donahoe of the *Daily Chronicle*, George Lynch of the same paper, Robert MacHugh of the *Daily Telegraph*, and Frederick Villiers, this time without bicycle but as always representing the *Graphic* whom he represented in the small wars up to 1914 and the First World War and who was the only war artist present at the capture of Port Arthur. Ellis Ashmead Bartlett went for the *Daily Telegraph*; during the First World War he was selected by the National Press Association to represent the London Press in the Dardanelles in 1915 and at General Joffre's Headquarters in 1916. Bennet Burleigh arrived in Japan with Melton Prior but found it almost impossible as all movement was forbidden. Melton Prior wrote:

> Here I am still with all the other correspondents, and it looks as though we shall be kept here ever so long yet. We are, of course, all mad at the delay, but personally I think the Japs are right not to let us loose in Korea to telegraph news for the benefit of the Russians. At last I have received a police pass for this town, and I shall be able to sketch anywhere. I am awfully pleased at it, as I have had such trouble up to the present, and have been nearly arrested three times for sketching soldiers. Mr. Williams of the *Sphere* was here three weeks before war broke out and got his permission quite easily, but as soon as war started the whole thing changed, and they are awfully secretive about everything and frightened to death at our giving away the movements of troops.

The correspondents managed to get some news through the official

Russo-Japanese War: General Kuroki at the battle of Sha-Ho observing the enemy positions, watched by General Wheeler, a well-known military correspondent.

Japanese paper the *Jiji Shimpoo*, and were as always content to be entertained.

> The Rothschild of Japan, a Mr. Mitsui, head of the house of Mitsui, gave us correspondents a great dinner at the Mitsui Club on Sunday last, the 21st, followed by a magnificent entertainment, with conjuring, dancing (Geisha girls) and a short Japanese play. It was a great evening.

Japanese censorship of news was strictly adhered to and, as was becoming their national characteristic, organization was perfect. Correspondents were divided into two categories, into two laps as it were, to be able to go to the front. Every day, each expected orders, but they never came and when they did they were usually countermanded. Melton Prior wrote to the editor of the *Illustrated London News*:

> Since writing you last I have had a great trouble here about going to the front. In the first place the Japanese Government asked Sir Claude Macdonald to send in the names of eight of the most important correspondents to go with the first column,

and my name was written fourth or fifth on the list, and, of course, we all thought this was all right, and I made arrangements the same as the others. But later on the Japs seemed to have altered their minds, and have now decided that no artist of any kind is to go with this first column, and I am to go with the second.

Other correspondents included Richard Harding Davis, complete with his bath-tub, typewriter, and camera, who A. G. Hales of the Daily News noted was, 'ever conspicuous in his checked coat with revolver slung on his hip'. Tom Clarke represented the *Daily Mail* and *Chicago Tribune*, Lionel James, *The Times*, Francis MacCullagh, a moustached Irishman, the *New York Herald*, and Raymond Recouly the French newspaper *Le Temps*.

With the Russian forces in Korea was Jack London. He later recounted staying in a Korean village when the head man came to see him. Having little or nothing to fill his dispatches, he received the chief and was astounded to be told that the entire village had turned out to greet him. He thought that his literary fame had travelled further than he had dreamed. Mounting the podium, the chief asked the bewildered correspondent to remove his false teeth, which London obligingly did but found to his dismay that he had after half an hour and almost thirty 'encores' to 'insult' his host by leaving.

Although the colonial wars were over for Britain, correspondents still found stories from the French and Italian North African campaigns as well as the Portuguese and South American Revolutions, and the so-called Fez Revolt of 1912. The revolutions in South America were followed mainly by an American press corps but the *Daily Chronicle* sent their veteran 'correspondent of comfort', as A. G. Hales called him, Richard Harding Davis. Melton Prior was on hand for the *Illustrated London News*, Florence O'Driscoll for *The Times*, and Charles William Domville-Fife also of *The Times* who kept his newspaper informed of events in Paraguay.

The North African campaigns conducted by the French and Italians were the last of the African colonial wars; Italy, by arrangement, being allowed her 'Place in the sun', while France continued to subdue by colonial rule. It was the age of revolutions in Europe and war correspondents profited from them. In Portugal, William Arthur Moore represented *The Times*, as he had done during the Turkish Revolution of 1909. He was later to report the revolution in Portugal, Persia in

Balkan Wars: Mr. Grant, one of the twelve *Daily Mirror* correspondents, taken prisoner by the Bulgarians after being mistaken for an Austrian.

Balkan Wars: Mr. Wyndham, correspondent of the *Daily Mirror,* talking to a Montenegran officer.

George Lynch, war correspondent, demonstrating the special gloves he patented for handling barbed wire.

Ellis Asmead Bartlett, war correspondent in the Balkans and during the First World War, in *tenue du campaigne.*

Frederick Villiers and a French military correspondent (note the armband) having their boots cleaned by French Moroccan troops after leaving the front line.

1912, the Balkan Wars and to accompany the British Expeditionary Force in their retreat from Mons in 1914. For four years he served in the Rifle Brigade and later covered the North-West Frontier campaign of 1919 and 1920. Born in 1880, he served as Lord Mountbatten's public relations advisor during 1944-6, and was at the age of seventy a war correspondent during the Korean War in 1950.

Britain had few if any colonial troubles but correspondents, ever catering for the public demand, searched and found news in the expeditions of the French and Spanish and Italians, who were imposing their rule in North Africa. Although these campaigns were avidly followed by a new brand of war correspondent, with some of the 'veterans', even the news-reading public now realized that an era had passed and that colonial campaigns were over. Europe would now be the focal point of 'hot' news, whose troubles would lead to the greatest and costliest confrontation in history.

# Epilogue

Even during the early twentieth century with its modern methods of communications, and in spite of strict censorship, war correspondents still found occasions to obtain scoops. During the Balkan Wars of 1912-13, after the numerous and frequent arrests of journalists, such as Thomas Grant, one of the twelve *Daily Mirror* war correspondents, a number of French and British newspapermen risked the threat of sanctions to get their news home. The classic example was the manoeuvre carried out by Bernard Alfieri, director of the office of *L'Illustration* and head of the *Daily Mirror* office. Thomas Grant of the *Mirror*, having pictures of a sensational nature, notified an agent in Tripoli. He managed to send an uncensored dispatch to a correspondent in Malta who in turn informed Alfieri. Alfieri, the master of 'hot news', immediately sent a boat to Tripoli on the pretext of repatriating British subjects and took the negatives on board. He personally took the pictures from Malta to Marseilles and overland through France to Calais where he embarked for England. Arriving at Dover, he took the first train to London, resulting in a *Daily Mirror* scoop, in the true Archibald Forbes tradition.

One correspondent presented himself at the telegraph office in the guise of a high-ranking Bulgarian official and duly sent his dispatch to London while he watched the trembling clerks. He spoilt the effect, however, by offering to pay and gave himself away. He was arrested and deported.

While the Balkan troubles provided suitable fields for adventuring war correspondents who still travelled in a certain style, and reported news in a well-defined way, the autumn of 1914 would see the start of total war, and a very different style of soldiering and reporting.

The method of waging war might change as well as the method of reporting it, but as long as man fights his fellow man, there will always be a place for the war correspondent, whatever his medium, because today's news will always be tomorrow's history.

# Bibliography

Atkins, J. B. (1911). *The Life of William Howard Russell.* (2 vols.). John Murray.

Ayerst, David. (1971). *The Biography of a Newspaper.* Collins.

Baldick, Robert. (1964). *The Siege of Paris.* Batsford.

Baynes, Hopkinson, Hunt and Knight. (1971). *Scoop, Scandal and Strife.* Lund Humphries.

Bennett, E. N. (1899). *The Downfall of the Dervishes.* Methuen and Co.

Bond, Brian. (1967). *Victorian Military Campaigns.* Hutchinson.

Burleigh, Bennett. (1898). *Sirdar and Khalifa.* Chapman and Hall.

Burnham, Lord. (1955). *Peterborough Court.* Cassell.

Churchill, Randolph. S. (1966). *The Young Churchill.* William Heinemann.

Creswicke, Louis. (1900). *South Africa and the Transvaal War.* T. C. & E. C. Jack.

Farwell, Byron. (1973). *Queen Victoria's Little Wars.* Allan Lane.

Forbes, Archibald. (1894). *Barracks, Bivouacs and Battles.* Macmillan & Co.

Forbes, Archibald. (1871). *My Experiences of the War between France and Germany.* Macmillan & Co.

Fleming, Peter. (1959). *The Siege of Peking.* Rupert Hart-Davis.

Gardener, Brian. (1966). *Mafeking.* Cassell.

Grey, Elizabeth. (1971). *The Noise of Drums and Trumpets.* Longmans.

Hensman, Howard. (1882). *The Afghan War 1879—80.* W. H. Allen & Co.

Henty, George Alfred. (1874). *The March to Coomassie.* Tinsley Bros.

Henty, George Alfred. (1868). *The March to Magdela.* Tinsley Bros.

Hohenberg, John. (1964). *Foreign Correspondence.* Columbia University Press.

Hozier, Captain H. M. (Editor). (1871). *The Franco Prussian War.* William Mackenzie.

Labouchère, Henry. (1872). *Diary of the Besieged Resident in Paris.*

Lehmann, Joseph. (1972). *The First Boer War.* Jonathan Cape.

Lloyd, Alan. (1964). *The Drums of Kumasi.* Longmans.

May, John Henry. (1970). *The Music of the Guns.* Jarrolds.

Morris, Donald. (1966). *The Washing of the Spears.* Jonathan Cape.

Nolan, E. H. (1857). *The History of the War against Russia.* J. S. Virtue.

Norris-Newman, Charles L. (1880). *With the British in Zululand throughout the War of 1879.* W. H. Allen & Co.

Parrit, Lieutenant-Colonel B. A. H. (1970). *The Intelligencers.* The Intelligence Corps.

Prior, Melton. (1912). *The Campaigns of a War Correspondent.* Edward Arnold.

Roberts, Lord F. S. (1900). *Forty-One Years in India.* Macmillan & Co.

Russell, W. H. (1860). *My Diary in India 1858—9.* Routledge, Warne and Routledge.

Stauman and Hageman. (1964). *The War Despatches of Stephen Crane.* Peter Owen.

Stanley, H. M. (1874). *Coomasie and Magdela.* Sampson Low.

Steevens, G. W. (1900). *From Capetown to Ladysmith.* William Blackwood & Sons.

Steevens, G. W. (1897). *With Kitchener to Khartum.* William Blackwood & Sons.

Stewart, A. T. Q. (1972). *The Pagoda War.* Faber and Faber.

Various authors. (1896). *Battles of the Nineteenth Century.* Cassell.

Vizetelly, E. A. (1914). *My Days of Adventure: The Fall of France 1870—71.*

*Who's Who.* 1848—1972 editions. A. & C. Black.

Wilson, H. W. (1900—01). *With the Flag to Pretoria.* Harmsworth Brothers.

Wilson, H. W. (1902). *After Pretoria, the Guerilla War.* Harmsworth Brothers.

Wood, F. (Editor). (1972). *Young Winston's Wars.* Leo Cooper Ltd.

Younghusband, G. J. & E. (1895). *The Relief of Chitral.* Macmillan & Co.

'How we lost Gordon.' Charles Williams. *Fortnightly Review*, March 1885.

'Images of War'. Exhibition Catalogue. National Army Museum. December 1973.

'La Guerre Russo-Japonaise'. *Revue Universelle.* 1904.

'Le Reportage Sous la Mitraille'. *Lectures pour Tous.* February 1913.

'Round the World with Swash and Buckle'. Robert Waldron. *American Heritage.* August 1967.

'Scandal'. Annual Report. National Army Museum 1972-3.

'The British Empire' (part work). B.B.C./*Time-Life.*

'The Genesis of a Profession'. S. T. Sheppard. *The United Services Magazine.* March 1907.

'The Rise and Fall of Henty's Empire'. John Springhall. *Times Literary Supplement.* 3 October 1968.

'The War Correspondent'. *Saturday Review*, 27 June 1885.


Newspapers and periodicals mentioned in the text in the British Library, British Newspaper Library, Victoria and Albert Museum and Wilkinson-Latham Collection.

# Index